FINANCIAL DERIVATIVE INVESTMENTS

An Introduction to Structured Products

FINANCIAL DERIVATIVE INVESTMENTS

An Introduction to Structured Products

Richard D. Bateson

University College London, UK

Imperial College Press

ICP

Published by

Imperial College Press
57 Shelton Street
Covent Garden
London WC2H 9HE

Distributed by

World Scientific Publishing Co. Pte. Ltd.
5 Toh Tuck Link, Singapore 596224
USA office: 27 Warren Street, Suite 401-402, Hackensack, NJ 07601
UK office: 57 Shelton Street, Covent Garden, London WC2H 9HE

British Library Cataloguing-in-Publication Data
A catalogue record for this book is available from the British Library.

FINANCIAL DERIVATIVE INVESTMENTS
An Introduction to Structured Products

ISBN-13 978-1-84816-711-7
ISBN-10 1-84816-711-3

Printed in Singapore by B & Jo Enterprise Pte Ltd

Preface

Although I started thinking about a book on derivative based investments years ago, the possibility of lecturing on a finance course at University College London (UCL) led to its final realisation. The idea was to write a short, understandable, practical book based on my experience of trading and structuring exotics, rather than present a purely mathematical approach. To achieve this I have included many term-sheets of actual trades and relegated as much mathematics as possible to the appendices. I have witnessed at first hand the development of the equity, interest rate and credit derivative markets and I have seen many good and bad products fall in and out of fashion. Hopefully, this book will prove both instructive for students and useful for anybody involved in the capital markets as an investor, product structurer or salesman.

My thanks to Professor Steve Bramwell at UCL for his encouragement, and to my much loved family for putting up with all those hours when "dad was down in the shed working on his stupid book".

Dr. Richard Bateson
Esher, Surrey
September 2010

Contents

Guide to Acronyms

ABS	Asset backed security
ATM	At-the-money
BHP	Bramwell–Holdsworth–Pinton
CDO	Collateralised debt obligation
CDS	Credit default swap
CLN	Credit linked note
CME	Chicago Mercantile Exchange
CMS	Constant maturity swap
CPPI	Constant proportion portfolio insurance
CS01	Present value of 1 basis point credit spread
DJ	Dow Jones
EBITDA	Earnings before income, taxes, depreciation and amortisation
EM	Emerging market
ETF	Exchange traded fund
EURIBOR	Euro Interbank Offered Rate
FRA	Forward rate agreement
FRN	Floating rate note
FTD	First-to-default
FTSE	Financial Times all shares index 100
FX	Foreign exchange
HJM	Heath, Jarrow and Morton model
HNW	High net worth
HY	High yield
IFA	Independent financial advisor
IG	Investment grade

IPE	International Petroleum Exchange
IRR	Internal rate of return
ISA	Individual Savings Account
ISDA	International Swaps and Derivatives Association
ITM	In-the-money
JTD	Jump to default
LBO	Leveraged buyout
LCDS	Loan credit default swap
LIBOR	London interbank offered rate
LMM	LIBOR market model
MTN	Medium term note
NC	Non-call period
OTC	Over-the-counter
OTM	Out-of-the-money
P&L	Profit and loss
PDE	Partial differential equation
PPN	Principal protected note
PV	Present value
PV01	Present value of 1 basis point
RPV01	"Risky" present value of 1 basis point
S&P	Standard and Poors
SIPP	Self-invested personal pension
SPC	Special purpose company
SPV	Special purpose vehicle

Glossary of Notations

The most commonly used notations in alphabetical order with non-Latin symbols at the end. Some have several uses but are distinguishable from their context.

a	Mean reversion parameter. Drift factor on binomial tree.
B	Basket value. Debt value. Bond price.
C,c	Fixed coupon.
D	Discount factor.
f	Forward interest rate. Floating rate. LIBOR. An option price.
h	Accrual factor. Coupon period. Interest period.
K	Strike price of an option.
L	Survival probability. LIBOR.
M	Month. Financing or repo discount factor.
$M( )$	Multivariate cumulative normal distribution.
$N( )$	Cumulative normal distribution.
P	Price of an option. Price of a discount bond.
Pr	Probability.
Q	Cumulative default probability.
q	Dividend yield of an equity. CDS premium.
R	Interest Rate. Swap Rate. Redemption amount. Recovery rate.
r	Risk free interest rate. Spot rate.
S	Underlying asset price. Usually an equity price.
s	Credit spread.
T	Time to maturity (in years).
t	Time in the future. Current time $t = 0$.
V	Value or price of a swap. Option value. Option payoffs.
X, x	Currency. Funding spread.

y   Yield of a bond. Return of an equity.

Z, z   Normally distributed random variable. Zero rate.

χ   Probability indicator function (equals 0 or 1).

φ( )   Normally distributed. A Gaussian distribution.

φ( )   Gaussian probability density.

λ   Hazard rate or Poisson coefficient.

μ   Drift of underlying asset.

ν   Volatility of bond or discount bond.

ρ   Correlation coefficient.

σ   Volatility of underlying asset.

Chapter 1

Introduction

1.1 Introduction

The recent "credit crisis" of 2007–2010 has unfortunately re-emphasised that many investors have not clearly understood the nature and risks involved in structured investments. The products investment banks have marketed to investors have become significantly more complex over the last 10–15 years. As new derivatives technologies have evolved, the risks involved in each generation of product have changed. From structured notes in the mid 1990s, reverse convertibles in the ".com" tech crash, collateralised debt obligations (CDOs) amidst the US corporate scandals and more recently the notorious "CDO–squared" (CDO^2) containing subprime mortgage collateral. In all cases, supposedly sophisticated financial investors demonstrated a lack of understanding of the pricing, risks and underlying principles involved in these products.

In this book, I attempt to demystify the world of derivative investments from a balanced, independent viewpoint. As *caveat emptor* applies to all investments (particularly to those structured by the well known investment banks), it is critical for today's investor to have an educated understanding. Many structured products are good investments, but also many are extremely bad, indeed toxic. It is better to be an informed investor than to simply follow the fads and fashion or a slick derivatives salesman.

The world of derivatives has become dominated by increasingly complex financial mathematics that is totally impenetrable by nearly everybody. Even deciphering the term-sheets on some products is enough to give one a headache. I have tried to describe the principal aspects of structured products in the simplest way possible by including many examples of common trades I have experienced. The range of products presented should provide a good overview of the main concepts involved in derivative based investments. Although a few equations are necessary, the majority of the mathematics is confined to the Appendices for those who are interested.

1.2 The Case for Derivative Investments

The recent evolution of derivatives technology by the leading investment banks has led to the development of a wide range of different investment products aimed at both retail and institutional investors. Derivatives are contracts that reference "real" underlying assets, which allow tailored solutions to speculation and investment in a wide range of different asset classes ranging from equities and interest rates to credit and commodities. Until relatively recently only "cash" investment could be readily undertaken by investors in these markets, for example by buying bonds or shares. Sometimes it was possible to sell "short" to profit from a declining market or obtain leverage by borrowing against a cash position.

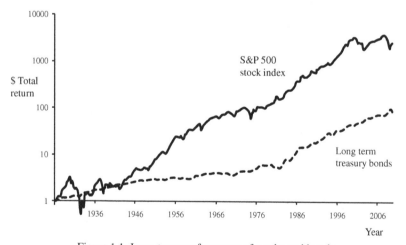

Figure 1.1: Long term performance of stocks and bonds.

However, with the advent of derivatives a range of different structured products has arisen to appeal to different categories of investors with varying risk/reward profiles and market views. Derivative products can now provide a range of alternative investments for the same underlying cash instrument allowing an investor to employ different strategies and risk profiles at different times in various markets. Although the very long term trend of equities has been upwards (Fig. 1.1, logarithmic scale) and equities have outperformed both cash and bonds, their performance has been volatile, with long periods of almost no growth. Consider the historical performance of different asset classes in Fig. 1.2 over different timescales. Over the last 10 years equities have significantly underperformed government and corporate bonds and even cash in the bank. Rather than be consistently long equities, structured products can provide investment solutions to range-bound and bearish markets, provide capital protection in uncertain situations, enhance yield when interest rates are low and provide exposure to other markets, such as corporate credit, when opportunities present themselves.

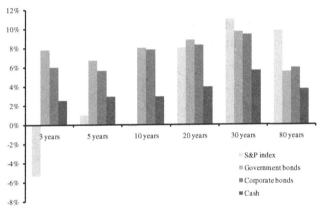

Figure 1.2: Total annualised return on different asset classes.

For example, instead of just simply purchasing an individual share where the investor is exposed to 100% of the underlying price movement, has no income except for dividends and may provide a capital loss, numerous alternatives are now possible. The investor might instead purchase a *capital guaranteed product* that provides, say, 80% of the positive growth of the underlying equity but guarantees to redeem 100% of the original investment amount even if the equity has fallen in value. If the investor prefers an income product he may purchase a *reverse convertible,* where the equity upside is sacrificed to provide a high annual coupon. Many other variations exist in which risk and return are modified by changing the underlying, modifying the maturity of investment, increasing and decreasing leverage and converting income to capital gain (or *vice versa*).

In this book we will outline the broad principles of designing and pricing different structured products using derivatives across a range of asset classes. We will illustrate with the most popular investment products of the last few years and concentrate on the common themes and problems involved.

1.3 Investment Criteria

Structuring investment products with derivatives allows the tailoring of products to different investor market views. Also, the product risk/reward profile can be optimised for different parts of the market cycle. Figure 1.3 outlines the main investment criteria, from the investor's viewpoint, in the design of a product.

Figure 1.3: Investor investment criteria.

Several important factors must be considered. Is the instrument designed for income or capital gain? Does it include a capital guarantee?

What is the range of maturities required? Is the product itself diversified or must it be held as part of a wider portfolio of products? What is the underlying asset class? What sectors to invest in? Does it incorporate the investors or analyst market views? Is the risk/reward appropriate for the investor? Are the fees reasonable and what is secondary liquidity like if it is to be redeemed or repurchased early? Is it easy to explain and understand? Also, particularly for retail products what will be the taxation implications (for example eligibility for ISAs in the UK)?

As can be seen, the design of a new investment product is a complex process even if just the investor's perspective is taken into account. In fact, the ability of the investment bank to price, hedge and provide a fair and reliable "after sales service" is just as important. The last point should not be underestimated since the bank and its distributors do not wish to suffer from reputational problems and litigation issues by structuring and selling unsuitable products particularly to the retail public.

Table 1.1: Overview of product demand for different asset classes.

	Retail investors	High net worth (HNW)	Institutional investors
Equity:			
Income	✔	✔	✔
Capital protected	✔	✔	
Basket capital protected	✔	✔	
Interest Rates:			
Capped floaters		✔	✔
Range notes		✔	✔
Callables			✔
Credit:			
Credit linked note (CLN)	✔	✔	✔
First-to-default CLN		✔	✔
CDO senior notes			✔
CDO equity		✔	✔
Other:			
Fund linked	✔	✔	✔
CPPI notes	✔	✔	✔
Hybrids		✔	✔

1.4 Types of Investors

Investors can be broadly grouped into three main categories: *retail* (which is you, me and the rest of the "unsophisticated" public), *high-net-worth* individuals (HNW) (a polite term for very rich people who are typically clients of private banks including entrepreneurs, lottery winners, landed gentry, Russian oligarchs and oil-rich sheiks) and *institutional* investors (banks, insurance companies, corporate, funds and pension funds, hedge funds, etc.). Generally institutional investors are categorised as the most sophisticated and informed investors and trade in the most complex structured products across a large number of asset classes. In recent years, however, particularly in Europe, a wide range of increasingly complex equity-linked product has been sold to the mass market retail. Different types of structured product have been popular with different investor groups in various countries. Table 1.1 attempts to provide a simplified overview for various popular products.

1.5 Families of Structured Products

We can broadly divide the universe of derivative based structured products into their main underlying risk: equity, interest rate or credit linked and other less common underlying assets such as funds, currencies (FX) and commodities (Fig. 1.4). Although there is some cross-over between these different classes in the form of "hybrid" product this classification works quite well.

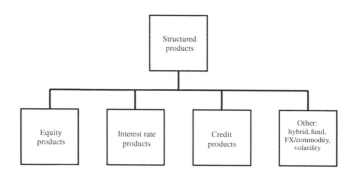

Figure 1.4: Main families of structured investment products.

1.5.1 *Structured equity products*

Equity-linked products, due to the volatile nature of equities, often provide the highest risk and return of any structured products. They appeal to retail and high net worth investors who are looking to outperform the return of their regular cash bank deposits. Such investors are often frequent equity investors and compare these returns to mutual funds and other stock market-linked investments. Products are usually either designed for income or capital gain and structured on single underlyings (index or individual equities) or baskets of stocks or indices. The most common products are reverse convertibles for income and capital guaranteed growth (and income) products for risk adverse investors. These are purchased in the form of notes and funds or simply equity-linked deposits.

The development of the market for structured equity product varies widely across Europe, but the UK, France, Germany, Italy, Benelux and Switzerland have been big growth markets. In the UK *independent financial advisors* (IFAs) have marketed a range of products including 3–5 year FTSE reverse convertibles and protected growth bonds with various features, such as barriers and auto-callables. Over £15bn of structured products were sold to UK retail and high net worth accounts in 2009. In France markets are traded in *warrants* (long-dated call options), reverse convertibles, capital guaranteed DJ Eurostoxx 50 and CAC index notes and sector specific baskets (e.g. technology, sustainability etc.). Some products have become extremely complex and difficult to understand such as the Société Générale (SocGen) products, for example the "Fuji" and "Himalaya". Despite the complexity, these products often succeed due to the high headline coupon, the capital guarantee and great marketing. In Switzerland the private banking and HNW sector is a major investor for all manner of structured products.

1.5.2 *Structured interest rate products*

Interest rate products or structured notes are mainly favoured by institutional investors who are looking for low risk and low yield enhancement. By incorporating interest rate views into structured notes it is possible to boost returns typically 50–200bp per annum (1bp = 1 basis point = 0.01%) above cash. Mostly, these products are capital guaranteed since the institutional investors don't generally want to put capital at risk and are only willing to risk coupon payments. Coupons can be capped, linked to barriers and ranges or issuer calls to provide moderate increases in yield. Some notes, such as dual currency notes, are also linked to FX levels.

1.5.3 *Structured credit products*

More frequently in recent years investors are willing to take corporate or sovereign credit risk in an attempt to boost income or in some cases provide capital gain. These products appeal to institutional, HNW and increasingly to retail investors. The credit asset class has taken a bit of "pummelling" amidst the 2007–2010 credit crisis but in fact corporate defaults outside the highly *leveraged buyout* names (LBOs) and a few long term distressed sectors, such as automotive, has remained low. Correlation products such as *first-to-default* and *collateralised debt obligations* (CDOs) have been extremely popular as a means to provide higher leverage and increased yield. Capital protected products are also common where more risky underlying assets, such as *high yield* (HY) and *emerging market* (EM) credits and even CDO first loss tranches are often linked to a coupon in a structure where the capital guarantee is provided by a much higher rated (AAA/AA) credit.

1.5.4 *Other types of structured investment products*

Although the asset categories of equities, rates and credit encompass the vast majority of structured products, other forms of derivative based investment products exist. Instead of an equity index an actual managed fund (equity, fixed income, hedge fund of funds etc.) can be used as the underlying and various *fund options* constructed around this to provide capital guaranteed and other structures. A cheaper alternative to fund options is the *constant proportion portfolio insurance* (CPPI) structure, which allows participation in the growth of an underlying fund whilst providing a capital guarantee. Other investments can be structured around FX and commodities using a similar methodology to equities, for example a capital guaranteed note linked to basket, currencies, crude oil prices, or even referencing a commodity based *exchange traded fund* (ETF). Also more recently, pure volatility (in the form of *volatility swaps*) can be used as an underlying, although, in my experience, this is a product that is only commonly used by specialised institutional investors, such as hedge funds. Lastly, the various different asset classes, such as equities and FX, can be combined in the form of *hybrid products* which is a growing sector that we shall briefly discuss in Chapter 10.

1.6 Evolution of Derivatives Technology

The development of structured derivative based products has been driven by advances in derivatives technology. In particular, the application of theoretical models together with their practical adaptation and implementation has allowed bank trading desks to build risk management systems to price and hedge complex derivatives or "exotics".

The development of model driven trading and risk management has coincided with the advent of the relatively inexpensive computers and notably the PC, allowing derivatives trading to become a lot more mathematical. Originally the emphasis was on nice, clean closed form solutions. Rapidly, products have become far more complex and mathematically intractable requiring numerical calculations such as simulations, "trees" and multi-dimensional finite difference grids to solve the differential equations involved. The future technological evolution will probably involve use of more complex "real" distributions and correlation structures.

Without these advances in computer technology, pricing and hedging derivatives trading books would have been computationally too time-consuming for effective risk management. Even today, virtually every derivatives trader will tell you his "book" takes too long to value and calculate the hedging parameters or "greeks". The most sophisticated correlation based equity basket products and delta hedged CDOs require *Monte Carlo simulation* of large numbers of underlying variables. These calculations necessitate computational short cuts and approximations for pricing.

The competition between the investment banks and the desire to innovate new products led to an "arms race" mentality in the market. New pricing models, computational algorithms and investment in computational hardware and software are continually in progress particularly in the most lucrative product sectors (equity, credit and hybrids at the time of writing). Figure 1.5 shows (from my totally biased personal viewpoint) the evolution of derivatives technology of the past 20 years from simple equity derivatives to the complex CDO models with hundreds of different corporate credit curves and large numbers of correlations. Here we shall briefly outline the main technological developments behind the different type of underlying.

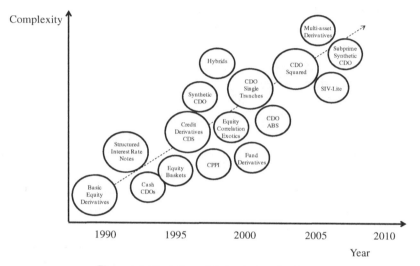

Figure 1.5: Evolution of derivatives technology.

1.6.1 *Equity derivative technology*

Equity derivative technology is perhaps the oldest and, thus, currently the most developed in terms of complexity of product. Most of the underlying models are relatively simple and based on the Black–Scholes model which was invented in the late 1970s. This basic model allowed for the pricing and hedging of exchange traded and *over-the-counter* (OTC) single stock and index based options in the 1980s. Investment banks began to use Black–Scholes to hedge large options books and the notion of hedging parameters or "greeks" became more widespread.

In the 1990s, equity based structured investment products were developed with longer dated options allowing capital guaranteed products to be produced. Initially, targeting institutions and then retail investors the products focused on indices (S&P 500, FTSE 100, etc.) and baskets of stocks. The baskets of stocks were generally treated using a single factor approximation, where the basket value replaces the stock price in the Black–Scholes model. Barrier and cross currency *quanto* technologies were also developed.

In the late 1990s bull market, several new types of product became popular. Perhaps the most popular product of all time was and still is the *reverse convertible bond* in its many guises. In its purest form it was just a bond with a *put option* sold by the investor to increase the coupon. The reverse convertible produced a wide range of variants including barriers, auto-calls and increased leveraged.

Later, complex long-dated products based on multiple equities and indices were developed that were computationally intensive to price and hedge. These included products based on the *worst* performing stocks in a basket (including the SocGen "Altiplano", "Everest" and "Himalaya" products) and various *rainbow* products. Optically attractive to investors with high coupons and capital guarantee, these products generated high margins for investment banks and were extremely successful.

The derivative leaders in this growing and high margin market came and went in waves, entering the business, making significant profits and then suffering from a "blow-up" or mishap in some part of the business. Banker Trust (now merged into Deutsche Bank) was a pioneer and UBS/SBC (before the Swiss bank merger) a second generation leader. The French banks and notably Société Générale, particularly for correlation products, took up the lead but now the technology is fairly widespread amongst many market counterparties.

1.6.2 *Interest rate derivative technology*

In the late 1980s, the *interest rate swap* market was developed. Interest rate swaps allow investors to exchange one set of cash-flows for another. For example, *swapping* fixed for floating rates for the next 15 years. This required banks to develop swap models that built interest rate curves from futures, deposits and the observable swap market to price and hedge swaps. The interbank cap/floor and swaption market developed over the same period with variants of the Black–Scholes model being used for pricing.

The structured swap market grew out of this in the early 1990s and a large structured note market developed targeted at institutional investors. Initially, rather naïve bond investors believing that yield enhancement was a low risk venture and with no understanding of the notion of forward rates, or how to calculate them, fuelled the market. Investment banks led by Bankers Trust invented a bewildering array of increasingly toxic products which led to a series of high profile investor losses including Orange County where Robert Citron lost $2.4bn in 1994 (it seemed a lot in those days!). After a couple of bad years where the negative reputation associated with the derivatives "D" word caused the product to fall out of favour, the market recovered and has flourished as investor understanding has increased.

The structured note market required the invention of a new class of models, more complex than those required for equities, which would describe the entire yield curve in a consistent manner. Although the Black–Scholes model had been used for the cap/floor and swaption market and could be applied to pricing some types of structured notes, it lacked an *arbitrage free* framework and new models were required. One factor models that described the movement of the spot rate (*Vasicek* and extended Vasicek, such as the *Hull–White model*) were developed and were highly successful, being fast, easy to implement and allowing pricing and hedging of options with early exercise dates (called *American* and *Bermudan* options) on trees and finite difference lattices. Multifactor models, such as the *Heath, Jarrow and Morton* (HJM) model, are now also commonplace. These describe more completely movements of the yield curve and allow certain calibration problems encountered with one factor models to be overcome. In recent years the *LIBOR* (*London Interbank Offered Rate*) *market model* (LMM) has been popular. Research in this area is still strong and the "ultimate" interest rate model remains to be discovered.

1.6.3 *Credit derivative technology*

Credit derivatives were first widely traded in the late 1990s, developing from the *asset swap* market into a more liquid *credit default swap* (CDS) market. Following several years of phenomenal growth a credit default swap market now exists for about 800–1000 global credits with a core of 400–500 liquid credits traded between the major institutions.

Historically, the rating given to a corporate and the bond it issued was a strong guide to pricing. The credit quality implied by the market could be gauged by the yield spread over government bonds or the interbank swaps curve. The development of the CDS market allowed default probabilities to be very easily derived from market spreads. A market standard pricing model seems to have developed, which is the *reduced form* or *hazard rate model* where defaults are described by a Poisson probability distribution process. Sometimes this is also called the *par recovery* model since bond credit losses are based on an amount relative to par (100%).

Correlation based products, for example *first-to-default* baskets where the payoff is dependent on the first default in a basket of credits, have been around since the start of the CDS market. Today, the market standard pricing model has effectively become the *normal copula* or *Gaussian copula* model where default times of different credits are modelled using a multivariate normal distribution. With increasingly competitive pricing between banks and the realisation that low probability "tail risk" is an important factor in modelling rare correlated defaults, the development of more sophisticated models to price and hedge these correlation risks remains a topic of current research.

For large structured credit portfolio trades, such as synthetic collateralised debt, obligations investors relied for many years on *credit ratings*. These ratings are supplied mainly from Moody's, S&P and Fitch and provide as a market guide to pricing. The rating models rely on historical default data and not default probabilities implied from the CDS market. Banks relentlessly exploited this arbitrage between market pricing and the ratings based approach to generate large profits in structured trading desks. Some transparency was provided for investors by the CDS market for *tranched* indices (tranche = "slice" in French). Innovations such as synthetic CDOs, delta hedging of single CDO tranches, CDOs of ABS (*asset backed securities*) led to the ultimate CDO arbitrage: the "CDO-squared" (CDO^2) just before the 2007 "credit crunch". It remains to be seen how this market recovers in the next few years, although at the time of writing the first few CDOs are starting to be printed once again. A miniscule *collateralised loan obligation* (CLO) volume of $1.5bn has been achieved for the first 8 months of 2010 compared with a peak of $90bn per annum pre-credit crunch.

1.7 Introduction to Structuring Investment Products

As a first example we will consider how an equity capital protected note might be structured for investors. The "term-sheet" designed to include the most important terms of the transaction for investors, is shown below in Example 1.1. From the term-sheet we can see that the Euro denominated 7 year note is issued by an "A" rated *issuer* at an issue price of 100% for 10 million notional (10mm). The *issuer* is usually a financial institution and is the borrower of the Euro 10mm proceeds of the note issue. It is *zero coupon* and thus pays no coupon but at maturity pays 100% plus 80% of the upside of the Dow Jones Eurostoxx 50 equity index as measured form the issue date.

Example 1.1

EUR PROTECTED BULL NOTES ON DJ EUROSTOXX 50	
ISSUER	: A rated Issuer
CURRENCY	: EUR
NOTIONAL	: 10mm
MATURITY	: 7 year
ISSUE PRICE	: 100%
UNDERLYING	: Dow Jones Eurostoxx 50
COUPON	: Zero coupon
PARTICIPATION	: 80%
REDEMPTION	: Each Note will be redeemed at maturity at an amount depending on $EUROSTOXX_{final}$, the closing price of the Underlying 3 business days before the Maturity Date. The Redemption Amount will be equal to $$100\% + Participation \times Max\left(\frac{EUROSTOXX_{final}}{EUROSTOXX_{initial}} - 100\%, 0\right)$$ where $EUROSTOXX_{initial}$ is the opening price of the Underlying on the Issue Date.

Thus, if the index rises 50% the investor will receive 100%+80%×50% = 140%. If the index falls he receives a minimum of 100%, so is 100% capital protected. The capital guaranteed bond is structured in the following way (see Fig. 1.6):

1. The investor pays *par* (100%) to the issuer and receives a note. The issuer has effectively borrowed 100% or Euro 10mm for 7 years until maturity.

2. During the life of the note the issuer pays a floating rate funding e.g. 3 month LIBOR (or more precisely the Euro equivalent called EURIBOR) plus a funding level of x basis points per annum ("bppa") to the *swap provider* or *swap counterparty*. The funding level will depend on the credit worthiness of the issuer and could be structured to include fees. The issuer pays the interest for borrowing the 100% to the swap provider rather than the note-holder.

3. At maturity the note redeems an amount dependent on the final level of the Eurostoxx index ("Index Final") relative to the level of the index on the issue date ("Index Initial"). The swap provider pays the derivative payoff of 80% times the maximum of (Index Final – Index Initial)/(Index Initial) and zero to the issuer. The issuer redeems the guaranteed principal amount of 100% plus the payment from the swap provider to the investor.

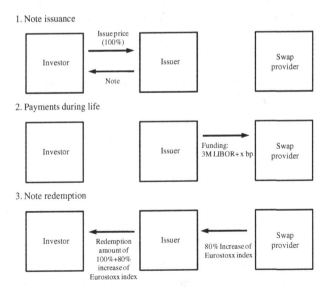

Figure 1.6: Issue of a protected bull note on DJ Eurostoxx 50.

1.8 Issuing Structured Notes

Most investors will buy a note or a bond when they invest in a structured product. These can be issued by a credit worthy financial or corporate issuer or a *special purpose company* or *vehicle* (SPC or SPV). Other common investment possibilities exist, for example retail investors can invest in a structured fund, bank deposit or certain institutions enter into a specialised insurance contract.

All the above forms of investment are simply different delivery mechanisms for an underlying financial swap contract. The swap provider is an investment bank or swap house that will structure and hedge a derivative that will be embedded in a swap contract with the issuing entity. The swap contract will be documented in a *swap confirmation* using a standard format and with the IDSA (International Swaps and Derivatives Association) market definitions.

The leading structured swap providers depend somewhat on the type of underlying derivative. The ranks have been thinned somewhat by the recent credit crisis. The demise of Lehman, who was prolific in retail equity products in 2002–2007, produced major problems for numerous investors both as a swap counterparty and an issuer. Similarly AIG Financial Products was a market leader for interest rate derivatives and Bear Stearns was also a major player in the structuring of CDOs and both of these have also disappeared.

- Equity derivatives: Société Générale, BNP Paribas, JP Morgan, Deutsche Bank, UBS, Goldman...

- Interest rate derivatives: JP Morgan, Barclays, CSFB, UBS, BNP Paribas...

- Credit derivatives: JP Morgan, Morgan Stanley, Deutsche Bank, CSFB, Goldman, Barclays...

1.8.1 *Financial or corporate issuers*

Highly rated (AAA, AA and sometimes A rated) financial institutions and corporations will issue structured bonds or notes to investors. By issuing a structured note the issuer will be able to borrow funds at an advantageous funding level compared with the issuer's existing borrowing programmes.

An *arranger* (generally an investment bank or broker) will design a structured product, find the investors and approach both the issuer and a swap provider (investment banks or swap house) who will provide the underlying structured swap contract.

Examples of numerous past frequent issuers include most highly rated mainstream financial institutions: Abbey National (Santander), Barclays, Northern Rock (!), Deutsche Bank, West LB, etc.

Most frequent issuers will use a *medium term note* (MTN) programme for issuing structured notes. This has the advantages of reduced documentation (standard form documents for note *pricing supplement* and *swap confirmations*), quick note settlement (typically 2–4 weeks), wide range of issue sizes (USD 1–2mm to 100mm typical) and low cost.

Issuer funding targets will depend on the credit quality of the issuer, maturity, currency and size of issue and current credit environment. Pre-credit crisis typically for 5 years term funding levels might range from LIBOR minus 15–20bp for a AAA issuer to LIBOR plus 20–60bp for a lower A rated issuer. Funding level should be directly related to the market spread of vanilla bonds of the issuer or the credit default swap referencing the issuer, but this is very often not the case as issuers will try to derive value from the issuance of structured bonds with the arranger.

1.8.2 *Special purpose vehicles (SPVs)*

A frequent alternative to a financial issuer is to use a special purpose company (SPC) or special purpose vehicle (SPV) as the issuer. In the US special trusts can also be used. SPVs can be multipurpose issuers with their own MTN programme or single use issuers.

In a nutshell, SPVs are companies incorporated in tax favourable jurisdictions (Cayman islands, Gibraltar etc.), who have a *trustee,* an *administrator*, no personnel except a board of directors, a tax exempt shareholder (who is usually a registered charity!) and possess no assets except investments of proceeds of the note issuance and swap contracts that may be entered into.

Proceeds of note issuance are used to purchase *collateral,* which is used as security for redemption of the notes (see Fig. 1.7). Collateral usually consists of highly rated short term instruments or highly rated bonds with a similar maturity to the notes issued by the SPV. The investor assumes the credit risk of the collateral but receives the extra spread that the collateral may offer. This may provide a funding advantage over financial issuers of an equivalent rating to the collateral.

As with a financial issuer the SPV enters into a structured swap with a swap provider to provide the characteristics of the structured note. The swap is funded by the SPV paying the interest paid on the collateral. In the event of default of the underlying collateral the swap provider will have a senior claim on the collateral above the note investors if it is owed money under the swap contract.

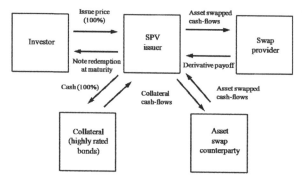

Figure 1.7: Typical special purpose vehicle (SPV) issuer.

In a similar fashion to an SPV products can be structured as actual funds (generally closed ended) whose only investments are cash (or suitable collateral) and the swap contract. Typical jurisdictions have been Luxembourg and Ireland. Investors buy units in the fund rather than purchasing a note or bond.

1.9 Structured Product Fees

Structured product fees are a very nebulous area and one of the major disadvantages for most investors is the complete lack of transparency of fees incorporated into different products. Generally speaking we can divide fees and costs into: (i) distributor fees, (ii) issuance costs and (iii) swap provider margins.

The *distributor fees* are charged by the selling agent or intermediary, for example the IFA or private bank, who directly market and sell the product to the retail or HNW investor. Typically for an equity linked product of say 5 years maturity this might be between 2–5% upfront. Some products which are structured as, say, funds the fees might be higher since a per annum fee is charged. A well known Belgian insurer uses an effective funding rate of LIBOR minus 1% per annum, providing almost 1% per annum of fees which could amount to 7–8% on longer maturity products. This may seem a large amount, but compare this with mutual funds, which if not discounted might be, around 2–5% front loaded and then 1% per annum, or hedge funds, which might be 2–5% upfront and then 2% per annum with a 20% performance fees. For an institutional investor purchasing directly from the issuer/swap provider this level of fees is generally bypassed. Also, for short dated equity products and lower volatility underlying assets, such as interest rate and credit products, fees are understandably much lower. A recent innovation are liquid, exchange listed equity products which allow retail investors to bypass distributor margins by buying cheaply through their broker. For example, SocGen has listed a range of index linked auto-callables on the London Stock Exchange (LSE).

Issuance costs depend on the issue size, maturity, credit rating and method of issuance. An efficient MTN programme will have relatively low costs compared with structuring a one-off fund (which may include custody fees, administrator fees, stock exchange listing etc.). Typically costs might range between 10–50bp per annum.

All the above fees actually ignore the swap provider margins or the profit made by the bank trading desk. The margin taken by the bank is the price at which the derivative is traded relative to the theoretical model price. If possible conservative volatilities and correlations will be used, and for long dated products where hedging risks are important, large reserves may be taken which are released into the trading book *profit and loss* (P&L) account over several years. The overall upfront profit would typically be 2–3% but could range from 0.5% for short dated, competitive products to 5–6%+ or more for longer dated complex products which involve large model risk. It is important to realise that in hedging the product the bank often takes risks which cannot be completely hedged. Sometimes for difficult to hedge products the traders might make a complete mess of the dynamic hedging strategy and all those theoretical upfront profits may evaporate very quickly.

Structured Products – Perfect Solution or Impossible Dream?

A particularly negative article from a major IFA and SIPP provider (with the above title) outlined the main objections to retail structured products: (i) the cost of capital protection, (ii) the quality of capital guarantees, (iii) the fixed term nature of the product and "lock-ins", (iv) the lack of dividends and (v) the lack of transparency.

The article was written by a market bull so perhaps if you are bullish over the next few years then it is obviously preferable to invest in a diverse pool of equities, index tracker or a well run mutual fund. However, if you are risk adverse or think that a bear market is possibly around the corner, then a capital guarantee has its uses. Imagine the effect of a multi-decade Japanese style bear market on a long only portfolio.

Obviously, capital guarantees are only worth anything if the guarantor or counterparty is credit worthy. Lehman Brothers bankruptcy caused many problems for investors since it issued many structured notes. Regulators should ideally ensure that only highly rated, stable financial institutions can act as issuers to retail investors and not potentially over-leveraged investment banks and brokers.

Although most retail structured products have a fixed term (say 3–5 years) there is in principle no reason why tight bid/offers cannot be made to investors wishing to exit early. Most trading desks will offer two-way prices and defer their margin over the life of a trade. The high early redemption cost comes mainly from greedy advisors and intermediaries who wish to upfront distribution margins. A step forward is a recent exchange listed product that allows higher liquidity and lower distribution margins for retail investors.

The lack of dividends is a "red herring", since as we shall see implied dividends are incorporated into pricing of structured products and the investor does not miss out on them.

Mutual funds and hedge fund investments provide little transparency for most investors. Just buying a "black box" fund on the basis of a historical straight line performance or low Sharpe ratio is dangerous (remember Bernie Madoff?). On the contrary, structured products offer a very clearly defined payoff linked to market observables, such as indices. Just remember you have to understand the product and don't stick "all your eggs in one basket". The UK's leading private bank recommends its clients to diversify by having 25% of their portfolios in structured products.

Chapter 2

Introduction to Swap Finance

2.1 Introduction

All structured products are based on the concept of swaps of various forms. The simplest swap is a fixed/floating interest rate swap, where fixed rates are exchanged for floating rates with a swap counterparty. More complex swaps with embedded options are required for developing derivative investments but first we will review the fundamental concepts of simple interest rate swaps.

2.2 Zero Rates and Discount Factors

If cash is placed on deposit with a financial institution it will accrete over time as interest gradually accumulates. If $1 is placed in an account with a guaranteed annual interest rate r for t years the investor will receive on maturity a compounded amount equal to:

$$\$1 \times (1+r)^t.$$

If the interest is compounded on a continuous basis we can use *exponential* compounding and we have:

$$\$1 \times e^{rt}.$$

Importantly, the annualised and continuously compounded interest rates are not exactly equivalent and in any practical application we must be careful in moving between them (Appx A.1). In this book, for ease of understanding we will not in general distinguish them and often we will

21

prefer the continuously compounded interest rate, since this allows easy mathematical manipulation and is heavily used in option pricing.

In general, the interest rate r will depend on several factors including the credit worthiness of the financial institution and maturity of the deposit. For transactions between most highly rated (AAA/AA/A) financial institutions, the annual interest rate is fairly standardised and there exists an effective interbank market rate or *zero rate* $z(0,t)$ for any given maturity t. This zero rate can be derived from various instruments traded between banks and include short term bank deposits, zero coupon bonds, futures and forward contracts and interest rate swaps.

Thus, the *present value* (*PV*) today (at time 0) of \$1 received in t years can be calculated using $z(0,t)$ the t year zero rate or annualised zero coupon rate.

$$P_{discount}(0,t) = \$1 \times \frac{1}{\left(1+z(0,t)\right)^t} = \$1 \times D(0,t). \tag{2.1}$$

Here $P_{discount}(0,t)$ is the value of a discount bond that pays \$1 at maturity. The factor $D(0,t)$ is known as the *discount factor*. Sometimes it is known as the "riskless" discount factor since it is used for discounting cashflows that are paid by highly rated issuers or counterparties. Figure 2.1(a) shows an example of a zero curve as a function of maturity T. The usual shape is upwards sloping but can be flat or inverted, depending on market conditions. The discount factor curve is always a decreasing function of time (Fig. 2.1(b)).

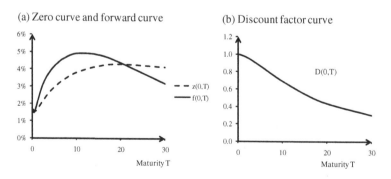

Figure 2.1: Zero curves and discount factors.

Frequently in financial calculations continuously compounded discount factors are used as an approximation due to their ease of manipulation. The discount factor in Eq. (2.1) when continuously compounded becomes an exponential function of time and zero rate

$$D(0,t) = e^{-z(0,t)t}.$$
(2.2)

2.3 Forward Rates

The *forward rate* is the interest rate that is used for compounding or discounting between two future dates. The current zero curve contains information on the market expectation of forward rates.

Consider the current 2 year discount factor $D(0,2)$. This can be written as a function of the known 1 year discount factor $D(0,1)$ and the discount factor between years 1 and 2, $D(1,2)$. The discount factor $D(1,2)$ is based on the current 1 year forward rate written as $f(0,1,2)$.

$$D(0,2) = D(0,1)\,D(1,2)$$
$$= \frac{1}{(1+z(0,1))}\frac{1}{(1+f(0,1,2))}.$$

More generally, we can write the simply compounded forward rate at time t between T and $T+h$ as a function of two discount factors. The time interval h is usually associated with an accrual period, such as the coupon period on a bond.

$$f(t,T,T+h) = \frac{1}{h}\left(\frac{D(t,T)}{D(t,T+h)} - 1\right).$$
(2.3)

In certain interest rate derivative models the notion of the "instantaneous" forward rate $f(t,T)$ is used. This is effectively the limit of the forward rate as the time interval h tends to zero, making the instantaneous forward rate related to the slope or gradient of the zero curve. For a positively sloped zero curve the forward curve will always lie above the zero curve as in Fig. 2.1(a).

2.4 Present Valuing Cash-flows and Bonds

Using the notion of discount factors $D(0,t)$ from Eq. (2.1) it is easy to calculate the present value today of a series of cash-flows paid on various future dates. Each cash-flow or coupon is present-valued using the relevant point on the discount factor curve.

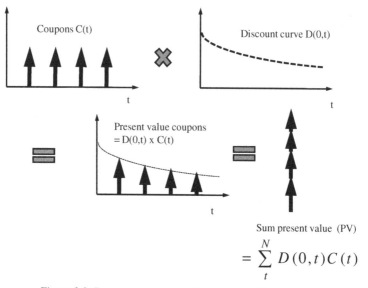

$$= \sum_t^N D(0,t)C(t)$$

Figure 2.2: Present valuing cash-flows using a discount curve.

Consider an investment that pays fixed rate coupons C on dates t_i ($i=1,2,..,N$) until maturity T as in Fig. 2.2. The total present value is given by the sum of the coupons C multiplied by the individual discount factors from the times t_i when the future coupons are paid.

$$P_{cash-flow}(0,T) = \sum_i^N C\,D(0,t_i). \tag{2.4}$$

This gives the present value of an annuity of rate C. Often it is useful to think of the value of an annuity where C = 1bp or 0.01%, which is called the PV01. If we include a principal amount paid at maturity T we can price a fixed rate bond as:

$$P_{bond}(0,T) = \sum_{i}^{N} C D(0,t_i) + D(0,T), \qquad (2.5)$$

where the ith discount factor is given as:

$$D(0,t_i) = \frac{1}{\left(1+z(0,t)\right)^{t_i}}. \qquad (2.6)$$

In general, whereas swap and derivative traders make use of zero rates and construct zero curves, bond traders prefer to work in terms of yields. For bond prices observable in the market, a yield y for a given bond can be determined and for a set of bonds of different maturities and for a given issuer a yield curve can be established. The yield can be interpreted as an effective discounting rate and will for most bond issuers lie above the zero curve due to issuer risk of default or credit risk. If we assume y is the yield of the bond (so $z(0,t) = y$ for a given maturity of bond T) we can rewrite Eq. (2.5) in annualised form as the well known yield equation for a bond:

$$P_{bond}(0,T) = \sum_{i}^{N} \frac{C}{(1+y)^{t_i}} + \frac{1}{(1+y)^{T}}. \qquad (2.7)$$

Here we have considered a coupon paid annually but coupons for a fixed rate bond are also usually paid on a semi-annual basis. If h is the *accrual period* corresponding to a coupon period for a bond of annualised coupon C the coupon paid at the end of the accrual period is given as Ch. In calculating actual interest accrued over a given period several common *date conventions* are used to modify the accrual period. The convention used generally depends on the type of security being considered. The three most popular conventions for exactly calculating the interest paid over a given coupon period are Actual/Actual, 30/360 and Actual/360 and are outlined in Appx (A.2).

The market or *quoted* price for a bond is not the actual price the purchaser will pay. The quoted price does not include accrued interest since the last coupon and is known as the *clean* price. Since the buyer of the bond will receive the next coupon paid by the bond the purchaser must actually pay the *cash price* or *dirty price* which includes any accrued interest since the last coupon date.

2.5 Floating Rate Instruments

The market rate used for short term investments of less than 1 year is usually expressed in terms of a market standard floating rate for example the LIBOR or EURIBOR for Euro rates. These rates are typically quoted as annualised rates for over-night, 1 day, 1 week, 1 month, 3 months, 6 months etc. investment periods. For most floating rate financial instruments 3 month or 6 month rates are commonly used and these correspond to coupon payment periods. For most of this book we will use LIBOR rather than EURIBOR for simplicity to denote floating rates.

Consider a very basic *floating rate note* (FRN) which pays a floating rate coupon f at the end of each coupon period h. We shall assume that the reference or accrual period h is the same for all coupons. The floating rate used for the ith coupon period is usually fixed at the prevailing market rate at the beginning of each coupon period t_i. The floating rate thus corresponds to the forward rate between t_i and t_i+h at time t_i.

The present value today of the FRN is given by the expected value of the future floating cash-flows plus the principal at maturity. Now, in general we don't know what the future forward rates will actually be. It can be shown that to avoid market arbitrage we can consider the future forward rates $f(t_i,t_i,t_i+h)$ to be set equal to today's expected forward rates $f(0,t_i,t_i+h)$. The assumption that today's forward rates are realised simplifies valuation for most cases and is true when a payment is made at the end of the fixing period as with FRNs. If we write the ith forward rate as $f_i = f(0,t_i,t_i+h)$ then in analogy with Eq. (2.4) we can write the FRN value as the present value of the sum of N expected floating rate coupons $f_i h$ plus principal:

$$P_{FRN}(0,T) = \sum_{i}^{N} D(0,t_i + h) f_i h + D(0,T). \qquad (2.8)$$

By substituting from the definition of the forward rate Eq. (2.3), we can show that the value of this FRN, which is exposed to no credit risk, is equal to par (100%). This is a very useful result in financial calculations and demonstrates, what all FRN investors know, that the value of an FRN is insensitive to the level of or changes in interest rates since any changes in floating rates are cancelled by changes in discount factors.

2.6 Interest Rate Swaps

An interest rate swap is simply where a series of fixed (or floating rate) payments is exchanged into a series of floating rate (or fixed rate) flows with a market counterparty. The most common form of interest rate swap is the fixed/floating swap and standard market swap rates are quoted in the interbank market for maturities commonly between 1–20+ years for all major currencies. Figure 2.3 shows a *payer's swap* where a fixed rate is paid in return for a floating rate on the same principal amount.

Valuation of a fixed/floating swap is easy using the present value approach outlined in the last few sections. Consider a swap where we pay a fixed rate C plus principal and receive a floating rate plus principal. Usually, different coupon periods will apply for the fixed and floating legs, for example 3 month floating and 6 month fixed. Assume that we have $j=(1,...,N)$ floating coupons with accrual periods h_j and $i=(1,...,M)$ fixed rate coupons with coupon period l_i. Since the principal amounts are the same on both sides of the swap they cancel and we can write:

$$V_{swap}(0,T) = PV\ Floating\ Leg - PV\ Fixed\ Leg$$

$$= \sum_{j}^{N} D(0,t_j + h_j) f_j h_j - \sum_{i}^{M} D(0,t_i) C l_i . \qquad (2.9)$$

For a market rate swap with initial *mark-to-market* value zero we can derive the fair market coupon or annualised *swap rate* $R(0,T)$ for maturity T. Rearranging the above equation to solve for the swap rate $R(0,T) = C$ we have:

$$R(0,T) = \frac{\left[100\% - D(0,T)\right]}{\sum_{i}^{M} D(0,t_i) l_i}. \qquad (2.10)$$

The market swap rate $R(0,T)$ is the swap level that is conventionally quoted in the market and is the annualised fixed rate paid or received on a market swap with a given maturity T.

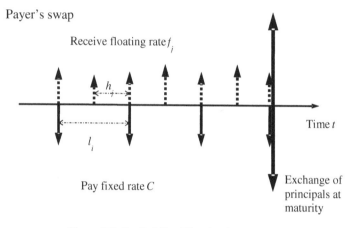

Figure 2.3: Typical fixed/floating interest rate swap.

The simplest swap is the fixed/floating swap, but many other common swaps can exist, ranging from *step-up* and *amortising swaps* where the notional of the swap can "step up" or down during the life of the trade to *currency swaps* where the two legs of the swap are denominated in different currencies. Most follow the methodology described above but some require slight adjustment to the conventional rates used, for example *convexity* and *quanto* adjustments, for correct valuation (Appx A.3).

2.7 Funding Legs for Structured Swaps

As discussed in Section 1.7, structured products are usually based on a swap where the issuer or borrower pays a *funding leg* of a series of floating rate cash-flows plus a fixed rate spread to a swap counterparty in return for a derivative payoff (Fig. 2.4). The derivative payoff is either at maturity for a capital gain structure or periodically during the life for an income structure.

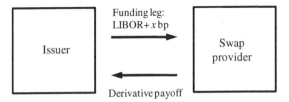

Figure 2.4: Issuer funding leg in a structured swap.

Following Eq. (2.8) the funding leg with N payments can be written as:

$$V_{funding}(0,T) = \sum_{j}^{N} D(0,t_j + h_j)(f_j + x)h_j, \qquad (2.11)$$

where x is the funding spread of the issuer. The funding spread will depend on issuer credit quality and is probably negative since it may include fees on an annual or upfront amount.

2.8 Forwards and Futures

2.8.1 *Forward contracts*

A *forward rate agreement* (FRA) or *forward* is an agreement to buy or sell an asset at a certain specified time in the future at a certain price called the *delivery price* or *strike K*. The advantage of a forward is that it is not necessary to trade the physical cash underlying with all the associated costs that may be involved e.g. custody, stamp duty etc. It is a bilateral OTC contract between two counterparties and is not traded on an exchange. Forward contracts can be written on a wide range of assets including stocks, indices, commodities and interest rates. Some are actually physically settled with delivery of an actual asset and some are simply cash settled.

If the delivery price is K and the price of the asset is $S(T)$ on the maturity date T the buyer of the forward has a long position and a payoff equal to $S(T)-K$ at maturity. Thus, if $S(T)>K$ the buyer will make money and if $S(T)<K$ he will lose money (Fig. 2.5).

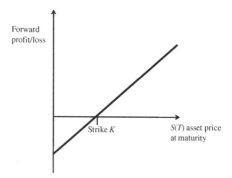

Figure 2.5: Forward contract payoff.

At an earlier time $t<T$ it is possible to provide a rational pricing for the forward contract. If we consider that an asset that pays no income then, for no arbitrage opportunities to exist, the forward price F is given by the expected price of the asset on the maturity date T, discounted back to time t. Using the discount factor between t and T, we can write:

$$F(t,T) = S(t)e^{r(T-t)}.$$

$$(2.12)$$

Here we have assumed that r is a constant, continuously compounded interest rate. If the underlying asset has a known income flow q, for example dividends, the value of the forward contract must be reduced and is given by:

$$F(t,T) = S(t)e^{(r-q)(T-t)}.$$

$$(2.13)$$

These results can be checked with a simple no-arbitrage argument. Assume that at time t we (i) borrow S dollars at rate r then (ii) buy the asset at value $S(t)$ and simultaneously (iii) sell the forward $F(t,T)$. With this strategy we will make a profit of:

$$-S(t)e^{(r-q)(T-t)} + S(T) + (F(t,T) - S(T)).$$

For a no-arbitrage market this must be equal to zero so the fair value of the forward is given by Eq. (2.13). Knowing the value of a forward is important in determining future asset prices for pricing options with future payoffs.

2.8.2 Futures contracts

A *futures* contract is similar to a *forward* but is exchange traded. It has an observable price and is *marked-to-market* daily by the exchange. Also, there is a daily settlement process between counterparties with daily margining to reduce the credit risk between buyer and seller. Futures can exist on a huge range of underlying assets from equity indices to wild hogs.

Of particular interest to us is the Eurodollar futures contract for short-term USD interest rates. The Eurodollar rate is also known as the LIBOR (London Interbank Offered Rate). There also exists similar financial contracts for other currencies, for example Euro Sterling contracts for Sterling LIBOR rates and EURIBOR contracts for Euro interest rates. Originally the Eurodollar interest rate was the rate of interest earned on Euro dollars deposited by one bank with another. This rate is generally slightly higher than the US government Treasury bill rate due to the credit risk of the depositary bank. The liquidity of the Eurodollar futures contract extends out to several years with contracts maturing every 3 months.

The Eurodollar contract is based on the buyer being able to enter a 90 day Eurodollar deposit at the maturity of the contract. If $P_{Fut}(0,T)$ is the price of the futures contract the contract value at today $t=0$ with maturity T is defined as:

$$\$10,000\left[100 - \frac{90}{360}(100 - P_{Fut}(0,T))\right]. \qquad (2.14)$$

Thus the implied 90 day forward rate implied from the futures contract is given by:

$$f_{Fut}(0,T,T+h) = \frac{100 - P_{Fut}(0,T)}{100}, \qquad (2.15)$$

with $h = 90/360 = 0.25$. Due to daily margining and settlement there is an effect called *convexity* which means that in general the forward rate derived from futures contracts is not exactly the true forward rate. This is especially true for maturities beyond a couple of years where up to 25–75bp difference can be observed for 5–10 years. A common convexity correction is discussed in more detail in Appx (A.4). The forward rates derived from first few Eurodollar contracts are often used in building the USD zero coupon curve.

2.9 Building Zero Curves

Until now we have assumed that we know what the zero curve $z(0,t)$ for a given currency is and by using Eq. (2.3) we can evaluate forward rates and discount factors to price bonds, FRNs and swaps. However, the zero curve is not an observable in the market and each bank or financial participant must calculate their own internal zero curve for pricing.

Generally, market LIBOR are used to calculate zero rates for shorter maturities up to 1.5–2 years and then market swap rates can be used for longer maturities via a "bootstrapping" technique (see Fig. 2.6). The "bootstrapping" technique uses the shorter maturity contract to determine the forward rate from the next higher maturity contract (Eq. 2.3). Futures contracts can be used for intermediate maturities. Finally, an interpolation technique is required which can provide "smooth" forward prices. The entire procedure is fairly complex and time consuming and since high accuracy (down to less than 1bp) is required some researchers spend many years programming, perfecting and maintaining their banks zero curves. Luckily information sources such as Bloomberg and Reuters provide almost "market standard" zero curves as part of their analytics packages and built in swap pricing algorithms.

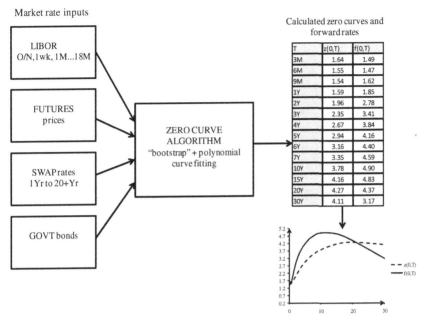

Figure 2.6: Building a market zero curve.

The Forth Bridge Zero Curve

The company zero curve was a bit like painting the Forth Bridge in Scotland – it was never finished since as soon as you got to one end you had to start all over again. There were always modifications to be made, maintenance to be carried out and extra things to include. One of the "quants" seemingly made an entire, well paid career specialising in it and he still can't tell you the perfect way to build it. Which instruments to use? How many futures contracts? What pricing source? How to interpolate the long maturities? How to get a smooth forward rate curve for those interest rate derivative models? Should you "bootstrap" from one end or do everything simultaneously? Different assumptions in different currencies? Also, when you implement the new version you also have annoyed traders on your back if their P&L moves against them suddenly. Frankly, it is all a bit of a nightmare if super accurate trading is required, so to dodge the issue and avoid potential arguments sometimes it is easier to use the standard curves on Reuters and Bloomberg.

Chapter 3

Pricing Equity Options

3.1 Call and Put Options

Options are traded on a huge variety of underlying assets including stocks, indices, long and short term debt, currencies (FX), commodities and futures. Standardised options are exchange traded for example at the LIFFE, CME and IPE exchanges whilst others, particularly those that are more complex, long dated or more illiquid are traded on an *over-the-counter* (OTC) basis with financial counterparties. Here we are interested in options on individual equities or equity indices. The most basic type of options are *call* and *put* options.

Buying a *call option* allows the purchaser to buy the *underlying* asset at a pre-agreed fixed price (the *strike price*) on the *maturity* date. Obviously, the holder of the option will *exercise* the call option and profit if the underlying rises above the strike price. Conversely, he will decide not to purchase the underlying asset if the underlying lies beneath the strike at maturity. A call option is thus suitable for an investor who is "bullish" and feels the underlying will rise in value whilst limiting downside risk.

A *put option* is essentially the inverse of a call option. Purchasing a put option allows the purchaser to sell the underlying asset at a fixed price or strike price at the maturity date. Thus, if the underlying asset falls in value beneath the strike, the holder will exercise the put option and make a profit. A put option allows an investor to take a bearish view on the underlying.

The payoff at maturity for a call option is thus

$$Payoff_{Call} = Max(S(T) - K, 0), \qquad (3.1)$$

35

where $S(T)$ is the value of the underlying on the maturity date T and K is the strike price. For a put option the payoff is similarly given by

$$Payoff_{Put} = Max(K - S(T),0).$$ (3.2)

These maturity payoff profiles are shown in Fig. 3.1 below.

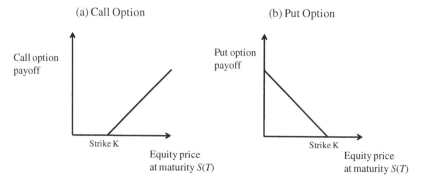

Figure 3.1: Call and put option payoffs at maturity.

Notice that buying a call and selling a put is equivalent to a forward contract with strike K. This is called *put-call parity* and is actually even true before the maturity date.

$$Payoff_{Call} - Payoff_{Put} = Max(S(T) - K,0) - Max(K - S(T),0)$$
$$= S(T) - K.$$

The amount paid for an option is called the *premium*. The premium is the sum of the *intrinsic value* and the *time value*.

Premium = Option Value = Intrinsic Value + Time Value.

The intrinsic value is effectively the value of the option if it could be exercised today and is thus $Max(S(t)-K,0)$ for a call option, where t is the current time $t < T$. This is illustrated in Fig. 3.2. For a call option if the price of the underlying is above the strike ($S > K$) the option is said to be *in-the-money* (ITM) and has positive intrinsic value. Call options where $S < K$ are *out-of-the-money* (OTM) and have zero intrinsic value.

An option for which the underlying trades at exactly the strike $S = K$ is termed *at-the-money* (ATM).

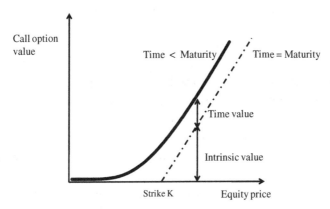

Figure 3.2: Intrinsic value and time value for a call option.

The time value is the value placed on the probability of the option moving into the money or of further increasing in value before the maturity date. Thus a call option which is OTM even though it has zero intrinsic value will still have residual time value due to the fact that the underlying may rise and finish above the strike before the maturity date. As an option reaches expiry or the maturity date the time value falls to zero and the option price converges to the intrinsic value.

Options that can only be exercised by the holder on a fixed maturity date are termed *European* options. Many options can be exercised at any time before maturity and are called *American* options. *Bermudan* options are exercisable only on predefined dates for example annually. In general simple European call options have exactly the same price as American options.

The factors influencing the premium of an equity option are as follows:
- The current stock price.
- The strike level.
- The time to maturity or expiry.
- The volatility of the underlying stock price.
- The current interest rate.
- The future dividends paid by the stock.

We can see that some of these factors: equity price, dividends and volatility are properties of the equity underlying itself and others, such as strike and maturity are parameters of the option structure.

3.2 Modelling Stock Prices

The underlying stock prices used in options pricing are commonly modelled by relatively simple *stochastic* or randomised processes. These random processes or "random walks" are identical to those used to describe *diffusion* processes in physics, like thermal diffusion or random movement of particles in *Brownian* motion. Typically, these models are described as *Markov* processes, where only the present value or price of the underlying variable is used to determine the future evolution of the price. Any historical information or past history is irrelevant in predicting future price changes. The assumption of these random walk processes governing price movements is a key feature of financial "efficient" market models and the "foundation" of all derivative pricing models. In general, this is a good assumption for deep, liquid equity markets, but are obviously not true for more inefficient markets where information flow and liquidity are constrained, for example small cap stocks, equity special situations and probably many credit markets.

Stock prices are most frequently modelled as *geometric* Brownian motion. For each small discrete time period Δt the change in stock price ΔS is related to an overall drift μ and a random change Δz

$$\frac{\Delta S(t)}{S(t)} = \mu \, \Delta t + \sigma \, \Delta z. \tag{3.3}$$

Here σ is the volatility per unit time of the stock price $S(t)$ at time t. The random variable Δz is randomly distributed with mean 0 and variance Δt, so we can write $\Delta z \sim \phi(0, \Delta t)$. Thus, for each time step Δt the random variable $\Delta z = \Delta t^{1/2} Z$ where $Z \sim \phi(0,1)$ is a number drawn from a standardised normal distribution with mean 0 and variance 1. A normal distribution gives the characteristic "bell" shape of Fig. 3.3. The distribution is symmetric and the central maximum corresponds to a cumulative probability of 0.5. The cumulative normal distribution N is defined such that $Pr(Z \leq z) < N(z)$.

The expected relative equity return $\Delta S/S$ over time period Δt is equal to the drift over the period $\mu \Delta t$ and the variance of the return $\sigma^2 \Delta t$. The relative change $\Delta S/S$ in $S(t)$ is normally distributed $\phi(\mu \Delta t, \sigma^2 \Delta t)$ but the absolute change ΔS is called *lognormally* distributed. This means that stock prices cannot go negative (Appx B.1).

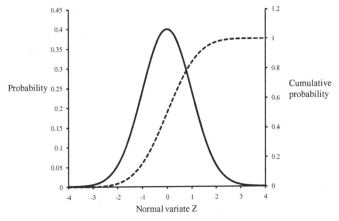

Figure 3.3: Normal distribution and cumulative normal distribution.

Using this model we can estimate volatilities from the variance of historical price data. Typically equity indices might have annualised long term volatilities of around 15–20%, blue-chip equities approximately 20–30% and TMT (technology, media, telecom) equities 30–60%. In option pricing however, for consistent market pricing, volatilities are implied from the market price of equity options traded on an exchange or between banks. We shall discuss this in more detail later.

3.3 The Black–Scholes Equation

The famous Black–Scholes pricing equations for call and put options were first published in the landmark paper by F. Black and M. Scholes in 1973 and Merton in the same year. Scholes and Merton were subsequently awarded the Nobel Prize in 1997. The success of these equations has led to them being the industry standard pricing model for European options on a wide variety of underlying assets ranging from equities and equity indices to currencies and commodities.

Real Markets and the BHP Distribution

Now the use of the normal distribution in financial statistics is essentially a first order assumption. It is a pretty robust assumption, provided movements or fluctuations are not too big and remain not much greater than the standard deviation. This simplification leads to analytic tractability, for example in Black–Scholes, where the equation of state leads to lognormal movements in stock prices and indices. Real financial market returns, however, have "fat tails" meaning extreme events or movements occur far more than usual. Also real return distributions are often asymmetric with tendency to fall faster than they rise and many of these "tail" effects are captured in the implied market volatility smile of equity options.

There is, however, a little known but better probability distribution: the Bramwell–Holdsworth–Pinton (BHP) distribution, where the "B" is named after my friend Steve Bramwell; recent discoverer of "magnetricity" and "magnetic monopoles". This distribution has only one free parameter (the standard deviation) and manages to fit the return distribution of major market indices down to an incredible 4–5 orders of magnitude. The distribution was originally derived for dealing with fluctuations in magnetism in 2-dimensional magnets, but since it is based on a universal statistical behaviour for a class of bounded physical systems, it bizarrely describes exactly diverse phenomena, such as the height of the river Danube, turbulence, trees burnt in forest fires, animal distributions in game parks...and more recently stock markets.

The Black–Scholes analysis is dependent on several major assumptions that are assumed to apply in efficient, deeply liquid markets. These assumptions include:

1. The stock price follows geometric Brownian motion with a constant volatility as Eq. (3.3).
2. The volatility is constant and not dependent on time and price level of the underlying.
3. There are no transaction costs, bid/offer spreads or taxes.
4. Short selling of securities is possible.
5. Trading and hedging is continuous and not discrete.

Although these assumptions are only a theoretical ideal a more detailed analysis on the effect of bid/offer spread, discrete hedging and other "real world imperfections" shows that the Black–Scholes analysis is remarkably robust. Most effects can be accommodated by slightly modifying the volatility used in the calculation (Appx B.17–B.18).

Now Eq. (3.3) is used to derive Black–Scholes equations (Appx B.3). The key argument in deriving these equations is the concept of *risk neutrality* in options pricing. The argument is that if we can instantaneously hedge an option with an amount of equity over a small time period Δt, we can always make a portfolio of options plus a certain amount of equities, independent of the movement of the equity ΔS. The portfolio of option plus equity is thus hedged against random price movements and "instantaneously riskless" over the period Δt. Obviously, for a hedged portfolio in an efficient market the investor in the portfolio cannot earn more than the risk free interest rate r. Thus, we can set the riskless portfolio return to be r. This means that in Eq. (3.3) we can replace μ by r, the risk free interest rate. The key argument is presented in Fig. 3.4 where we form a riskless portfolio by being long an option and selling an amount (called a *delta* amount) of equities against it. Thus, all option contracts can in fact be valued using the risk free rate instead of the observed market drift of the underlying stock. This effect is known as *risk neutral valuation*. It is a very important result since it means that all investors for the purposes of derivative valuation can be considered as being *risk neutral* and in the *risk neutral world* the expected return on all investment assets is the risk free rate. It simplifies derivative analysis and means that any solutions or prices we derive are valid in the real world. A more detailed analysis is contained in Appx (B.3).

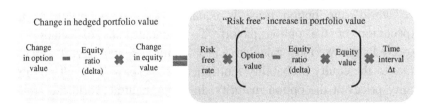

Figure 3.4: The risk neutral argument.

Since the growth rate μ of the stock can be replaced by the risk free interest rate r, the risk neutral process for the stock price is now given from Eq. (3.3) as

$$\frac{dS(t)}{S(t)} = r\,dt + \sigma\,dz.$$

(3.4)

This assumes $\Delta t \to dt$ in the continuous differential limit of small time intervals. The process can be integrated over time t to give the value for the result for the stock price at any future time which follows a lognormal distribution

$$S(t) = S(0)\,e^{(r-\frac{\sigma^2}{2})t + \sigma\sqrt{\Delta t}\,Z},$$

(3.5)

where $Z \sim \phi(0,1)$ is normally distributed (Appx B.4). The random value of the stock price $S(t)$ at later time t is given from the initial value of the stock price $S(0)$. Notice the drift term is not just related to the interest rate r but includes an additional term related to the volatility $-\sigma^2 t/2$. If we wish to include a continuous dividend, this is simple, since from the definition of a forward Eq. (2.13) we must replace r by $(r - q)$ so the effective drift in the risk neutral world is reduced by an amount q.

3.4 The Black–Scholes Option Pricing Equation

Although it is not entirely necessary for the understanding of the rest of this book, it is worth attempting to understand the origins of the Black–Scholes option pricing equation. We shall attempt to outline the concepts with the minimum of mathematics, but unfortunately some is necessary. More details are contained in Appx (B.5).

The fundamental concept in options pricing is that in an "arbitrage free world" the option price is equal to the present value of the expectation of the option payoff. To calculate this expectation or expected value we must calculate a probability weighted payoff which is equal to the equity probability multiplied by the payoff for all possible equity prices at the option maturity. In a risk neutral world the equity lognormal probability distribution is given by Eq. (3.5) and present value discounting will use the risk free rate r.

Consider a call option with final payoff $Max(S(T)-K,0)$ at maturity T. In Fig. 3.5 we show the probability distribution for the final stock price $Pr(S(T))$. This probability distribution is lognormal and is centred about the forward price of the stock. The forward price is obviously slightly different than the initial price due to the drift term in Eq. (3.5). Now for an option with, for example strike $K = 150\%$, the only non-zero payoffs are in the tail of the distribution (the shaded area). To calculate the probability weighted payoff we must multiply the payoff $(S(T)-K)$ in this region by the probability. Effectively, this amounts to an integration over probability $Pr(S(T))$ multiplied by payoff $Max(S(T)-K,0)$ to obtain the expected value. This expected value must then be discounted back to today using a discount factor $D(0,T)$ to give the present value of the expected payoff.

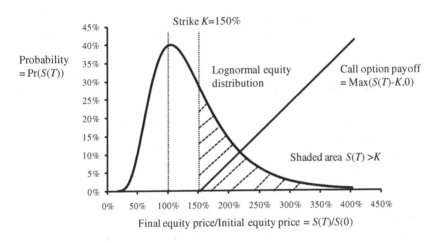

Figure 3.5: Black–Scholes call option valuation.

Mathematically we can write this integral as

$$P_{Call}(0,T) = D(0,T) \int_{K}^{\infty} Pr(S(T))(S(T) - K)\, dS(T). \qquad (3.6)$$

Using Eq. (3.5) we can perform this integration to arrive at the Black–Scholes call option price (Appx B.5).

$$P_{Call}(0,T) = S(0)\,N(d_1) - e^{-rT}K\,N(d_2), \qquad (3.7)$$

where N is the cumulative normal distribution and

$$d_1 = \frac{\ln(S(0)/K) + (r + \sigma^2/2)T}{\sigma\sqrt{T}} \qquad (3.8)$$

$$d_2 = d_1 - \sigma\sqrt{T}.$$

The value of the put option can be derived in a similar way and results in

$$P_{Put}(0,T) = e^{-rT}K\,N(-d_2) - S(0)\,N(-d_1). \qquad (3.9)$$

The above equations can be easily modified to include equity dividends. From our discussion in Chapter 2 we had for the forward Eq. (2.13) indicating we can replace $S(0)$ with $S(0)e^{-qT}$ for a stock paying a continuous dividend q.

3.5 Market Implied Volatility

The key unknown variable in using the Black–Scholes equation remains the volatility. We could use historic volatilities but since the market prices for equity options are readily quoted in the market we can invert Eq. (3.7) and Eq. (3.9) to calculate *implied* volatilities for different strikes K and maturities T. We shall denote these implied volatilities as $\sigma(K,T)$.

Now it turns out that the implied volatility $\sigma(K,T)$ is not a constant value but constitutes rather a concave surface in K and T. For a given maturity T it exhibits a "smile" or curvature for different strikes K. This effect is often most pronounced for indices and is demonstrated for the DJ Eurostoxx50 Index in Fig. 3.6. Generally, the *volatility smile* is greatest for shorter maturities and flattens out for longer maturities. The slope at any point is called the *skew*. The volatility surface itself evolves with time and is in itself a dynamic random variable. The smile reflects the fact that the Black–Scholes model is a simplification and does not truly model reality. The future distribution of stock prices implied from the market is obviously not lognormal due to numerous possible effects including supply/demand, worries about a future market crash, etc.

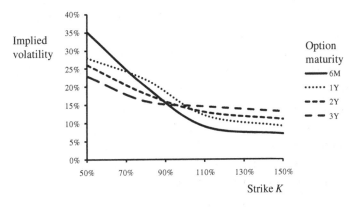

Figure 3.6: Typical DJ Eurostoxx 50 equity index volatility smiles.

The Auto Vol Surface Terminator

I had a friend who was a derivatives pioneer and his goal (now realised to be practically impossible) was to price his bank's entire equity derivatives exotics book on a consistent basis using one volatility surface constructed automatically from daily market volatilities. No human intervention. The human was taken out of the loop just like in Arnie's Terminator film. The theory looked great, the system was built, his superior's suitably impressed (if you can take a subjective trader out of the loop so much the better!) and everybody signed off on the methodology. The "D-day" for going live arrived, the machine was plugged in and took over. For the first few weeks it was great, everything was stable and it worked perfectly. Then the market and volatility surface moved in a peculiar way that was a bit unexpected and then, day after day the system started to slowly haemorrhage money. He hoped it would come back and explained it was a short term "glitch" but things got progressively worse and, after creating a big hole in the P&L, the system was unplugged and thrown away. After a couple of years of trading no exotic options, they went back to doing things manually the old way with different trades, having different manual vols in a totally inconsistent and theoretically unpleasing way.

Thus, a major shortcoming of the Black–Scholes model is that we cannot use one consistent volatility. Our practical approach becomes one of using conservative estimates and volatility bounds. This is particularly troublesome for many exotic options that include barriers, cliquets and forward starting options. Fortunately, most exotic structured products have longer maturities where the volatility curve starts to flatten but nevertheless estimating and trading volatility is the major skill of traders. Unfortunately, it is often impossible to tell whether the initial volatility estimate was correct until at maturity and a thorough audit is made of the P&L of a particular trade along with the associated hedges many years after the trade was initiated...and who bothers to actually do that.

In an attempt to fit the volatility smile in a more theoretically pleasing way various schemes have been attempted and these are described in Appx (B). Simple variations of the Black–Scholes process including skewed probability distributions and jump-diffusion processes exist (Appx B.14). Another alternative is to use an implied volatility model where local volatilities from the volatility surface are used to price options using a deformed binomial tree (Appx B.15). Lastly, stochastic volatility models where the volatility follows a stochastic process remain the subject of much research (Appx B.16).

3.6 Option Price Sensitivities – "The Greeks"

From the Black–Scholes pricing formula we can calculate the sensitivity of the option price to different market parameters. Although the stock price and time to maturity are the major underlying variables in the Black–Scholes analysis, the assumption that interest rates and volatilities are constant is clearly an approximation. In practice rates and volatility will change over time and influence the value of the option.

The price of any derivative can be expanded as a series to changes in the various underlying pricing parameters or sensitivities (Appx B.8). These sensitivities have been given several well known names and are collectively known as the "greeks". The major greeks are:

- Delta – the sensitivity of the option price to changes in the underlying price.

- Gamma – the change of delta with respect to changes in the underlying and thus the first derivative of delta.

- Vega – the sensitivity to changes in implied volatility.

- Theta – the change in price of the option with time and thus a measure of the decay of time value.

- Rho – the sensitivity to interest rates.

Here we will describe the major greeks for simple vanilla call and put options but in practice for exotic options more complex greeks can be derived but they are evaluated in a similar manner but generate different profiles.

3.6.1 *Delta*

Delta or Δ is the sensitivity of the option price to the movements in the underlying stock price and is arguably the most important greek. Thus, for each call option we can sell Δ amount of stocks against it to hedge against movements in the underlying price. The delta is the gradient or slope of the option price versus the equity price (see Fig. 3.7). Mathematically, it is calculated as the first derivative with respect to the equity price $\partial P_{call} / \partial S$.

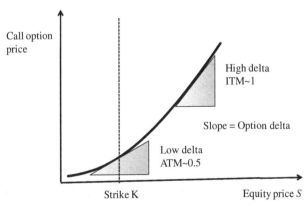

Figure 3.7: Call option deltas equal the gradient $\partial P_{Call} / \partial S$.

For an option deeply out-of-the-money the delta is close to zero, whereas for an option deeply in-the-money, the delta approaches 1 to reflect the fact that it is certain to be exercised and behaves like the underling equity. An option that is at-the-money has a delta close to 0.5. A typical delta profile is shown in Fig. 3.8(a).

3.6.2 Gamma

A hedge in delta is only an instantaneous hedge and as the underlying stock price moves the delta will gradually change according to the gamma. The delta should thus be recalculated and re-hedged on a periodic basis or when the underlying price has moved significantly to remain delta neutral.

The gamma is the rate of change of delta with respect to the equity price and is the same for a call and a put option. Thus, the gamma is the second order differential of the option price. Since the rate of change of delta is always positive, gamma is always positive. The gradient of delta is highest at-the-money and this provides a maximum for gamma. Gamma approaches zero for deeply in-the-money or out-of-the-money options (Fig. 3.8(b)).

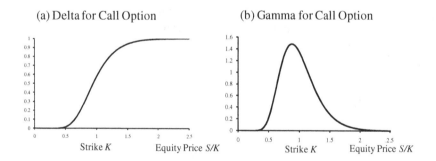

Figure 3.8: Call option delta and gamma.

3.6.3 Vega

The vega is the change in option price with respect to implied volatility so $\partial P_{Call}/\partial \sigma$. It is the same for calls and puts and always positive for the holder of the option who has "bought vol" and is thus "long vol". Vega has a maximum at-the-money (Fig. 3.9(a)) and can be hedged using other options which themselves have an offsetting vega.

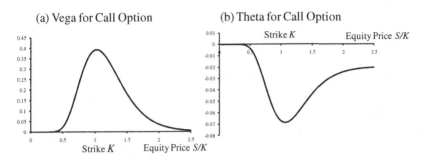

Figure 3.9: Call option vega and theta.

3.6.4 *Theta*

Theta is a measure of the change in time value of an option and by convention is always negative for the holder of an option. It is not really a parameter which is hedged but merely expresses the impact of *time decay* on the price of an option. For an at-the-money call theta is largest (see Fig. 3.9(b)).

3.6.5 *Hedging portfolios using greeks*

The sensitivities or greeks can be used to *dynamically* hedge the value of an option or a portfolio of options and stocks against market movements. For a portfolio, the aggregate sensitivities (deltas, gammas, vegas...) must be considered. For example, to hedge the portfolio against small movements in the stock price, the overall portfolio delta must be set close to zero. This is achieved by varying the weights ω_i of the M instruments (stocks and options) comprising the portfolio each with delta Δ_i ($i = 1,2,...,M$).

$$\Delta_{portfolio} = \sum_{i=1}^{M} \omega_i \Delta_i = 0 \qquad (3.10)$$

Similarly, the portfolio gamma and vega can be hedged if there exists several different option contracts with which to hedge. In practice, most options traders will hedge the portfolio delta and trade the gamma and the vega.

3.7 Numerical Methods

Closed form solutions of Black–Scholes equation can be found to value a wide range of European style options. For more exotic options, and in particular American and Bermudan style options with early exercise features, various numerical methods can be used. Although the computational calculation time for these numerical techniques is somewhat slower than for closed form solutions, they provide great flexibility and provide the ability to calculate a wide range of option types.

The randomised equity process given by Eq. (3.4) is essentially a diffusion process. It is possible to establish a *partial differential equation* (PDE) for any type of option involving the equity price as an underlying (Appx B.3). This differential equation is called the Black–Scholes PDE and can be solved using various numerical methods subject to different boundary conditions (which describe different payoff functions). The three major numerical techniques which are most commonly used are:

- Binomial tree
- Monte Carlo simulation
- PDE lattice techniques

In reality, the binomial tree is a very simple form of PDE lattice technique but often is viewed as distinct in the market. Here we shall describe briefly the two former techniques and provide a more detailed mathematical explanation of all three techniques in Appx (B.9–B.13).

3.7.1 *Binomial trees*

The *binomial tree* is perhaps the simplest numerical technique used to solve the Black–Scholes PDE and is widely used for pricing simple American and Bermudan options and options that evade a closed form solution. It is not really suitable for path dependent options, such as *lookbacks,* where Monte Carlo simulation is the preferred method. The advantage of the binomial tree is that it is robust, simple to debug, and can be quickly implemented even within a spreadsheet.

Consider the movement of a stock of price $S(t)$ at time t that can move with a *binomial* process to either a higher price $S(t)u$ with probability p or to a lower price $S(t)d$ with probability $(1-p)$ at a later time $t+\Delta t$. This *binomial fork* is shown in Fig. 3.10(a).

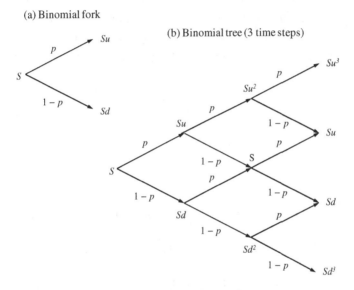

(a) Binomial fork

(b) Binomial tree (3 time steps)

Figure 3.10: Building a binomial tree.

We can find mathematical expressions for the branching probability p and the factors u and d by comparing the expected value and variance of this binomial process to that given by the Black–Scholes Eq. (3.4). To solve for p, u and d simultaneously, we can impose the condition $u = 1/d$. This condition allows the building of a *recombining* binomial tree, since an up movement followed by a down movement is equivalent to a down then an up movement $Sud = Sdu$ etc. This provides the following simple equations for the probability p and the multipliers u and d:

$$p=\frac{a-d}{u-d}, \qquad u = e^{\sigma\sqrt{\Delta t}}, \qquad d = e^{-\sigma\sqrt{\Delta t}}, \qquad a = e^{r\Delta t}. \quad (3.11)$$

Using, this result we can build a binomial lattice or tree of stock prices (Fig. 3.10(b)). This binomial tree can be used to value a range of different option contracts.

Consider the valuation of a simple call option. Usually the terminal node is set equal to the option payoff at maturity. At maturity T the exercise value of the option is known from the payoff and can be calculated for each terminal node as $V(T) = Max(S(T)-K,0)$. The common technique is then to "roll-back" in time the option value from the terminal time slice to the previous earlier time slice. This is done by working out the discounted average payoff each node at time t from the two connected later nodes at time $(t + \Delta t)$ using the probabilities p and $(1-p)$ and applying a discount factor for one time slice (see Fig. 3.11).

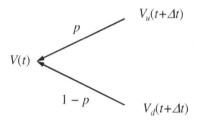

Figure 3.11: Rolling back through the tree at a node.

For an individual fork this can be mathematically written as

$$V(t) = D(t,t + \Delta t)\big[pV_u(t + \Delta t) + (1 - p)V_d(t + \Delta t)\big] \qquad (3.12)$$

where V_u and V_d are the option values at the later connected nodes. By rolling like this back though the tree an option value can be computed at every node and eventually when the first node at time zero $V(0)$ is reached the initial option value is given. This process is detailed in (Appx B.9) and gives the value for a European option with no early exercise.

For an American option, early exercise can occur. At each node the roll-back value is compared with the intrinsic value at the node to see whether it is more profitable for an investor to exercise at the node or continue to hold the option. The value at the node during the roll-back is given by the maximum of the intrinsic value or the current option value.

Using this approach we can price many types of options, including, importantly, those with early exercise features, such as Bermudans and Americans (Appx B.9). The binomial tree can even be used to price *convertible bonds* if we assume rates and credit spreads are non-stochastic and have constant term structures (Appx B.10). Barrier options, due their discontinuous nature, can however present a problem and various solutions have been proposed to improve accuracy when dealing with these. Although these solutions are all a compromise between computational efficiency and precision, one technique is to distort the tree to actually place tree nodes on the barrier and another (which I prefer) is to use a separate interpolative procedure if a barrier lies between nodes. With the latter approach, it is even possible to build in a mini closed form or (log)normal distribution at nodes adjacent to the barrier which gives pretty much exact prices and greeks.

From the binomial tree we can directly approximate some of the greek hedging parameters, for example deltas can be calculated as the difference in option price between the two nodes on the second time slice. To include equity dividends on the tree we must rebuild the tree slightly. Several approaches are available depending on whether we wish to use known continuous dividends, proportional dividends or absolute dividends. The simplest is for continuous dividends as in Black–Scholes where the drift parameter a must be modified to include a continuous dividend q by replacing r with $(r-q)$ in Eq. (3.11).

The method for tree building above assumes that interest rates are flat over time. Over short time horizons this is a good approximation when equity volatilities are the dominant feature in pricing. However, sometimes it is important to include some form of term-structure for interest rates. The simplest way to include the rate term-structure is to substitute the constant interest rate r at each time slice with the forward rate.

We have described a binomial tree for one stochastic variable but it is obviously possible to extend easily to at least one more dimension having therefore two stochastic variables by building a *three-dimensional* or *3D tree*. Correlation between the two underlying assets can be included and the 3D tree can be used to value a range of options with two underlying equities such as spread options and exchange options (Appx B.11)

3.7.2 *Monte Carlo simulation*

Monte Carlo simulation is a very simple and highly flexible approach to pricing options. It is well suited to path dependent and barrier options, where information for the final option payoff must be calculated and stored along each path. The technique is best suited to European style options and including American and Bermudan early exercise features is extremely complex to perform with reasonable computational efficiency.

In a Monte Carlo simulation a *future path* of the stock price is simulated from the Black–Scholes equation and the option payoff for the individual path recorded. By generating a large number of paths and possible payoffs an average or expected payoff can be statistically established and the option price estimated.

In the simplest form of Monte Carlo the basic Black–Scholes lognormal stock process is discretised into small time intervals Δt. Assume that each simulation path contains N equal time steps of interval Δt such that at the maturity of the option $T = N\Delta t$. We simulate each path by generating a series of independent normally distributed random variables $Z \sim \phi(0,1)$. The stock price for time t_{i+1} is given from the previous time step t_i by

$$S(t_{i+1}) = S(t_i) + \Delta S(t_i))$$
$$= S(t_i)\left[1 + (r-q)\Delta t + \sigma\sqrt{\Delta t}\, Z_i\right]. \qquad (3.13)$$

This method is fine for small time steps Δt but an alternative and more accurate method is to use Eq. (3.5) to jump accurately large distances or steps in time if required – for example just simulating at coupon dates or averaging dates (Appx B.12).

Consider pricing a call option using Monte Carlo. At maturity the payoff can be computed for each path and stored. After M simulations we can then work out the average payoff and discounting this back to time zero gives the option payoff. This is written mathematically as the discounted average payoff of the M paths

$$P_{Call}(0,T,K) \sim \frac{D(0,T)}{M}\sum_{j}^{M} Max(S_j(T)-K,0), \qquad (3.14)$$

where the sum is over the payout of the *j*th path for $j=(1,2,...,M)$. This process is shown schematically for a few paths in Fig. 3.12.

Valuing puts and calls is trivial and the real power of Monte Carlo is calculating path dependent options and options with path dependent resets and barriers. *Lookback options* are easy since we can store the maximum or minimum value along each path (Appx B.12.1). Similarly for *average rate options* we can include time steps at each desired averaging point for each path (Appx B.12.2).

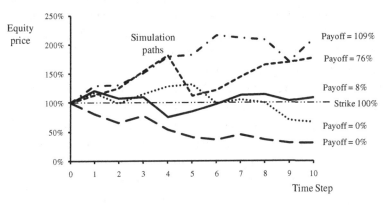

Figure 3.12: Monte Carlo valuation of call option with five sample paths.

With a standard Monte Carlo simulation the standard computational pricing error ε is inversely proportional to the square root of the number of simulation paths. If σ_{obs} is the observed variance of the discounted payoff the standard error is

$$\varepsilon \propto \frac{\sigma_{obs}}{\sqrt{M}}. \tag{3.15}$$

In addition, the error increases approximately linearly with the number of "dimensions". By dimensions we mean the number of stochastic variables or number of fixings to some degree. Thus, a 5 year monthly lookback option or a 5 year basket option with 10 stocks will take significantly longer to converge to than a vanilla call option. Once the number of dimensions becomes large and the accuracy required is high, the time demanded for computation can become impractical. Various "speed-up" algorithms have been developed and can be applied. These include fancy named algorithms such as Brownian bridges, antithetic variables, control variates, quasi-random number sequences and weighted Monte Carlo. My favourite technique is quasi-random numbers and in particular Sobol sequences, which are outlined (along with most of the other techniques) in the great book by W. Press *et al.* (see Further Reading).

Since evaluating greek hedging parameters (delta, gamma, etc.) requires calculating small changes in option prices, great care is required when using Monte Carlo. The simplest approach is to perturbate the inputs slightly and recalculate using the same stored random number sequences.

We previously noted that pricing American and Bermudan options using Monte Carlo is very complex. So-called *American Monte Carlo* has come a long way in the last few years though and is becoming more widespread in solving certain problems (particularly in interest rate pricing of Bermudan swaptions). For early exercise we need to work out the current option price at every point and compare the intrinsic option value to see whether it is worth exercising the option. Unfortunately, Monte Carlo is a forward moving process (a forward simulation that advances in time), so it is difficult to obtain the current option price unless we perform a mini Monte Carlo at each simulation point. If you do this, however, it results in a "bushy" Monte Carlo with a huge number of simulation paths. Several methods are used to get round this problem and most involve determining the *exercise boundary* – the boundary (or surface) in the underlying variables with time at which it is efficient to exercise the option. A few Monte Carlo simulations can be used to estimate this boundary and then through suitable interpolation a continuous boundary can be constructed. The estimated exercise boundary is then used in the full-blown Monte Carlo to price the option. Sounds simple but estimating the exercise boundary is fairly non-trivial and instrument specific.

3.8 Digitals and Barrier Options

Digital call options (sometimes called *binaries*) are extremely popular and have a discrete or digital payoff at maturity should the underlying lie above the strike. Digital puts are the opposite and payoff should the underlying fall below the strike at maturity.

In their simplest form, *barrier call* options payoff if the underlying rises above the strike at any time during the life of the option and not just at maturity as with digitals. Usually, the barrier is specified as being monitored continuously or on a daily basis. Since we can assign a strike to both the barrier and a strike to the final payoff function many forms of barrier options can be constructed. For example, a *knock-out call* option may have call with strike K_1 that disappears, should the underlying fall below a certain strike K_2.

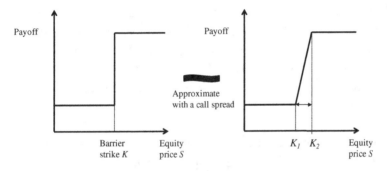

Figure 3.13: Approximating digitals with call spreads.

Both digitals and barriers are included in many investment products. Black–Scholes closed forms exist for digitals and continuous barrier options and these are detailed in the Appx (C.5–C.6). However, actually trading barriers can be very difficult due to their discrete nature which can render hedging extremely problematic. Consider a digital option close to maturity where the underlying is close to the strike. The trader might have to pay out a large sum if the option finishes above the barrier or zero otherwise. The greek parameters become meaningless in such a situation since the slope of the payoff (the delta) is theoretically infinite at the strike. One common technique for dealing with this is to over-hedge by approximating the digital call option as a *call spread* (see Fig. 3.13). If, for example the digital strike is 100% we can approximate with a "95/100%" or say "98/102%" call spread and apply a suitable volatility smile to the two options composing the call spread. Obviously, this leads to conservative prices but building spread options into digital and barrier models makes hedging much easier.

3.9 FX Options and Quantos

Until now we have considered all instruments that are priced in the same currency but often many products involve investing in indices or equities that are denominated in a foreign currency. Imagine a Euro (EUR) denominated investor that wishes to invest in the FTSE index which is denominated in Sterling (GBP). The traditional route is to take currency risk on his investment by (i) converting EUR to GBP, (ii) buying the FTSE index in GBP, (iii) at maturity sell the FTSE in GBP and (iv) convert the GBP proceeds back into EUR. In doing so the investor is exposed to both volatility on the FTSE index and the GBP/EUR exchange rate. The alternative is to hedge the FX risk and invest just in the actual price risk of the FTSE. The actual FX rate becomes irrelevant as is effectively locked-in at its initial level. Investments which hedge this FX risk are termed *quantoed* products and in practice most structured products are automatically *quanto* the underlying.

Fortunately, quanto pricing is practically very easy in the Black–Scholes framework although perhaps conceptually a bit difficult to understand (Appx B.20). A modified Black–Scholes model can be used to price currency options if we recognise that a cash investor in a foreign currency receives an interest rate or yield in a foreign currency which is analogous to holding a dividend paying equity (Appx B.19).

On this basis, if we wish to eliminate currency risk for investors, we must modify the drift in the Black–Scholes equity equation to retain risk neutrality. If ρ is the correlation between the FX rate and the equity price for a quantoed equity we must modify the equity dividend yield to be

$$q^* = (q + r - r_f + \rho \sigma_{FX} \sigma_f), \qquad (3.16)$$

where r is the domestic currency interest rate and r_f the foreign interest rate. The FX rate process has a volatility of σ_{FX} and σ_f the foreign equity volatility (that is being quantoed). Fortunately, the quanto correlation term is usually is quite small using correlations obtained from historical data. By replacing the dividend yield with Eq. (3.16) in all the previous Black–Scholes equations we can simply price quanto products where all the FX risk has been removed for investors.

Chapter 4

Equity Structured Products

4.1 Introduction

There exists an extremely wide range of equity derivative based products available to the investor. In this chapter we shall focus on popular products that have one underlying asset – either an equity or an index. Single name products can be primarily distinguished by whether they are structured for income or capital gain and whether they have a capital guarantee of some form.

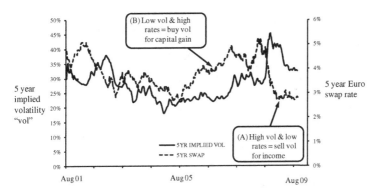

Figure 4.1: DJ Eurostoxx50 equity index historic implied volatilities and 5 year swap rates.

It is interesting to consider at which point in the market cycle certain products are a good investment from a relative value point of view. If implied volatilities are high "selling", volatility or "vol" by selling options is the best trade. If interest rates are low this favours buying reverse convertibles or other yield products where coupon is enhanced through selling options, for example (A) in Fig. 4.1.

However, if interest rates are high, then capital guaranteed structures look more attractive since the zero coupon bond which provides the capital guarantee is cheaper. This allows a larger amount of option to be purchased creating a higher *participation* in the index performance. If option volatility is relatively low then, this further increases the amount of option that can be purchased. Thus capital gain products with capital guarantees are favoured by high rates and low volatilities, for example (B) in Fig. 4.1.

4.2 Reverse Convertibles

The *reverse convertible* note is one of the most successful structured equity products of recent years in Europe and Asia providing high income but with no capital guarantee. Most major banks propose a range of reverse convertibles on different underlying stocks and indices to both their retail and institutional client bases.

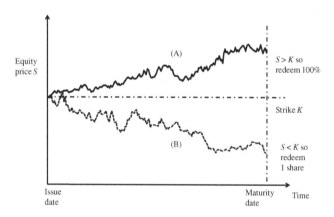

Figure 4.2: Possible reverse convertible redemptions.

Reverse convertibles are generally short dated (3 months to 1 year maturity) on single stocks and up to 3–5 years on indices. The investor effectively sells a put on an underlying share or index to provide an enhanced fixed coupon. They are non-capital guaranteed investments exposing the investor to capital loss, should the underlying fall. Typically, for short dated reverse convertibles on single stocks the nominal size of each note is equal to the initial underlying share price on the issue date. If the underlying share has not fallen by the maturity date the investor is redeemed at 100% plus a large fixed coupon (Fig. 4.2 scenario A). Should, however, the share have fallen by the maturity date the investor is redeemed physically with one share plus the high coupon (Fig. 4.2 scenario B). Although physical settlement is most common some reverse converts are structured to be cash settled and this is always true for those on indices and for retail products where it is too complex to deliver the physical underlying.

Example 4.1

16.0% USD REVERSE CONVERTIBLE NOTES ON ALCATEL	
ISSUER	: AA rated Issuer
CURRENCY	: USD
MATURITY	: 1 year
ISSUE PRICE	: 100%
UNDERLYING	: ALCATEL
ANNUAL COUPON	: 16.0%
DENOMINATION	: 100% × $ALCATEL_{initial}$, the opening price of the Underlying on the Issue Date.
REDEMPTION	: Each Note will be redeemed at maturity as follows depending on $ALCATEL_{final}$, the closing price of the Underlying 3 business days before the Maturity Date.
	If $ALCATEL_{final} > 100\% \times ALCATEL_{initial}$ at 100%.
	If $ALCATEL_{final} < 100\% \times ALCATEL_{initial}$ with 1 share (physical settlement).

The attraction for the investor in buying a reverse convertible is to monetise a potential capital gain by selling market volatility to provide a large fixed coupon *C*. This is particularly appealing in bullish or moderately bullish markets. In addition, if the underlying share should fall a cushion is provided by the large coupon and the investor's *break-even* is (100% – present value of fixed coupon *C*) of the initial share price (Fig. 4.3). If a share should fall, physical settlement has the advantage that the investor can hold the share until it recovers. Example 4.1 shows a short dated (1 year) single stock reverse convertible on a highly volatile tech stock (Alcatel or now Alcatel–Lucent) paying a high 16% annualised coupon. The present value of the investor coupon was approximately 15% so the investor break-even point is a 15% fall in Alcatel over 1 year.

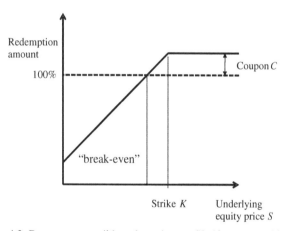

Figure 4.3: Reverse convertible redemption profile if coupon paid at maturity.

The present value of the extra coupon paid to the investor above the risk free rate is approximately equal to the premium of the put option sold in the structure. Thus a high coupon will be obtained for expensive options on highly volatile stocks such as TMT (telecoms, media, technology) sectors. The investor is short volatility and if implied volatility increases before maturity the value of the notes will fall. Figure 4.4 shows generic examples of annualised coupons for different volatilities and maturities. Assuming standard fees (say 1% per annum fees) and flat rates (3%) we see that the coupon falls rapidly with maturity and there is no great extra enhancement beyond 2–3 years. Higher volatility TMT stocks and short dated reverse converts offer very large enhancements (5–8%) relative to lower volatility indices.

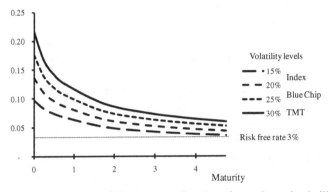

Figure 4.4: Reverse convertible coupon as function of maturity and volatility.

4.2.1 *Structuring reverse convertibles*

A reverse convertible note on a single stock is structured with the cash-flows shown schematically in Fig. 4.5.

1. Issuance and swap

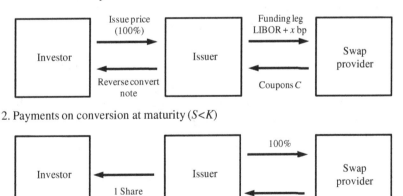

Figure 4.5: Reverse convertible structure on one share.

Reverse Switzerland

The amount of global savings wealth concentrated in Switzerland is truly mind boggling. For example over 30% of the world's global hedge fund investments go through this tiny country. It was also for us the biggest market for structured equity products and particularly reverse convertibles. There are hundreds of different private banks and wealth managers from small family offices or pools of just 20 clients to the larger well-known banks scattered across Switzerland. It used to be as simple as ring and email a few, advertise your retail/HNW deal in the newspaper and a sizable trade would be done as all these private bankers piled in. Traditionally conservative and risk adverse, I could never understand why they loved the reverse convertible so much, but I guess the paltry Swiss interest rates versus the mega coupons of short dated 1–3 month tech stock reverse convertibles answered that. With fees and the shape of the volatility and rate curve it was slightly more beneficial to do slightly longer maturities. However, I learnt that the appeal from the private bank's perspective was to sell as short-dated as possible since every 1–3 months they would receive a new commission on placing a new deal – so best to keep rotating your clients' money.

The *redemption amount* at maturity for a reverse convertible paying a coupon C at maturity is thus given by

$$R_{\substack{reverse \\ convert}} = 100\% - Max(K - S(T),0) + C, \qquad (4.1)$$

where K is the initial strike (usually $K = 100\%$ for at-the-money) and $S(T)$ the final stock price at maturity. The issuer swap structure is shown schematically in Fig. 4.5. If we assume that N coupons are paid before maturity we can write the *issuer swap* as

$$V(0,T) = Issuer\ funding + Put\ option - Coupons$$

$$= V_{funding}(0,T) + P_{put}(0,T,K) - C\sum_{j}^{N} D(0,t_j), \qquad (4.2)$$

where $P_{put}(0,T)$ is the value of the put option for maturity T. The issuer funding swap is the present value of LIBOR cash-flows and funding spreads (Appx C.1).

4.2.2 *Discount reverse convertibles*

Reverse convertibles can also be structured in a zero coupon form as discount notes or certificates with a sub-par (less than 100%) issue price. This results in the initial price of each note being lower than that of the underlying share. Discount reverse convertibles are attractive since the investor believes that at worst he is buying shares at a significant "discount" to their value today. In Example 4.2 the issue price is 79% of the value of the SAP share (a software company) on the issue date.

Example 4.2

EUR DISCOUNT REVERSE NOTES ON SAP		
ISSUER	:	AA rated Issuer
CURRENCY	:	EUR
MATURITY	:	1 year
ISSUE PRICE	:	79%
UNDERLYING	:	SAP
ANNUAL COUPON	:	Zero coupon
DENOMINATION	:	$100\% \times SAP_{initial}$, the opening price of the Underlying on the Issue Date.
REDEMPTION	:	Each Note will be redeemed at maturity as follows depending on SAP_{final}, the closing price of the Underlying 3 business days before the Maturity Date.
		If $SAP_{final} > 100\% \times SAP_{initial}$ at 100%.
		If $SAP_{final} < 100\% \times SAP_{initial}$ with 1 share.

The redemption amount at maturity is as before

$$R_{\substack{reverse \\ discount}} = 100\% - Max(K - S(T), 0). \qquad (4.3)$$

The swap structure is valued, since it is a zero coupon note, as

$$\begin{aligned} V(0,T) &= Issuer\ funding\ + Put\ option \\ &= V_{funding}(0,T) + P_{put}(0,T,K). \end{aligned} \qquad (4.4)$$

which is initially positive and provides the initial issue price of

$$P_{\substack{reverse \\ discount}}(0,T) = 100\% - V(0,T) \ < 100\%.$$

The price of each note is given by multiplying the issue price by the denomination of each note (initial value of one share on the issue date) (Appx C.2).

4.2.3 Knock-in reverse convertibles

Obviously, the main obstacle for many investors in buying reverse convertibles is the lack of capital guarantee. To provide increased capital protection for the investor the reverse convertible can be structured with a put option that is only activated, should the underlying share price fall *below* a certain barrier level at any time before maturity. This *knock-in* put will typically have a strike ATM but have a *barrier level* or *knock-in level* set at some 80–90% of the initial stock price. Thus, the stock must fall by some 10–20% before the put is activated. This increased security for the investor leads to a coupon that is usually slightly reduced from that offered by a vanilla reverse convertible.

A K_1 strike put with K_2 knock-in level is shown schematically in Fig. 4.6. Three example paths are shown: path (a) finishes above the strike K_1, so is redeemed at 100%; path (b) redeems 100% since the knock-in barrier at K_2 has not been hit even though it finished below strike K_1; and finally (c) which hits the knock-in barrier K_2 and activates the put so that a share (less than 100% value) is physically redeemed at maturity.

Example 4.3

13.0% EUR KNOCK-IN REVERSE CONVERTIBLE NOTES ON DEUTSCHE TELEKOM		

ISSUER : A rated Issuer

CURRENCY : EUR

MATURITY : 1 year

ISSUE PRICE : 100%

UNDERLYING : Deutsche Telekom

ANNUAL COUPON : 13.0%

DENOMINATION : $100\% \times DTEL_{initial}$, the opening price of the Underlying on the Issue Date.

KNOCK IN LEVEL : $80\% \times DTEL_{initial}$

REDEMPTION : Each Note will be redeemed at maturity as follows depending on $DTEL_{final}$, the closing price of the Underlying 3 business days before the Maturity Date and $DTEL_{min}$ the <u>lowest</u> daily closing price of the Underlying observed between the Issue Date and 3 business days before the Maturity Date.

If $DTEL_{final} > 100\% \times DTEL_{initial}$ redeemed at 100% whatever the level of $DTEL_{min}$.

If $DTEL_{final} < 100\% \times DTEL_{initial}$ redeemed with 1 share if $DTEL_{min}$ is lower or equal to the Knock-in Level,
or 100% if $DTEL_{min}$ is higher than the Knock-in Level.

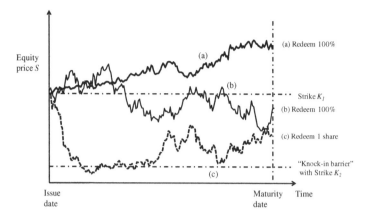

Figure 4.6: Knock-in reverse convertible scenarios.

A theoretical Black–Scholes closed form price can be evaluated for a *knock-in put* and this is detailed in Appx (C.3). However, the closed form is for continuous observation and although some knock-in reverse convertibles are documented as such others are based on the daily or weekly close. For such discrete observation dates and to include the effects of barrier "immunisation" in hedging, a lattice pricing approach is often used. Pricing levels approaching the theoretical closed form value are observed in the OTC market but in general most banks will try to reduce or "immunise" the discontinuity with a sloping barrier or *put-spread* in the model (see the discussion on pricing digitals and barriers in Section 3.8) resulting in a price slightly below the closed form value.

Bond Fund Reverse Convertibles

The fact that reverse convertibles notes could be considered by many investors to have the same rating as the issuer (AA say) was a great selling point despite being completely crazy misuse of rating. I knew many Middle East investors that would buy reverse converts to spice up the yields on their highly rated fixed income bond funds. They looked stars for a few years and when finally the time came equities fell and they were redeemed in stock there was an easy solution – just transfer the equities to your global equity fund that you manage as well.

4.2.4 *Lock-up reverse convertibles*

Lock-up reverse convertibles incorporate a put option that is effectively deactivated or "knocks-out" should the underlying stock rise above some specified barrier level or *lock-up* level (typically 110% or 120%) at any time before the maturity date. Thus, if the stock rises significantly in value above the lock-up level the investor will be sure to receive 100% at maturity even if the stock subsequently falls below the strike. The benefit for the investor is that the stock might rally sharply during the life and he is protected, should it subsequently fall before maturity. In Example 4.4 a lock-up reverse convertible was issued on a highly volatile tech stock (JDS Uniphase) and despite the lock-up feature managed to achieve a very high coupon with a knock-out if the JDS rose by more than 20% at any time before maturity.

The lock-up feature is obtained by the investor effectively selling a *knock-out put*. As with the knock-in put a closed form solution is possible and we detail this in Appx (C.4). It, however, only applies to an abrupt, continuously observed barrier.

4.2.5 *Leveraged reverse convertibles*

To increase the fixed coupon payable to investors the reverse convertible can be *leveraged* by selling several put options with different strikes. The effect of receiving several put premiums enhances the coupon, but if the underlying falls significantly the erosion of the investor's capital can be very significant since there is a gearing to the rate of loss. Many combinations exist but due to their leveraged nature they are cash settled and consequently often structured on indices. In Example 4.5 we show a leveraged knock-in reverse convertible.

The notes in this example contain both a knock-in feature to protect the investor against small falls in the underlying index of up to 25% but offer a high coupon due to the increased leverage on the downside. Should the underlying index fall below 25% at anytime during the life and the final value of the underlying be below the strike, the loss of capital is very rapid. The investor loses 1% for each 1% fall up to 25% in the index and 2% loss for each subsequent fall beyond 25% (2× leverage). This payoff profile is shown in Fig. 4.7.

Example 4.4

17.25% EUR LOCK-UP REVERSE CONVERTIBLE NOTES ON JDS UNIPHASE		
ISSUER	:	A rated Issuer
CURRENCY	:	EUR
MATURITY	:	1 year
ISSUE PRICE	:	100%
UNDERLYING	:	JDS Uniphase
ANNUAL COUPON	:	17.25%
DENOMINATION	:	100% × $JDS_{initial}$, the opening price of the Underlying on the Issue Date.
LOCK-UP LEVEL	:	120% × $JDS_{initial}$
REDEMPTION	:	Each Note will be redeemed at maturity as follows depending on JDS_{final}, the closing price of the Underlying 3 business days before the Maturity date and JDS_{maxi} the <u>highest</u> daily closing price of the Underlying observed between the Issue Date and 3 business days before the Maturity Date. If JDS_{final} > 100% × $JDS_{initial}$ at 100% whatever the level of JDS_{maxi}. If JDS_{final} < 100% × $JDS_{initial}$ redeemed with 1 share if JDS_{maxi} is lower or equal to the Lock-up Level, or 100% if JDS_{maxi} is higher than the Lock-up Level.

Example 4.5

10.25% GBP LEVERAGED KNOCK-IN REVERSE CONVERTIBLE NOTES ON DJ EUROSTOXX 50	
ISSUER	: A rated Issuer
CURRENCY	: GBP
MATURITY	: 3 year
ISSUE PRICE	: 100%
UNDERLYING	: Dow Jones Eurostoxx 50, the opening price of the Underlying on the Issue Date.
ANNUAL COUPON	: 10.25%
KNOCK-IN LEVEL	: 75% × EUROSTOXX$_{initial}$
REDEMPTION	: Each Note will be redeemed at maturity as follows depending on *EUROSTOXX$_{final}$*, the closing price of the Underlying 3 business days before the Maturity Date and *EUROSTOXX$_{min}$* the <u>lowest</u> daily closing price of the Underlying observed between the Issue Date and 3 business days before the Maturity Date.

If *EUROSTOXX$_{final}$* > 100% × *EUROSTOXX$_{initial}$* at 100% whatever the level of *EUROSTOXX$_{min}$*.

If *EUROSTOXX$_{final}$* < 100% × *EUROSTOXX$_{initial}$* then, if *EUROSTOXX$_{min}$* is greater than or equal to the Knock-in Level 100%;
otherwise for every 1% fall in the Underlying upto 25% the redemption amount will be reduced by 1% and 2% for each 1% fall in the Underlying value beyond 25%. The minimum redemption amount is zero.

This is obtained through combining the sale of a 100% strike 75% knock-in put and a 75% strike 75% knock-in put. In addition to protect the swap provider against an extreme market fall two 37.5% strike 75% knock-in puts should also ideally be purchased since the investor cannot lose more than 100% of his capital. In reality these inexpensive deeply *out-of-the-money* puts would be probably priced in (including a large volatility smile effect) but not actually hedged by the swap counterparty. Also in the example the notes are in GBP but the Eurostoxx is a Euro denominated index which means that the puts should all be valued as *quanto puts* where the risk neutral drift term is modified by a correlation factor (see Section 3.9). The example redemption amount (subject to knock-in) is

$$
\begin{aligned}
R_{\substack{reverse \\ leveraged}} &= 100\% - Max\big(K_1 - S(T),0\big) - Max\big(K_2 - S(T),0\big) \\
&+ 2\,Max\big(K_3 - S(T),0\big),
\end{aligned}
\tag{4.6}
$$

where $K_1 = 100\%$, $K_2 = 75\%$ and $K_3 = 37.5\%$ (Appx C.7).

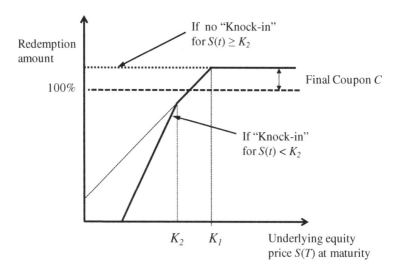

Figure 4.7: Leveraged reverse convertible payoff if "knock-in" event.

Example 4.6

GBP AUTO-CALLABLE FUND ON FTSE INDEX	
FUND	: Fund holding AA rated government bond collateral with A rated swap counterparty
CURRENCY	: GBP
MATURITY	: 5 year, subject to possible early redemption.
ISSUE PRICE	: 100%
UNDERLYING	: FTSE 100 Index
ANNUAL COUPON	: Zero coupon
REDEMPTION	: At the end of year 2 if $FTSE_{current} \geq FTSE_{initial}$ at 100% the fund is redeemed early at 113%.
	At the end of year 3 if $FTSE_{current} \geq FTSE_{initial}$ at 100% the fund is redeemed early at 120%.
	At the end of year 4 if $FTSE_{current} \geq FTSE_{initial}$ at 100% the fund is redeemed early at 126%.
	At the end of year 5 if $FTSE_{current} \geq FTSE_{initial}$ at 100% the fund is redeemed at 133%.
	At the end of year 5 if $FTSE_{current} < FTSE_{initial}$ but $FTSE_{current} \geq 50\% \times FTSE_{initial}$ the fund is redeemed at 100%.
	At the end of year 5 if
	$FTSE_{current} < 50\% \times FTSE_{initial}$ the fund is redeemed at less than par at $(100\% \times FTSE_{current}/FTSE_{initial})$,
	where $FTSE_{current}$ is the current closing Underlying level on the date tested.

4.2.6 *Auto-callables and extendibles*

A popular method for increasing the reverse convertible coupon is including *auto-callable* or *extendible* features. With an auto-callable the coupons are paid but if the underlying has risen above a predefined strike by the call date then the note is redeemed early at 100% plus coupon.

The call dates usually correspond with coupon payment or accrual periods. Obviously at the call date if the put option is deeply OTM then there is little possibility of it being exercised in the next coupon period so rather than pay the next coupon then the note is *auto-called*. The equivalent concept is the extendible, which was very popular in Japan, where short dated reverse converts extend in maturity if there was likelihood of the put option being deeper ITM at the next coupon date. In the UK, auto-callables are often termed *kick-out* products since the investor is "kicked-out" or redeemed early.

Example 4.6 shows a recent auto-callable reverse convertible on the FTSE index. This is structured as a fund rather than a note and called a "Defined Returns Fund". It is a 5 year fund but if the FTSE has risen in any year from year 2, the fund is redeemed early paying 100% plus a specified accreting coupon. To increase investor safety the fund has a 50% knock-in digital with 100% strike which is tested at maturity. The strike for calculating losses is set at 100% so a 49% fall in the index produces no loss whilst a 51% fall produces a 51% loss. Products incorporating a deeply out-of-the-money 50% strike have recently become very popular and one wonders if various investment banks, in the current economically uncertain environment, are effectively buying cheap "crash" protection off retail investors.

Black–Scholes closed forms exist for simple auto-callables and extendibles but for multiple extensions and different strike features we can use Monte Carlo simulation or lattices. Although Monte Carlo cannot be applied to most Bermudan callables since the auto-callables have "hard coded" call features simulation techniques can be used.

4.2.7 *Contingent coupon reverse convertibles*

By making the reverse convertible coupon contingent on some event such as a range it is possible to enhance the coupon further. Example 4.7 shows a recent product marketed to retail that is perhaps somewhat overcomplicated. It is similar to Example 4.6 but if the index lies in the range 85% to 105% of the initial index value, a large semi-annual coupon

Example 4.7

9.0% EUR EUROSTOXX CORRIDOR INCOME NOTES

ISSUER	:	AAA rated Issuer
CURRENCY	:	EUR
MATURITY	:	5 year, subject to possible early redemption
ISSUE PRICE	:	100%
UNDERLYING	:	Dow Jones Eurostoxx 50 Index
COUPON	:	4.5% payable semi-annually (9% pa) if at the end of each semi-annual period the Underlying lies in the range: $EUROSTOXX_{current} < 105\% \times EUROSTOXX_{initial}$ and $EUROSTOXX_{current} > 85\% \times EUROSTOXX_{initial}$, otherwise zero coupon is payable.
REDEMPTION	:	Each Note may be redeemed early at an amount depending on $EUROSTOXX_{current}$, the closing price of the Underlying at the end of every six months. If $EUROSTOXX_{current} \geq 105\% \times EUROSTOXX_{initial}$ the Redemption Amount will be equal to 104.5%. If not previously redeemed the notes will be redeemed at maturity at a value equal to: If $EUROSTOXX_{final} \geq 50\% \times EUROSTOXX_{initial}$ the Redemption Amount will be equal to 100%. If $EUROSTOXX_{final} < 50\% \times EUROSTOXX_{initial}$ the Redemption Amount will be equal to $(100\% \times EUROSTOXX_{final}/EUROSTOXX_{initial})$, where $EUROSTOXX_{initial}$ is the opening price of the Underlying on the Issue Date.

is paid (4.5% or 9% per annum equivalent). If the index rises above 105%, a coupon is paid and the notes are auto-called and redeemed early, but if the index is below 85% then no coupon is payable. There is protection, set at 50% as in the last example. The danger of this product is that the index falls early in the life of the product (below 85%) and never recovers, leaving the investor to receive no income for 5 years and a possible reduced redemption amount if the index falls by more than 50%.

4.2.8 Reverse convertible summary

Reverse convertibles provide a clever way of providing a high income whilst sacrificing capital protection. They are appealing to investors when interest rates are low and implied volatilities are high (see Fig. 4.1) and are most commonly structured on single stocks or indices. In Table 4.1 we summarise some of the main features that can be included in reverse convertibles. Other notable features that can modify the coupon are Bermudan issuer calls, averaging of underlying performance and reverse convertibles on two or more stocks (power reverse convertibles see Section 5.8.2). Perhaps the best investment strategy for reverse convertible investors is purchasing short dated, single stock reverse converts with physically settlement. This maximises the coupon for investors and if the underlying falls the investor just holds the stock and receives dividends until it eventually recovers. For cash settlement on an index a longer maturity 2–4 years may be preferable since it is likely that an index, will rise over several years whereas over shorter periods an unexpected principal loss maybe suffered.

Table 4.1: Common reverse convertible features.

Underlyings	Coupon Enhancement	Investor Protection
Single stock	High volatility	Low volatility
Small basket	Shorter maturity	Longer maturity
Index	Leveraged	Knock-out/knock-in
	Extendible/auto-call	Barrier protection

4.3 Protected Bull Notes

Protected bull notes allow the investor to benefit from the upside performance of the underlying index or stock whilst providing 100% capital guarantee of the initial investment amount should the market have fallen by the maturity date. These structures are the most popular structured equity product and have proved very popular with risk adverse investors who would like stock market exposure but are worried about long term capital risk.

The notes are structured through the effective purchase of a zero coupon bond to provide the capital guarantee and the purchase of an at-the-money call option on the underlying. Example 4.8 shows 7 year protected bull notes with a 70% *participation* in the upside of the DJ Eurostoxx 50 index.

Example 4.8

EUR PROTECTED BULL NOTES ON DJ EUROSTOXX 50
ISSUER : A rated Issuer
CURRENCY : EUR
MATURITY : 7 year
ISSUE PRICE : 100%
UNDERLYING : Dow Jones Eurostoxx 50
COUPON : Zero coupon
PARTICIPATION : 70%
REDEMPTION : Each Note will be redeemed at maturity at an amount depending on $EUROSTOXX_{final}$, the closing price of the Underlying 3 business days before the Maturity Date. The Redemption Amount will be equal to: $$100\% + Participation \times Max\left(\frac{EUROSTOXX_{final}}{EUROSTOXX_{initial}} - 100\%,\, 0\right),$$ where $EUROSTOXX_{initial}$ is the opening price of the Underlying on the Issue Date.

Unfortunately, in recent years with a low interest rate environment the zero coupon bond is very expensive and this, combined with the high implied volatility and consequent high cost of call options, leads to low participation in the performance of the underlying. To increase the participation, the notes are structured with long maturities (5–10 years) or incorporate partial capital guarantees (typically 90–95%). Frequently averaging of the underlying performance and overall performance caps are used to boost the participation (see below).

The redemption amount at maturity T is given by

$$R_{\substack{protected \\ bull}} = 100\% + \alpha \ Max\left(\frac{S(T)}{S(0)} - K, 0\right), \qquad (4.7)$$

where α is the *participation* of the performance in the underlying index and the call option is typically ATM with strike $K = 100\%$ (Appx C.8). Thus, as shown in Fig. 4.8 if the value of the underlying at maturity is less than the strike then 100% is redeemed but if the underlying is greater than the strike then 100% plus α of the upside or growth is redeemed.

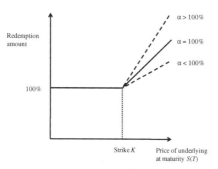

Figure 4.8: Redemption amount for protected bull note for different participation levels.

The issuer swap can be written simply as

$$V(0,T) = Issuer \ funding \ - \ Call \ option$$
$$= V_{funding}(0,T) - \alpha \ P_{call}(0,T,K) \qquad (4.8)$$

Since this must value to an amount equal to zero (although upfront fees may be included) we can determine the participation α. Figure 4.9 shows the idealised participation levels (ignoring fees) as a function of maturity for various volatilities and interest rates. For 5% swap rates participation rises rapidly until 3–4 years maturity then rises almost linearly with maturity. Lower volatilities (indices, funds and effective averaging) can provide almost 30–40% higher participation levels. The structure is very sensitive to fees and with 1% per annum fees over 5 years the participation could be reduced by 20–30% depending on the level of rates.

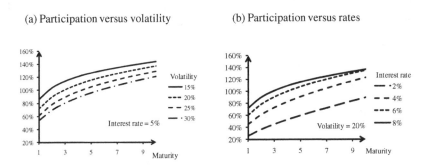

Figure 4.9: Equity bull protected note participation.

4.3.1 *Average protected bull notes*

Averaging the final value of the underlying over several fixing dates (for example quarterly observations over the last couple of years) can significantly reduce the cost of the call option by reducing the effective underlying volatility and thus increase the participation. Very often the averaging feature is marketed as "extra protection" for the investor in the event of a market fall just before the maturity date. Example 4.9 shows 7 year protected bull notes with a monthly averaging over the last 2 years before maturity. Figure 4.10 shows the simulated effect of this averaging. In the last 2 years the performance is smoothed and volatility reduced. This can protect the investor in a falling market (a) but reduce the upside in a rallying market (b).

The *average spot* call, or *Asian* call as it is frequently known, is priced as the arithmetic average over the averaging dates (Appx C.9). For options defined as arithmetic averages there exists no true analytical pricing equations. This is principally because the probability distribution of an arithmetic average of a series of lognormal distributions (which is assumed in Black–Scholes) is not analytically tractable. Instead, approximations are used where the first two moments of the probability

Example 4.9

EUR AVERAGE PROTECTED BULL NOTES ON CAC40

ISSUER	:	AA rated Issuer
CURRENCY	:	EUR
MATURITY	:	7 year
ISSUE PRICE	:	100%
UNDERLYING	:	CAC 40
COUPON	:	Zero coupon
PARTICIPATION	:	80%

REDEMPTION : Each Note will be redeemed at maturity at an amount depending on CAC_{final}, the monthly closing price of the Underlying averaged over the last 2 years before the Maturity Date. The Redemption Amount will be equal to:

$$100\% + Participation \times Max\left(\frac{CAC_{final}}{CAC_{initial}} - 100\%, 0\right),$$

where $CAC_{initial}$ is the opening price of the Underlying on the Issue Date.

---

distribution (effectively the mean and variance) for the Asian average option are calculated exactly and then it is assumed the distribution of the arithmetic average is a lognormal distribution with these first two moments. This allows an approximation using a Black–Scholes style formula which is detailed in Appx (C.10). Monte Carlo solutions can often be used to check these approximations, particularly for irregularly spaced averaging periods. Where averaging exists for the initial fixing the problem becomes more complex and closed form approximations are not applicable and we must resort straight away to Monte Carlo. Some structures which I call "super average" products have crazy averaging schemes such as weekly or monthly averaging over the life of the product or taking daily averages every month and then taking an overall weighted average of some form and unfortunately these products are computationally very intensive unless short cuts can be found.

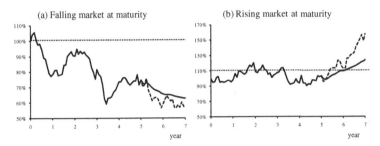

Figure 4.10: Effect of monthly averaging performance in the last 2 years showing that averaging reduces volatility.

4.3.2 *Capped protected bull notes*

With a *capped* structure the overall performance of the notes is capped at a maximum value whatever the gain of the underlying by selling a second call with an out-of-the-money cap with strike K_2, where $K_2 > K_1$ (see Fig. 4.11). This allows the participation to be boosted although, unfortunately, the enhancement is often not as good as expected due to the large smile effect applied to the second call option.

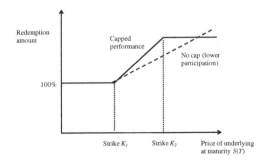

Figure 4.11: Redemption amount for capped protected bull notes.

Example 4.11

GBP CAPPED PROTECTED BULL NOTES ON FTSE 100

ISSUER	:	AA rated Issuer
CURRENCY	:	GBP
MATURITY	:	8 year
ISSUE PRICE	:	100%
UNDERLYING	:	FTSE 100
COUPON	:	Zero coupon
REDEMPTION	:	Each Note will be redeemed at maturity at an amount depending on $FTSE_{final}$, the monthly closing price of the Underlying averaged over the year before the Maturity date. The Redemption amount will be equal to:

$$100\% + 100\% \times Min\left[Max\left(\frac{FTSE_{final}}{FTSE_{initial}} - 100\%,\ 0 \right), 70\% \right],$$

where $FTSE_{initial}$ is the opening price of the Underlying on the Issue Date.

The redemption value is then given by

$$R_{\substack{protected \\ bull\, capped}} = 100\% + \alpha \left\{ Max\left(\frac{S(T)}{S(0)} - K_1, 0 \right) - Max\left(\frac{S(T)}{S(0)} - K_2, 0 \right) \right\}, \quad (4.9)$$

which is priced as two calls and known as a call spread (Appx C.11). Due to the volatility smile we must use a different volatility for the deeply OTM option that is sold to provide the cap. Example 4.11 shows an 8 year structure with 100% participation and a 70% cap.

By combining a series of different call spreads a variety of different structures are possible for example different participation rates for different performance levels of the underlying or introducing a partial capital guarantee. A common theme is to introduce a minimum return but this obviously lowers the participation as in Example 4.12 where an FTSE linked deposit is given with a minimum return of 6.5% and only a 30% participation.

Example 4.12

GBP FTSE100 LINKED GUARANTEED DEPOSIT WITH MINIMUM RETURN

DEPOSIT	:	Deposit account with AA Rated Bank
CURRENCY	:	GBP
MATURITY	:	5 year
INITIAL DEPOSIT	:	100%
UNDERLYING	:	FTSE 100
INTEREST	:	Zero interest
REDEMPTION	:	Each Note will be redeemed at maturity at an amount depending on $FTSE_{final}$, the monthly closing price of the Underlying. The Redemption amount will be equal to:

$$100\% + Max\left[6.5\%, 30\%\left(\frac{FTSE_{final}}{FTSE_{initial}} - 100\%\right)\right],$$

where $FTSE_{inital}$ is the opening price of the Underlying at the start of the investment term.

4.4 Protected Cliquet Notes

In a *cliquet* structure the performance of the underlying index over each cliquet period (typically annually) is paid to the note-holder either at the end of each cliquet period or at maturity. The strike for each cliquet period is thus fixed by the value of the underlying at the start of each period. The product can be structured as an income product or for capital gain.

For a simple *cliquet call* with cliquet period between times t_{i-1} and t_i the payoff can be written as

$$Payoff_{\substack{cliquet \\ call}} = Max\left(\frac{S(t_i)}{S(t_{i-1})} - K, 0 \right), \qquad (4.10)$$

where typically the strike K is 100% for an ATM cliquet call. The payoff is shown in Fig. 4.12(a). Cliquet calls can be evaluated using simple Black–Scholes formula for a *forward starting* option (Appx C.13).

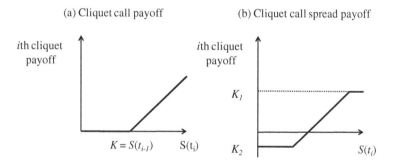

Figure 4.12: Cliquet and cliquet call spread payoffs.

Since, however, a series of cliquet calls is too expensive to incorporate in a capital guaranteed structure, a series of cliquet call spreads is used. This provides a cap and a floor on the performance of each cliquet period (see Fig. 4.12(b)). Now the most important thing in correctly pricing a cliquet call spread is the volatility smile applied to the two different strikes for each cliquet period and in particular the forward level of volatility and form of the smile relevant for forward starting options. In the general absence of a complete volatility surface or a correctly calibrated stochastic volatility model to check assumptions this relies on the expertise and judgement of the derivatives trader and knowledge of where similar structures are priced in the market. Large losses have been incurred by various banks for mispricing the forward starting volatility effect in these structures. Generally, we can carefully apply conservative bounds to the forward volatility skew that should be used.

Example 4.13

EUR PROTECTED CLIQUET NOTES ON DJ EUROSTOXX 50
ISSUER : AA rated Issuer
CURRENCY : EUR
MATURITY : 8 year
ISSUE PRICE : 100%
UNDERLYING : Dow Jones Eurostoxx 50
COUPON : Zero coupon
REDEMPTION : Each Note will be redeemed at an amount equal to 100% plus $$Max\left[\sum_{i=1}^{8} Max\left(-3\%, Min\left(\frac{EUROSTOXX_i}{EUROSTOXX_{i-1}} - 100\%, 10\%\right)\right), 15\%\right],$$ where $EUROSTOXX_i$ for $i=1,...,7$ is the closing price of the Underlying averaged over 10 business days at the beginning of each annual period. $EUROSTOXX_i$ for $i=8$ is the closing price of the Underlying averaged over 10 business days before the end of the annual period.

To provide structures that are more optically pleasing to investors final caps and floors on the overall payout at maturity can be added to the cap and floor on each cliquet period. These more complex structures often meet with great success and are generally priced using a Monte Carlo simulation. A typical structure might have a form of payout given by

$$R_{\substack{protected \\ cliquet \\ cap\,floor}} = 100\%$$

$$+ Max\left[\sum_{i}^{N} Max\left(K_2,\, Min\left(\frac{S(t_i)}{S(t_{i-1})} - 100\%,\, K_1\right)\right),\, K_3\right], \quad (4.11)$$

where K_3 is the overall floor at maturity over the N cliquet periods. This type of capital guaranteed structure is illustrated in Example 4.13 where the investor can receive between -3% and 10% of each annual performance of the underlying at maturity but will receive a minimum guaranteed redemption of 100% plus 15%.

4.4.1 *Reverse cliquets*

An alternative income structure has been the *reverse cliquet* structure. These notes are usually shown in fully capital guaranteed form and consist of the investor selling a series of cliquet puts to enhance the return of the notes. The maximum total loss of the series of cliquet puts is floored at the total coupon that would be payable to the investor at maturity if the underlying never fell in value over any cliquet period. Usually, a minimum coupon payable is also included, should the underlying fall significantly in value. In Example 4.14 a maximum coupon of 30% is payable at maturity and a minimum of 10%. Notice that in each cliquet period if the equity falls the final payout is correspondingly reduced but if the equity rises then the payout is not increased again.

Optically these products show a very high potential coupon whilst remaining capital guaranteed – in the example 30%. Obviously it is very unlikely that the investor will actually receive this high coupon and will most likely receive 10%. As with a reverse convertible, the investor is short volatility so the price of the notes before maturity decreases as the implied volatility increases. Valuation of these products is performed using a Monte Carlo simulation due to the overall cap and floor usually using a conservative volatility structure since adjustments for volatility smile and maturity effects are complicated.

Example 4.14

EUR REVERSE CLIQUET NOTES ON OLIVETTI

ISSUER	:	AA rated Issuer
CURRENCY	:	EUR
MATURITY	:	6 year
ISSUE PRICE	:	100%
UNDERLYING	:	Olivetti
COUPON	:	Zero coupon
REDEMPTION	:	Each Note will be redeemed at an amount equal to 100% plus

$$Max\left[10\%, 30\% + \sum_{i=1}^{6} Min\left(\frac{OLIVETTI_i}{OLIVETTI_{i-1}} - 100\%, 0\% \right) \right],$$

where:

$OLIVETTI_i$ for $i=1,...,6$ is the closing price of the Underlying at the beginning of each annual period.

$OLIVETTI_i$ for $i=6$ is the closing price of the Underlying 5 business days before the Maturity Date.

4.4.2 *Scaled cliquet protected notes*

The cliquet concept can be adapted to give numerous complicated variants. Consider the *scaled* or sorted cliquet notes in Example 4.15. They are 100% capital guaranteed but each of the 16 quarterly cliquet performances is recorded. At maturity the performances are sorted with the 4 best given a 60% weighting and the 12 others a 100% weighting. The weighting of the 4 best (which are presumably positive returns) by 60% considerably reduces the cost of the option.

Other variants include *replacement cliquets,* where a number of cliquet returns are replaced with fixed coupons. A popular product is also the "Napoleon" cliquet which pays a high fixed coupon plus the worst cliquet period return. Since the worst period return is likely to be highly negative the initial fixed coupon advertised is very attractive to investors.

Example 4.15

EUR PROTECTED SCALED CLIQUET NOTES ON DJ EUROSTOXX 50

ISSUER	:	AA rated Issuer
CURRENCY	:	EUR
MATURITY	:	4 year
ISSUE PRICE	:	100%
UNDERLYING	:	Dow Jones Eurostoxx 50 Index
COUPON	:	Zero coupon
REDEMPTION	:	Each Note will be redeemed at an amount equal to 100% plus 60% of the sum of the 4 best quarterly performances plus 100% of the sum of the 12 other quarterly performances subject to a minimum of zero.

The performance for the ith quarterly period $(i=1,...,16)$ is defined as

$$\left(\frac{EUROSTOXX_i}{EUROSTOXX_{i-1}} - 100\% \right),$$

where

$EUROSTOXX_{i-1}$ is the closing price of the Underlying at the beginning of each quarterly period.
$EUROSTOXX_i$ is the closing price of the Underlying at the end of the quarterly period.

Example 4.16

<table>
<tr><td colspan="2">EUR PROTECTED "FUJI" NOTES ON NESTLE</td></tr>
<tr><td>ISSUER</td><td>: AA rated Issuer</td></tr>
<tr><td>CURRENCY</td><td>: EUR</td></tr>
<tr><td>MATURITY</td><td>: 8 year</td></tr>
<tr><td>ISSUE PRICE</td><td>: 100%</td></tr>
<tr><td>UNDERLYING</td><td>: Nestlé AG</td></tr>
<tr><td>ANNUAL COUPON</td><td>: The annual coupon paid will be between 9.0% and 0.0% depending on the lowest price of the underlying observed during the previous year $NESTLE_{mini}$

9.0% if $NESTLE_{mini} > 90\% \times NESTLE_{initial}$
otherwise
5.0% if $NESTLE_{mini} > 85\% \times NESTLE_{initial}$
otherwise
3.0% if $NESTLE_{mini} > 80\% \times NESTLE_{initial}$
otherwise
0.0% if $NESTLE_{mini} \leq 80\% \times NESTLE_{initial}$

where $NESTLE_{initial}$ is the opening price of the underlying on the Issue Date.</td></tr>
<tr><td>REDEMPTION</td><td>: Each Note will be redeemed at 100%.</td></tr>
</table>

4.5 Multi-Barrier Protected Notes

Several successful capital protected products have been structured using a series of multiple barrier options to generate high potential annual coupons. A typical example is the SocGen protected "Fuji" note where if the underlying has not fallen in each year below the initial value (fixed on the issue date) a very high annual coupon (8–10% typically) is paid. If the underlying price falls during any annual period below the initial value fixed on the issue date the coupon paid progressively steps down to towards zero. This structure appeals to investors since they are usually bullish over the long maturity (5–8 years) of the notes so even if there is a short term market correction the investors expect high coupons to be paid throughout most of the life of the notes. Example 4.16 shows a typical example with Nestlé (the confectionary and food company) as the underlying.

It is important to remember that the coupon is based on the lowest equity price in the previous year based on continuous observation and not just on the coupon date. This makes the option much cheaper since a sudden drop of the equity price during the year (even if it subsequently recovers) will trigger the barrier and reduce the annual coupon. Also it is important to pick a blue-chip equity with stable long term prospects and likely to rise in price over a period of several years. Distressed and speculative industrial sectors should be avoided. In the example, Nestlé was viewed as a stable, highly rated, blue-chip company with growth prospects.

The annual coupon can be written as a series of forward start barrier options for which we can use a closed form (Appx C.14). However, in practice a conservative valuation can be established using a Monte Carlo valuation with discrete observations and with each barrier represented as a put spread to smooth hedging.

4.6 Leveraged Bull Notes

Mixing the previous concepts we can provide products with leveraged upside participation but reduced or partial capital guarantees to the downside. Consider Example 4.17 marketed to retail investors as an "Enhanced Growth Plan" on the FTSE index. For a 6 year product the upside participation is 200% subject to a cap of 90% with a minimum of 25% return should the index rise by maturity. If the FTSE falls the notes redeem 100% except if the index falls by more than 50% when (as with Example 4.6) the entire fall of the index, from the issue date, is impacted on the redemption amount. The complex redemption profile is shown in Fig. 4.13 and can be decomposed into vanilla call spreads and digital options.

Example 4.17

GBP 2× LEVERAGED BULL NOTES ON FTSE 100

ISSUER	:	AA rated Issuer
CURRENCY	:	GBP
MATURITY	:	6 year
ISSUE PRICE	:	100%
UNDERLYING	:	FTSE 100
COUPON	:	Zero coupon
PARTICIPATION	:	100%
REDEMPTION	:	Each Note will be redeemed at maturity at an amount depending on $FTSE_{final}$, the closing price of the Underlying on the Maturity Date.

REDEMPTION (continued):

If $FTSE_{final} \geq FTSE_{initial}$ the Redemption Amount will be equal to

$$100\% + Max\left[25\%, Min\left(200\%\left(\frac{FTSE_{final}}{FTSE_{initial}} - 100\% \right), 90\% \right) \right]$$

If $FTSE_{final} < FTSE_{initial}$ and $FTSE_{final} \geq 50\% \times FTSE_{initial}$ the Redemption Amount will be equal to 100%.

If $FTSE_{final} < 50\% \times FTSE_{initial}$ the Redemption Amount will be equal to $(100\% \times FTSE_{final}/FTSE_{initial})$,

where $FTSE_{initial}$ is the opening price of the Underlying on the Issue Date.

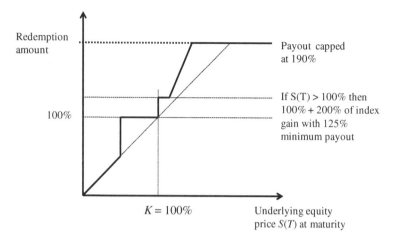

Figure 4.13: Redemption amount for leveraged FTSE notes.

4.7 Summary of Equity Structured Products

We have discussed a range of common equity structured products based
on a single underlying index or equity (see Fig. 4.14). These products
can provide income or capital gain and can incorporate capital protection
if longer maturities are considered. Most income structures are based
around the popular reverse convertible and numerous variants are
possible where the investor can trade-off coupon or yield for extra capital
protection (knock-in and knock-outs, etc.) or enhance the coupon
through taking extra risk (higher volatility equities, extendibles, leverage,
etc.). Most capital protected structures are in the form of bull notes with
different mechanisms (averages, caps, etc.) to increase participation.
Cliquets are a popular product but are too expensive to provide capital
guaranteed products unless caps, floors or other ingenious mechanisms,
such as sorting or averaging, are included. Selling expensive options in
the form of multi-barrier notes or reverse cliquets can provide capital
guaranteed structures like the Fuji with high headline coupons but with
reduced possibility of the investor actually receiving them. Lastly,
leveraged structures are possible but these generally require a sacrifice in
capital protection.

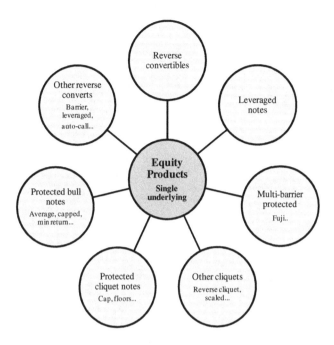

Figure 4.14: Summary of equity structured products.

Chapter 5

Basket Equity Products

5.1 Introduction

A large number of products for both retail and high net worth investors are structured using baskets of equities. For investors these products are appealing since they can invest in "themes" such as technology, sustainability, etc. and reduce the risk of investing in individual stocks through diversification. For the product structurer a new dimension of correlation between equity price movements is introduced. Correlation can allow changes in effective volatility to be produced, for example low correlation baskets allow lower overall volatility and higher participation levels in capital guaranteed structures.

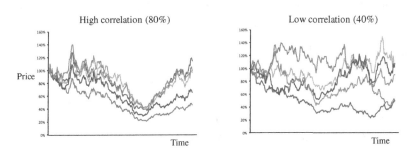

Figure 5.1: Correlation and dispersion effect in equity baskets.

Also, correlation effects can allow the innovation of new products linked to the *dispersion* of possible returns in the basket such as "best-of" and "worst-of" products. Figure 5.1 shows the effect of dispersion in a small basket with low and high correlation (Appx D.1). Here we shall review the most popular basket, and correlation products.

5.2 Basket Notes

Basket notes are retail investment products that allow investment in a pre-selected basket of stocks for a period of several years (generally 2–5 years). They are not capital guaranteed and can be directly replicated by investing in the basket of stocks so are in some sense similar to exchange traded funds (ETFs). Basket notes do, however, provide advantages for investors when:

(i)   The stocks are from markets that might be difficult to access for retail investors (for example emerging markets).

(ii)   The stocks are denominated in different currencies and cross currency risks can be hedged out or *quantoed.*

(iii)   Stocks can be selected by analysts and detailed research can be used to compile "optimum" baskets for tracking specific sectors (tech, pharmaceutical, etc.) or providing diversified low volatility baskets.

(iv)   Trading strategies can be associated with the baskets such as "momentum select" and "value select" strategies.

(v)   Include simple features such as averaging.

Here, Example 5.1 shows Euro basket composed of a theme of "cheap" or "value" pharmaceutical blue-chips but denominated in a mix currencies (GBP, USD, EUR, CHF) and quantoed into Euro.

5.3 Protected Basket Bull Notes

Protected basket bull notes are capital guaranteed notes comprising a zero coupon to provide the capital guarantee and a call option on an underlying basket of stocks or indices. The basket of stocks are usually chosen to be thematic or sectorial (high correlation $\rho \sim 70–90\%$) or diversified (low correlation $\rho < 60–70\%$). By selecting a diversified basket the implied volatility can be reduced significantly which can allow a higher participation. This effect is illustrated in Fig. 5.2 where the basket value (solid black line) in a 5 name basket has considerably lower volatility than the individual components. A basket, due to diversification, has a much lower volatility than its individual constituents. Most index baskets for this reason include the Nikkei 225 due to its lower correlation with the US and European indices.

Example 5.1

EUR PROTECTED BULL NOTES ON
A BASKET OF "VALUE" PHARMA STOCKS

ISSUER	:	A rated Issuer
CURRENCY	:	EUR
MATURITY	:	3 year
ISSUE PRICE	:	100%
UNDERLYING BASKET	:	An equally weighted basket composed of:

Glaxo Smithkline
Sanofi
Novartis
Pfizer
Wyeth

COUPON	:	Zero coupon
REDEMPTION	:	Each Note will be redeemed at maturity at an amount equal to

$$R = BASKET_{final},$$

where

$$BASKET_{final} = \sum_{i=1}^{5} \omega_i \frac{S_i(T)}{S_i(0)}$$

with
$\omega_i = 1/5$ is the weighting coefficient of the ith share ($i=1,...,5$).
$S_i(T)$ is the closing price of the ith share 5 business days before the Maturity Date.
$S_i(0)$ opening price of the ith share on the Issue Date.

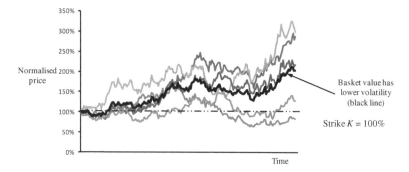

Figure 5.2: A diversified basket lowers volatility compared with constituents.

Example 5.2 shows a banking basket which clearly demonstrates the value of a capital guarantee. Before the credit crisis the financial sector was viewed as a boring, stable sector. Despite being a single sector basket the basket correlation allowed a 100% participation level well before the credit crisis. At the time it was not realised that a credit crisis would produce a very high simultaneous correlation across the whole of the European banking sector.

For a basket with N_B constituents with weightings ω_i the redemption amount is given as

$$R_{\substack{basket \\ protected}} = 100\% + \alpha \, Max\left(\sum_{i=1}^{N_B} \omega_i \frac{S_i(T)}{S_i(0)} - K, 0\right), \qquad (5.1)$$

where α is the participation and K the strike (Appx D.2). We can price the issuer swap as the funding leg minus the basket call cost

$$V(0,T) = V_{funding}(0,T) - \alpha \, P_{\substack{basket \\ call}}(0,T,K).$$

The investor in the protected basket bull notes is long, both correlation and volatility. Increasing volatility or correlation will increase the price of the option and the notes. Higher participations are achieved through using low correlation baskets with 5–10 constituents. Figure 5.3 shows it is easy to achieve 15–30%+ increases in participation using baskets.

Example 5.2

EUR PROTECTED BULL NOTES ON A BASKET OF EUROPEAN BANKS

ISSUER	:	A rated Issuer
CURRENCY	:	EUR
MATURITY	:	6 year
ISSUE PRICE	:	100%
UNDERLYING BASKET	:	An equally weighted basket composed of

Société Générale
Barclays
Deutsche Bank
Santander
Crédit Agricole
Crédit Suisse
Royal Bank of Scotland

COUPON	:	Zero coupon
REDEMPTION	:	Each Note will be redeemed at maturity at an amount equal to

$$R = 100\% + Max(BASKET_{final} - 100\%, 0),$$

where

$$BASKET_{final} = \sum_{i=1}^{7} \omega_i \frac{S_i(T)}{S_i(0)}$$

with
$\omega_i = 1/7$ is the weighting coefficient of the ith share $(i=1,...,7)$.
$S_i(T)$ is the closing price of the ith share 5 business days before the Maturity Date.
$S_i(0)$ opening price of the ith share on the Issue Date.

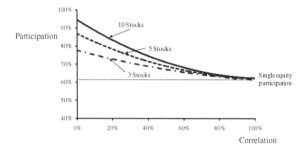

Figure 5.3: Typical effect of correlation on basket participation level.

Many variables are required to price basket products, including the relative weighting of every constituent of the basket, the initial spot rates, the dividend rates, volatilities and pair-wise correlations. Generally, the basket is priced using a single factor correlation method to simplify calculation.

Two major approaches are used for evaluating options on baskets. The first is the single factor technique where the dynamics of the basket are approximated by a single lognormal variable which is modelled by Black–Scholes (closed form or lattice) (Appx D.3). The first two moments (thus the mean and variance) of the multivariate basket distribution are each matched by a single factor. The matched growth rate and volatility are then used in the Black–Scholes equation. A conservative correlation number relative to that calculated from the pair-wise correlations is also employed. The second approach is to use a full blown multivariate modelling approach with a Monte Carlo simulation of the individual equities (Appx D.4). This is more computationally intensive but allows considerable flexibility.

5.3.1 *Average protected basket bull notes*

As with a single underlying equity, often averaging is used to reduce the cost of the basket call option and increase the participation. Averaging for the initial price fixing or, more importantly, the end of the option period for the final fixing has the effect of reducing the volatility of the option and hence the cost.

A closed form approximation can be used to evaluate this "averaging-out case" (Appx D.5). However, it is really an approximation

Example 5.3

<table>
<tr><td colspan="3">**EUR AVERAGE PROTECTED BULL NOTES ON A BASKET OF GLOBAL VALUE STOCKS**</td></tr>
</table>

ISSUER	:	A rated Issuer
CURRENCY	:	EUR
MATURITY	:	8 year
ISSUE PRICE	:	100%
UNDERLYING BASKET	:	An equally weighted basket composed of

Solvay	Sainsbury's
Lafarge	British Airways
Société Générale	Philip Morris
Daimler Chrysler	Ford Motor
Deutsche Lufthansa	Goodyear
Akzo Nobel	ENI
Unilever	Endessa

COUPON	:	Zero coupon
REDEMPTION	:	Each Note will be redeemed at maturity at an amount equal to

$$R = 100\% + Max(BASKET_{average} - 100\%, 0),$$

where
$BASKET_{average}$ is the arithmetic average of the basket value $BASKET_{value}$ over the 24 monthly Averaging Dates preceding the Maturity Date.

$$BASKET_{value} = \sum_{i=1}^{14} \omega_i \frac{S_i(t_j)}{S_i(0)}$$

with
$\omega_i = 1/14$ is the initial weighting of the ith share $(i=1,...,14)$.
$S_i(t_j)$ is the closing price of the ith share on the jth Averaging Date.

$S_i(0)$ opening price of the ith share on the Issue Date.
Averaging Dates are the final business day of the 24 months preceding the Maturity Date. The last $(j=24)$ Averaging Date is 5 business days before the Maturity Date.

of an approximation since first we approximate the basket as a single lognormal factor as discussed in Section 5.3 and then we impose the averaging to modify this single lognormal variable further to price an Asian option as in Section 4.3.1.

Unfortunately, this closed form approximation does not work for "averaging in" or when the averaging intervals are not equal. Monte Carlo simulation allows evaluation of the payoff but lots of fixings are sometimes required. For Example 5.3 there are $14 \times 24 = 336$ fixings for the full multivariate simulation. For big baskets with lots of fixings calculations can quickly become tedious and time consuming and various approximation methods must be implemented on a case by case basis. Sometimes "super-average" baskets based on average of monthly averages and other strange things are marketed but the overall concept is to compress the volatility down to increase participation.

5.3.2 *Capped protected basket bull notes*

As with a single underlying asset another popular method for reducing the cost of the basket call option is capping the basket return at a certain level. If K_I is the basket strike and K_L the cap level the redemption amount can be written as

$$R_{\substack{protected \\ basket cap}} = 100\% + \alpha Min[Max(B(T) - K_1, 0), K_L], \qquad (5.2)$$

where $B(T)$ is the basket value at maturity. This can be decomposed into a call spread so *long* a call strike K_1 and *short* a call strike $K_2 = K_1 + K_L$:

$$R_{\substack{protected \\ basket cap}} = 100\%$$
$$+ \alpha \{Max(B(T) - K_1, 0) - Max(B(T) - K_2, 0)\} \qquad (5.3)$$

Pricing this is relatively straightforward, except for determining the volatility to be used for the second call with the OTM strike. Typically the option is significantly OTM and smile effects will significantly reduce the value of the second option. An alternative structure that provides high participation is the individually capped basket call, where the performance of each constituent in the basket is capped.

Example 5.4

<table>
<tr><td colspan="2" align="center">EUR CAPPED PROTECTED BULL NOTES ON
A BASKET OF TELECOM STOCKS</td></tr>
<tr><td>ISSUER</td><td>: A rated Issuer</td></tr>
<tr><td>CURRENCY</td><td>: EUR</td></tr>
<tr><td>MATURITY</td><td>: 8 year</td></tr>
<tr><td>ISSUE PRICE</td><td>: 100%</td></tr>
<tr><td>UNDERLYING BASKET</td><td>: An equally weighted basket composed of
ATT
British Telecom
Vodaphone
France Telecom
Deutsche Telecom
Telecom Italia
Telefonica</td></tr>
<tr><td>COUPON</td><td>: Zero coupon</td></tr>
<tr><td>REDEMPTION</td><td>: Each Note will be redeemed at maturity at an amount equal to</td></tr>
</table>

$$R = 100\% + Min(Max(BASKET_{final} - 100\%, 80\%), 0\%),$$

where

$$BASKET_{final} = \sum_{i=1}^{N} \omega_i \frac{S_i(T)}{S_i(0)}$$

with

$\omega_i = 1/7$ the weighting coefficient of the ith share ($i=1,...,7$).
$S_i(T)$ is the closing price of the ith share 5 business days before the Maturity Date.
$S_i(0)$ opening price of the ith share on the Issue Date.

5.4 Protected Basket Cliquet Notes

This product is similar to the protected cliquet structure on a single underlying. The protected basket cliquet notes have a payoff typically linked to the sum of the annual performances of the basket. Generally, a cap and floor on each annual performance period is added. Capping the performance of each measurement period considerably reduces the cost of the option whilst still being appealing from an investor's point of view. Example 5.5 shows an "ethical" single stock basket with cliquet caps and floors on each period. The maximum annual return is set at 12%. The overall possible sum of the cliquets is limited to 8 x 12% with a floor of zero.

This product can be evaluated either as a closed form under a single factor approximation or via a Monte Carlo simulation (see Appx D.6). Protected basket cliquet notes are often popular with baskets of indices for example S&P500, Eurostoxx 50 and Nikkei 225.

Benelux Correlation

No trading desk really liked doing derivatives business with the Benelux institutions. Although they were prolific users of exotic derivatives of all asset classes the competition to get their business was extreme to say the least. They had standardised term-sheets and process and would ask about a million banks (a slight exaggeration) to price the deal for them. If as a trader you managed to get the deal it meant that your price was the "best" and therefore you probably had the "wrong" price or made an error somewhere (wrong volatility or correlation assumption or just stupidly read the term-sheet incorrectly). Particularly nasty were those correlation trades where there was no market observable for the correlation to be used. If you won one of those you had most likely been completely stuffed. The system they had invented was ruthless and left no morsels on the table for their counterparties. Since the system was so biased in their favour it was in a derivative salesman's interest to find "easier" clients. The preferred practice was (and still is) finding "naive capacity" or less informed investors to make some oversize profits to compensate.

Example 5.5

EUR PROTECTED CLIQUET NOTES ON
A BASKET OF ETHICAL STOCKS

ISSUER	:	A rated Issuer
CURRENCY	:	EUR
MATURITY	:	8 year
ISSUE PRICE	:	100%
UNDERLYING BASKET	:	An equally weighted basket composed of

Bilfinger & Berger	Xerox
Johnson & Johnson	British Telecom
Colgate Palmolive	Kingfisher
Deere & Co	

COUPON : Zero coupon

REDEMPTION : Each Note will be redeemed at maturity at an amount equal to

$$100\% + \sum_{j=1}^{8} Max\left(Min\left(\frac{BASKET(t_j)}{BASKET(t_{j-1})} - 100\%, 12\%\right), 0\%\right)$$

where

$$BASKET(t_j) = \sum_{i=1}^{N} \omega_i \frac{S_i(t_j)}{S_i(0)}$$

with
$\omega_i = 1/7$ is the initial coefficient of the ith share ($i=1,....7$).
$S_i(t_j)$ ($j=1,....7$) is the closing price of the ith share on the averaged over the last 5 business days of the jth year.
$S_i(t_8)$ is the closing price of the ith share 5 business days before the Maturity Date.
$S_i(0)$ opening price of the ith share on the Issue Date.

Example 5.6

15.0% EUR REVERSE CONVERTIBLE NOTES ON A FRENCH BANK BASKET		
ISSUER	:	AA rated Issuer
CURRENCY	:	EUR
MATURITY	:	1 year
ISSUE PRICE	:	100%
UNDERLYING	:	Basket composed of
		BNP Paribas 1 share
		CCF 1 share
		Société Générale 1 share
		Credit Agricole 1 share
ANNUAL COUPON	:	15.0%
DENOMINATION	:	$100\% \times BASKET_{initial}$, the opening price of the Underlying on the Issue Date.
REDEMPTION	:	Each Note will be redeemed at maturity as follows depending on $BASKET_{final}$, the closing price of the Underlying 3 business days before the Maturity date.
		If $BASKET_{final} \geq 100\% \times BASKET_{initial}$ at 100%.
		If $BASKET_{final} < 100\% \times BASKET_{initial}$ with 1 Basket (Physical Delivery) or its equivalent in EUR (Cash Settlement) at the issuer's choice.

5.5 Basket Reverse Convertibles

A reverse convertible on a basket is an interesting variant on the reverse convertible theme and it provides risk reduction and diversification for the investor. If the basket value has fallen below the strike on the maturity date the investor is redeemed (physically or in cash) the value of the basket. This diversification thus protects the investor should any single stock perform particularly badly.

The diversification effect obtained through using a basket does of course lower the volatility and hence the coupon compared with a single stock reverse convertible. Typically, basket reverse converts are structured on a particular sector so correlation and hence volatility remain high. A buyer of a basket reverse convertible is thus effectively short volatility and correlation. Increases in volatility and correlation will decrease the value of the notes. Example 5.6 shows a French bank basket where the issuer has the right to redeem physically in shares or cash should the basket have fallen in value at maturity.

The payoff of the basket reverse convertible can be written as

$$R_{\substack{reverse \\ basket}} = 100\% - Max(K - B(T), 0) , \qquad (5.4)$$

where the evaluation of the basket put can be carried out using a closed form under a single factor basket approximation. A high correlation basket will maintain a high volatility and hence a large coupon.

5.6 Protected Multiple Binary Notes

With *multiple binary notes* an enhanced coupon is paid if one or more underlyings finish above a particular strike level in any coupon period. A popular example is the *double binary cliquet notes* where both the two underlying indices (e.g. S&P 500 and DJ Eurostoxx 50) must rise in any given year for a high coupon to be paid (see Fig. 5.4).

The high coupon is produced by the lower joint probability of both events happening and although the correlation used in pricing is quite high (S&P 500/ DJ Eurostoxx 50 ~ 80–85%) large coupon enhancements are possible.

The double binary notes can be composed as a sum of a series of *double binaries* with one for each coupon period. The value of each double binary paying a fixed coupon can be calculated by considering the probability that both correlated stocks or indices rise in the same period. This can be evaluated using a Black–Scholes closed form solution for a digital binary. This closed form uses the joint probability distribution, which includes a correlation that both indices will finish above the strike at maturity. This joint probability distribution is described by the *bivariate normal distribution,* which is similar to the

Example 5.7

EUR 11% PROTECTED CLIQUET DOUBLE BINARY NOTES ON THE DJ EUROSTOXX 50 AND S&P 500	
ISSUER	: A rated Issuer
CURRENCY	: EUR
MATURITY	: 8 year
ISSUE PRICE	: 100%
UNDERLYING #1	: Dow Jones EUROSTOXX 50
UNDERLYING #2	: S&P 500
COUPON	: Each annual fixed coupon is dependent on the performance of the two Underlyings over the previous year with the jth ($j=1,...,8$) annual coupon payment equal to

$$Coupon\ (j)\ = 11\%$$
$$if\ \frac{S_1(t_j)}{S_1(t_{j-1})} > 100\%\ and\ \frac{S_2(t_j)}{S_2(t_{j-1})} > 100\%$$
$$Coupon\ (j)\ =\ 0\ \ otherwise$$

where
$S_i(t_j)$ ($j=1,...,7$) is the closing price of the ith Underlying ($i=1,2$) on the last business day of the jth year.

$S_i(t_8)$ is the) is the closing price of the ith Underlying ($i=1,2$) 5 business days before the Maturity Date.

$S_i(t_0)$ is the opening price of the ith Underlying on the Issue Date

REDEMPTION : Each Note will be redeemed at maturity at 100%.

normal distribution but with another dimension added to reflect the second underlying (Appx D.7). This methodology provides a theoretical valuation but in practice it proves better to smooth the discontinuity in the product by pricing as a *worst-of call spread* that we will discuss later in this chapter.

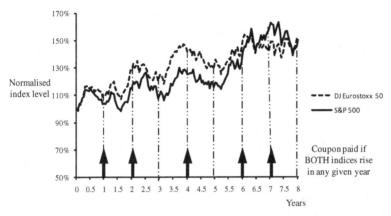

Figure 5.4: Double binary coupon simulation.

The double binary is a pure correlation product and although relatively insensitive to volatility is extremely sensitive to correlation. The investor is long correlation and as the correlation increases the value of the notes increases.

Double Binary System

We sold to a UK institutional investor a large index double binary (S&P, FTSE) at a great correlation making a tidy profit. We had even conservatively priced the digital payoff as a spread rather than being abrupt. Things were ok for a while and the option drifted far out of the money so there was almost no point hedging it. Then just before maturity both indices suddenly raced towards the strike and hovered incredibly close to the barrier. It made the trader sweat a bit since there was large gamma and it was proving impossible to hedge properly. Would we have to pay out a large sum of money and take a loss? Things were uncertain until the last minute but fortunately both indices finished below the strike.

Other multiple binary products are possible. The double binary can be referred to as a "2 in 2" product since there are two underlyings and both must finish above the strike. A "3 in 3" with three underlyings will provide a higher coupon. Some combinations, for example "3 in 4", can provide correlation sensitivity reversals which can lead to significant hedging problems. Usually if a correlation sensitivity is always in the same direction, we can assume a conservative estimate when we initially price the option.

5.7 Rainbow Notes

In a *rainbow note* the payout is based on the weighted sum of the returns of the underlyings in the basket ranked by performance. For example, for three underlyings something like 50% best performance, 30% second best and 20% worst ("50%/30%/20%") is common. Example 5.8 shows a rainbow option on three European indices.

The basic rainbow note is based on the forward price and there is no strike. The realised performances of stocks in the basket are sorted from the worst to the best and the rainbow option pays a weighted sum of these sorted returns.

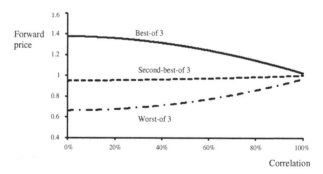

Figure 5.5: Example best-of forward versus basket correlation.

The rainbow option is generally priced using Monte Carlo simulation (Appx D.8). The individual stocks are simulated, sorted at the maturity date and the weights applied to attain the payoff. A complex closed form solution is possible for certain simplified products using copula techniques (see Appx G.13) but the majority of products traded include some form of averaging which generally means Monte Carlo is the only route. Figure 5.5 shows the behaviour of the price of a typical three name, 25% volatility rainbow forward versus correlation. Obviously at 100% correlation the *best-of* is equal to the *worst-of* forward. The best-of becomes very expensive as the correlation falls and the worst-of is very cheap for low correlation.

Example 5.8

EUR RAINBOW NOTES ON A BASKET OF EUROPEAN INDICES		
ISSUER	:	A rated Issuer
CURRENCY	:	EUR
MATURITY	:	5 year
ISSUE PRICE	:	100%
UNDERLYING BASKET	:	FTSE 100 CAC 40 MIB 30
COUPON	:	Zero coupon
REDEMPTION	:	The weight of each underlying in the Basket is defined at maturity depending on the ranking of the performance of each index between the opening price on the Issue Date and the closing price 5 business days before the Maturity Date. Each Note will be redeemed at maturity at an amount equal to $$R = 50\% \frac{S_1(T)}{S_1(0)} + 30\% \frac{S_2(T)}{S_2(0)} + 20\% \frac{S_3(T)}{S_3(0)}$$ where $S_i(T)$ is the closing price of the *i*th <u>best</u> performing index (*i*=1,2,3) 5 business days before the Maturity Date. $S_i(0)$ opening price of the *i*th <u>best</u> performing index on the Issue Date.

Example 5.9

EUR PROTECTED RAINBOW NOTES ON A BASKET OF INDICES

ISSUER	:	A rated Issuer
CURRENCY	:	EUR
MATURITY	:	5 year
ISSUE PRICE	:	100%
UNDERLYING BASKET	:	FTSE 100 CAC 40 MIB 30
COUPON	:	Zero coupon
REDEMPTION	:	The weight of each underlying in the Basket is defined at maturity depending on the ranking of the performance of each index between the opening price on the Issue Date and the closing price 5 business days before the Maturity Date. Each Note will be redeemed at maturity at an amount equal to

$$R = 100\% + 80\% \times Max \left(50\% \frac{S_1(T)}{S_1(0)} + 30\% \frac{S_2(T)}{S_2(0)} + 20\% \frac{S_3(T)}{S_3(0)} - 100\%, 0\% \right)$$

where

$S_i(T)$ is the closing price of the ith <u>best</u> performing index ($i=1,2,3$) 5 business days before the Maturity Date.

$S_i(0)$ opening price of the ith <u>best</u> performing index on the Issue Date.

Using the same pricing model many combinations are possible and the value of the option and the correlation behaviour will vary enormously. The same pricing model can be used to price a wide range of basket products including pure *worst-of* (0%/0%/100%) and *best-of* structures (100%/0%/0%).

5.7.1 *Protected rainbow notes*

A call option on the rainbow payout is also popular since it allows capital protected structures. Particularly popular are best-of and *second-best* notes although these options are expensive and participations are low unless averaging is used.

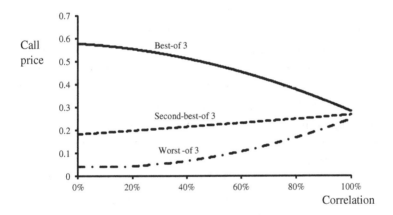

Figure 5.6: Example rainbow call price versus basket correlation.

The *rainbow call* is calculated by including a strike on the payoff of the rainbow basket at maturity (Appx D.8). In Fig. 5.6 we can see that the best-of call option is significantly more expensive than the second-best-of or worst-of call options and that the price increases with decreasing correlation. Typically the worst-of is 3–6 times cheaper than the best-of. This is the opposite correlation behaviour than for a normal basket call option and issuing some rainbow notes can hedge the correlation risk in trading books.

5.8 Worst-of Protected Notes

The worst-of option is an option on the worst performance in the basket of stocks or indices. It is a form of rainbow option and has proved very popular in recent years in the form of capital protected notes. The primary reason for its popularity is the high participations that can be obtained due to the very low cost of the option. As the number of stocks in the basket increases and the correlation decreases the option becomes cheaper. In Example 5.10 traded below the product is capital guaranteed and the worst-of option is so cheap that a 1% base annual coupon is payable. The payout is written as 200% plus the worst-of forward so if the worst performance over 10 years is −20% then the investor receives 180% at maturity. If it rises by 20% the investor receives 220%. This is very appealing for an investor who thinks he can pick a quality blue-chip basket in which all stocks will rise over 10 years.

The note is capital protected since the worst possible performance is potentially bankruptcy of a name with an effective −100% performance. In this sense it worth considering the worst-of option as an analogy for a *first-to-default* credit default swap introduced in Chapter 9. It is obviously important to avoid companies that are overleveraged or in distressed sectors such as autos and airlines and stick to quality investment grade names.

The most common form of the option pays the worst performance and has no strike (forward strike set at zero). The payoff of the actual option is given by

$$Payoff_{\substack{worst-of \\ forward}} = Min\left(\frac{S_1(T)}{S_1(0)}, \frac{S_2(T)}{S_2(0)}, ..., \frac{S_{N_B}(T)}{S_{N_B}(0)} \right). \tag{5.5}$$

Usually this is evaluated using a Monte Carlo simulation (see Appx D.9). However a closed form solution does exist for two underlyings based on the well known *exchange option* (see Appx D.10) and can be extended through a *normal copula* approximation to several underlyings in a similar fashion to a *first-to-default* basket in Chapter 9 (see Appx G.13). Figure 5.7 shows the worst-of forward price and demonstrates that adding up to about 10 names to the basket significantly reduces the worst-of price.

Example 5.10

EUR PROTECTED "WORST-OF" BULL NOTES ON A BASKET OF EUROPEAN BLUE CHIP STOCKS

ISSUER	:	A rated Issuer
CURRENCY	:	EUR
MATURITY	:	10 year
ISSUE PRICE	:	100%
UNDERLYING BASKET	:	An equally weighted basket composed of

Alcatel	BMW
Pinault Printemps	Hoechst
Peugeot	Vodaphone
Edison	Reed Elsevier
Telecom Italia	Telefonica

COUPON	:	1% per annum
REDEMPTION	:	Each Note will be redeemed at maturity at an amount equal to

$$200\% + Min\left[\frac{S_1(T)-S_1(0)}{S_1(0)},...,\ ...,\frac{S_i(T)-S_i(0)}{S_i(0)},...,\ ...\frac{S_{10}(T)-S_{10}(0)}{S_{10}(0)} \right]$$

where
$S_i(T)$ is the closing price of the *i*th share (*i*=1,...,10) 5 business days before the Maturity Date.
$S_i(0)$ opening price of the *i*th share on the Issue Date.

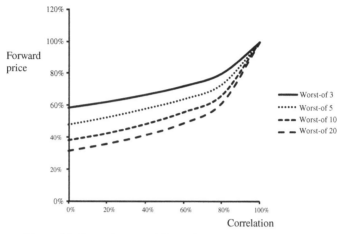

Figure 5.7: Example wrst-of forward versus basket correlation.

5.8.1 *Everest protected notes*

Everest protected notes were a very successful capital guaranteed product invented by Société Générale in the late 90s. During this period SocGen led a wave of innovative, best selling correlation products such as "Everest", "Atlas" and "Himalaya". More recent products of this type are usually variations of similar themes. Even with conservative correlation assumptions these products looked extremely attractive to investors (although very complex to understand).

The Everest notes pay high annual coupon linked to the worst performing stock in a basket of some 10–15 diversified blue-chip stocks. Investors were lured by the high headline coupon (often over 10%) and by the logic that although in the short term the worst performing stock of a basket of blue chips might fall slightly, over several years even the worst performing stock would probably rise in value. Typically these notes were issued with 6–10 year maturities.

Informed investors could take the view that over time most equities historically rise in value ensuring significant coupons at least in later years, whereas in the risk neutral Black–Scholes world, due to the volatility of the equities there is a high probability that at least one equity will fall considerably in value. In a sense this can be viewed as "risk neutral" versus "real world" arbitrage or simply an investor's view against the strong assumptions of the model.

Example 5.11

EUR PROTECTED "EVEREST" NOTES ON A BASKET OF EUROPEAN BLUE CHIP STOCKS

ISSUER	:	A rated Issuer
CURRENCY	:	EUR
MATURITY	:	10 year
ISSUE PRICE	:	100%
UNDERLYING BASKET	:	An equally weighted basket composed of

Alcatel	Smithkline Beecham
Carrefour	SAP
DaimlerChrysler	Vodaphone
Deutsche Bank	Reed Elsevier
Telecom Italia	Sonera

COUPON : The annual coupon paid in the *j*th year will index the worst performing share in the portfolio and be equal to

$$10\% \times Min\left[\frac{S_1(t_j)-S_1(0)}{S_1(0)},...,\frac{S_i(t_j)-S_i(0)}{S_i(0)},... \\ ...,\frac{S_{10}(t_j)-S_{10}(0)}{S_{10}(0)}\right],$$

where
$S_i(t_j)$ is the closing price of the *i*th share *(i=1,...,10)* 5 business days before the end of the *j*th year *(j=1,...,10)*
$S_i(0)$ opening price of the *i*th share on the Issue Date.

REDEMPTION : Each Note will be redeemed at maturity at 100%

In the Example 5.11 if the worst stock has fallen −25% from the issue date, then the annual coupon payable is 75% × 10% = 7.5%. For pricing the Everest paying a fixed coupon can be decomposed into a series of worst-of basket options for each of the annual coupon dates (Appx D.11).

5.8.2 *Power reverse convertibles*

Another application of the worst-of concept is the *power reverse convertible*. These are reverse convertibles where the coupon is enhanced by the investor effectively selling a very expensive put on the worst performing share in basket. Usually power reverse convertibles are only based on a basket of 2–4 stocks and the denomination of the notes is set so that physical delivery is possible. This allows the investor to hold the equity until it recovers if it has fallen beneath the strike (which is highly likely).

Although they offer a very high coupon the fact that they redeem the worst-of if the worst performing share falls below the strike makes them fairly toxic unless the shares are carefully chosen. Many power reverse convertibles were written on technology shares before the ".com" crash and presumably redeemed in shares although investors received a high coupon. The Example 5.12 shows a physically redeemed power reverse convertible on Deutsche Telekom and Nokia.

The power reverse can be valued as a put on the worst performing share with a strike K (typically 100%). This put is therefore extremely expensive and since the note-holder is a seller of the option this provides a high coupon. The redemption amount for N_B stocks in the basket is given as

$$R_{\substack{power \\ reverse}} = 100\% - Max\left(K - Min\left(\frac{S_1(T)}{S_1(0)}, \frac{S_2(T)}{S_2(0)}, ..., \frac{S_{N_B}(T)}{S_{N_B}(0)}\right), 0\right). \qquad (5.6)$$

For two stocks it is usual to value with a closed form solution whilst for a larger basket a Monte Carlo is better (Appx D.12). The maximum number of stocks in the basket I have seen is four.

Example 5.12

15.5% EUR POWER REVERSE CONVERTIBLE NOTES ON DEUTSCHE TELEKOM OR NOKIA		
ISSUER	:	AA rated Issuer
CURRENCY	:	EUR
MATURITY	:	2 year
ISSUE PRICE	:	100%
UNDERLYING	:	Deutsche Telekom AG 90 shares Nokia OYJ 40 shares
ANNUAL COUPON	:	15.5%
DENOMINATION	:	EUR 3600.
REDEMPTION	:	Each Note will be redeemed at maturity as follows, depending on $NOKIA_{final}$ and DTE_{final}, the closing price of the 2 underlyings 3 business days before the Maturity Date: If $NOKIA_{final} \geq$ EUR 90 and if $DTE_{final} \geq$ EUR 40 at 100% otherwise each Note is redeemed into the share that has declined most (40 NOKIA shares or 90 DTE shares).

5.9 Performance Select Protected Notes

Another popular basket product concept has been based around the idea of "performance select". During the life of the notes several stocks, usually the best or the worst, are removed from the basket. The payout at maturity is then based on the performance of either the remaining stocks or those removed from the basket depending on the product. Three widely sold products in Europe were the SocGen "Atlas" with the capital unprotected variant the "Kilimanjaro" and the "Himalaya". For maximum flexibility these require Monte Carlo pricing although, as previously mentioned, limited closed forms using a technique similar to the normal copulas for first-to-default CDS have been developed (Appx G.13).

The Min/Max Grand Prix Notes

The Everest product, based on the worst performing share in a basket, provided a high coupon with a capital guarantee – typically 10% coupon at the time. One day we had an eager salesman with a client involved in Grand Prix motorsports who wanted to buy a capital guaranteed product but it had to pay a much higher coupon than the Everest. Virtually impossible we said but eventually we came up with the craziest product I have ever devised: the "Min–Max" note (although it had a fancy marketing name). The large 16% coupons were linked to the difference between the minimum and maximum performance (since issue) of a basket of shares. We priced with conservative vols and correlation and included tidy profit. The client loved it and did a reasonable size trade despite the salesman dropping the coupon to 12% and increasing his sales margin at the last minute. Unfortunately, about one week after issuance Nokia (which was in the basket) crashed and the commodity based shares rallied ... reducing the coupon massively. Things looked bleak but eventually Nokia recovered enough to pay a reasonable coupon.

5.9.1 *Atlas protected notes*

With the "Atlas" protected notes the investor receives 100% plus a call on the performance of a basket of the remaining stocks at maturity. In the Example 5.13 below an initial basket of 21 stocks is used. After 5 years the 5 worst performing stocks are removed from the basket, leaving 16 stocks. On the 10 year maturity date the 6 best performing stocks are removed leaving only 10 stocks upon which the basket call performance is calculated.

Optically this looks attractive to the investor since he is avoiding the worst stocks although sacrificing the best at maturity. Also he has 100% capital guarantee and 100% participation at maturity. However, removing the five worst stocks in year 5 has actually little effect since so much can happen in the last 5 years. The call option is effectively almost a call on the worst 10 stocks in a basket of 16 stocks since the 6 best are removed at the end.

Practically pricing using Monte Carlo simulation is straight forward: in year 5 the stocks are sorted and the worst 5 removed and then at maturity the basket is sorted again and the 6 best are removed. The final basket value is based on the average performance since issue of the 10 remaining stocks.

5.9.2 *Himalaya protected notes*

The "Himalaya" product has a similar sorting concept to the Atlas. Example 5.14 shows a 6 year capital protected product with an initial basket of 12 stocks. Each year the two best performing stocks are removed from the basket and their average return calculated and recorded. All returns are calculated with respect to the values of the individual stocks on the issue date. At maturity the investor is redeemed 100% plus a call (70% participation in example) on the sum of all the yearly average returns. For the investor this seems appealing since he is receiving the returns of the best stocks every year.

5.10 Worst-of Knock-out Notes

Several complex products such as the Pulsar and Altiplano based on combining worst-of and knock-out options were developed where the worst share hits a barrier (set very low) to determine whether a coupon is paid. These products arbitraged investors' expectations of how stocks behave and how baskets of stocks are actually modelled to produce cheap options, hence large coupons, and capital guaranteed products.

5.10.1 *Pulsar protected notes*

The "Pulsar" note was a long dated, capital guaranteed product which allowed very high structuring and sales margins (8–14%!) whilst appearing optically attractive to investors in a low interest rate environment. The Pulsar is very difficult to understand completely and in fact I don't know how investors ever understood much about the product except the 10–12%+ potential coupon. Some very large trades were carried out, however, so here is an attempt at an explanation.

Example 5.13

EUR "ATLAS" PROTECTED NOTES ON A BASKET OF PHARMACEUTICAL STOCKS	
ISSUER	: A rated Issuer
CURRENCY	: EUR
MATURITY	: 10 year
ISSUE PRICE	: 100%
UNDERLYING BASKET	: An equally weighted basket initially composed of 21 pharmaceutical stocks: Abott Laboratories American Home Prods Amgen Biogen ... 21 stocks in total
BASKET SELECTION PROCESS	: 5 years before the Maturity Date the 5 shares demonstrating the worst performance are removed from the underlying basket. On the final valuation date 3 business days before the Maturity Date the 6 best performing shares are removed from the basket leaving 10 shares which are used to determine the final Basket value.
COUPON	: Zero coupon
REDEMPTION	: Each Note will be redeemed at maturity at an amount equal to $$R = 100\% + Max(BASKET_{final} - 100\%, 0),$$ where $$BASKET_{final} = \sum_{i=1}^{N} \omega_i \frac{S_i(T)}{S_i(0)} \quad \text{and}$$ $\omega_i = 10\%$ is the weighting coefficient of the ith share ($i=1,...,10$) remaining in the basket at the Maturity Date. $S_i(T)$ is the closing price of the ith share remaining in the basket 3 business days before the Maturity Date. $S_i(0)$ opening price of the corresponding ith share on the Issue Date.

Example 5.14

EUR "HIMALAYA" PROTECTED BULL NOTES ON A BASKET OF EUROPEAN BLUE-CHIPS

ISSUER	:	A rated Issuer
CURRENCY	:	EUR
MATURITY	:	6 year
ISSUE PRICE	:	100%
UNDERLYING BASKET	:	An equally weighted basket composed of

Adeco	France Telecom
Axa	L'Oreal
BMW	Pinault-Printemps
British Airways	Roche
Deutsche bank	Tesco
Endessa	Total

BASKET SELECTION PROCESS : At the end of each year the 2 <u>best</u> performing shares are <u>removed</u> from the basket and their average return to the removal date recorded. Thus for the ith year 2 stocks are removed and the average return $RETURN(i)$ calculated.

$$RETURN(i) = \frac{1}{2}\left(\frac{S_1(t_i)}{S_1(0)} + \frac{S_2(t_i)}{S_2(0)} - 200\% \right)$$

with

$S_j(t_i)$ is the closing price of the jth share (j=1,2) removed at the end of the ith year.

$S_j(0)$ opening price of the corresponding jth share on the Issue Date.

COUPON : Zero coupon

REDEMPTION : Each Note will be redeemed at maturity at an amount

$$100\% + 70\% \times Max(\sum_i^6 RETURN(i) - 100\%, 0).$$

Example 5.15

EUR "PULSAR" PROTECTED NOTES ON A BASKET OF EUROPEAN BLUE CHIP STOCKS

ISSUER	:	A rated Issuer
CURRENCY	:	EUR
MATURITY	:	10 year
ISSUE PRICE	:	100%
UNDERLYING BASKET	:	An equally weighted basket composed of

BASF	Nokia
BMW	Elsevier NV
Akzo Nobel	Novartis
Dresdner Bank	Telefonica
LVMH	Total Fina

COUPON	:	Zero coupon
KNOCK-IN EVENT	:	Between Year 6 and Year 10 , if the lowest daily closing price of any of the 10 underlying stocks ($STOCK_{min}$) is lower than or equal to 60% of their initial values ($STOCK_{min} \leq 60\% \ STOCK_{initial}$) then a Knock-in Event will occur.
REDEMPTION	:	Each Note will be redeemed at maturity as follows:

If the Knock-in Event has not occurred a redemption amount equal to 300% (annualised yield 11.6% equivalent)

If the Knock-in Event has occurred a redemption amount equal to 200% plus the return of the worst performing stock at maturity.

$$200\% + Min\left[\frac{S_1(T)-S_1(0)}{S_1(0)},...,\frac{S_i(T)-S_i(0)}{S_i(0)},...,\frac{S_{10}(T)-S_{10}(0)}{S_{10}(0)} \right],$$

where
$S_i(T)$ is the closing price of the *i*th share ($i=1,...,10$) 5 business days before the Maturity Date.
$S_i(0)$ opening price of the *i*th share on the Issue Date.

The Pulsar references an underlying basket of 10 or so diversified stocks as in Example 5.15. The investor will be paid 300% in year 10 (equal to an effective yield of 11.6%) except if any of the stocks during years 6–10 fall below 60% of their initial values. If any stock has fallen this low, then the investor will be paid at maturity 200% plus the performance of the worst performing stock at maturity. Notice importantly that the stock falling below the 60% barrier is not necessarily the worst stock at maturity (a fact missed by many investors). Thus if stock A is 55% of its initial value in year 7 and rises to 110% by maturity, whilst stock B falls by 20% over the 10 years, the notes will redeem 200%–20% = 180%. If stock B falls to 0 then the redemption amount is equal to 200%–100% = 100%. The product can be decomposed into:

(i)   a zero coupon bond redeeming 100% at maturity.
(ii)   a worst-of, knock-out digital paying 200% with a barrier at 40% of the initial stock price of each stock.
(iii)   a worst-of, knock-in forward on the worst-of with a knock-in at 40% and forward strike at the initial stock price.

Some products have also been structured with (iii) being a knock-in Asian call on the worst of rather than a forward (Appx D.13).

The value can be determined by Monte Carlo simulation. However, due to the continuous barrier, long maturity and large number of stocks in the basket the simulation is computationally quite complex, particularly to calculate deltas and gammas on the individual stocks. In general the barrier can be approximated as a discretely sampled barrier and the effect of convergence to a continuous barrier can be investigated to provide a bound on pricing error.

With about 10+ stocks and long maturities the knock-out digital is very cheap (since it is expected to knock-out). The knock-in forward on the worst-of is also inexpensive for a diversified basket since it is probable, under Black–Scholes, that at least one stock will have fallen considerably by maturity. For most hedging scenarios a knock-out will occur but is easy to imagine future equity paths that although theoretically possible to hedge are in fact a complete nightmare to hedge practically. To cover this risk, sufficient profits must ideally be made on the trade.

Investors are long correlation, since as correlation rises both the value of the digital and the worst-of forward increases. The price sensitivity to correlation assumptions is very high and the key factor in pricing.

Example 5.16

EUR "NEPTUNE" PROTECTED NOTES ON A BASKET OF EUROPEAN BLUE CHIP STOCKS		
ISSUER	:	A rated Issuer
CURRENCY	:	EUR
MATURITY	:	10 Years
ISSUE PRICE	:	100%
UNDERLYING BASKET	:	An equally weighted basket composed of
		BASF Nokia
		BMW Elsevier NV
		Akzo Nobel Novartis
		Dresdner Bank Telefonica
		LVMH Total
COUPON	:	12% annual coupon is payable except if during the previous year the <u>lowest</u> daily closing price of <u>any</u> of the 10 underlying stocks ($STOCK_{min}$) is lower than or equal to 50% of their initial values ($STOCK_{min} \le 50\%\ STOCK_{initial}$) as determined on the Issue Date then no coupon will be payable.
REDEMPTION	:	Each Note will be redeemed at maturity at 100%.

5.10.2 *Altiplano and Neptune protected notes*

The SocGen "Altiplano" protected notes are based on the technology used to price the Pulsar. The notes have just one worst-of knock-out coupon at maturity and a guaranteed minimum coupon if there is a knock-out. Thus, a large coupon is paid provided that no stock in the underlying basket of stocks falls at any time below a predetermined barrier level (Appx D.14). This provides an easier to understand and more transparent product than the Pulsar. A variant of the Altiplano is the "Neptune" that featured a series of annual worst-of knock-out coupons.

5.11 Summary

Equity basket or correlation products provide an extremely wide range of investment products (see Fig. 5.8) ranging in complexity from simple basket products to worst-of barrier products such as the Pulsar. They can be structured to provide a range of different risk profiles. By using a diversified basket effective volatility can be lowered resulting in higher participations in capital guaranteed products. High income products can be produced by selling expensive options such as worst-of puts to enhance coupons whilst retaining capital guarantees.

The products are notoriously difficult to price and hedging after issuance is problematic since many underlying assets must be monitored over very long maturities. Trading basket products, due to the limitations of the models and the correlation assumptions imposed, becomes an "art form" and requires the most skilful traders, if the theoretical upfront profits on trades are to be locked in until product maturity.

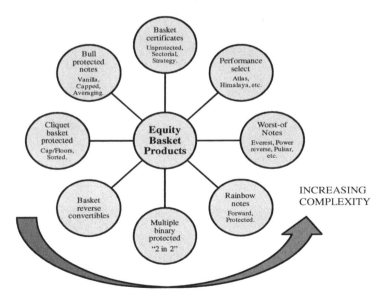

Figure 5.8: Equity basket products.

Chapter 6

Pricing Interest Rate Products

6.1 Introduction

Beyond the simple present value discounting approach used to value swaps and bonds we require interest rate models to value option based structures where the payout is determined by the level of interest rates.

Interest rate derivatives can range from simple call and put options on the level of floating rates or LIBOR such as *caps* and *floors* to more complex structures where the payout might include numerous "exotic" features such as ranges and barriers, choosers, ratchets etc. This wide range of products will be described in more detail in the next chapter. To correctly value them demands a variety of complex interest rate models.

In the early 1990s there was a rapid expansion in the interest rate derivatives markets as investors purchased *structured notes* to provide increased income in what was viewed then as a low rate environment. Although debacles linked to structured notes such as the California Orange County bankruptcy demonstrated that investors did not fully understand the risks involved in these new products, the advent of the structured note market led to a rapid evolution in interest rate derivatives technology. Interest rate structured notes are generally more suitable for institutional investors since retail investors prefer higher returns than the typical 50–200bp yield gains obtained in structured interest rate products.

Modelling interest rates is far more demanding than equity derivatives for which Black–Scholes is the relatively simple market standard for all products. Although as we have seen the nature of equity structured products has become increasingly complex (equity baskets, increased correlation products etc.), interest rate products are generally simpler in design but the actual modelling of the interest rate process is far more difficult for several reasons.

Firstly, the probabilistic distribution followed by interest rates is complicated. In one sense rates are bounded; they rarely rise extremely high (<15–20% for most economies) and are essentially never negative. In addition, today's forward interest rate curve describes the market expectation of future rates and this must be included in any model.

Secondly, unlike for equity products where only one variable, the spot equity price, is modelled, for many interest rate products the entire term structure of interest rates is required in valuation. The evolution of the term structure or zero curve is a complex process and can exhibit parallel shifts, twists, inversion and slope changes. In general, since an entire range of liquid instruments (futures, swaps, bonds, etc.) can be more or less continuously traded along the interest rate curve, any curve movements within the model must be "arbitrage" free to be financially consistent.

Lastly, the volatilities of the various parts of the interest rate curve are markedly different. In general, the short end is more volatile than the long end and a maximum volatility can be exhibited at intermediate maturities.

6.2 Approaches to Modelling Interest Rates

Although there has been a rapid evolution in complexity of models over the last few years, a pragmatic approach and a good rule of thumb is to use the simplest model that describes the key features of the derivative being modelled. It is easy to build a complex model including many stochastic or random factors but calibration, stability and successful implementation of the model becomes much more difficult. The model can quickly become a "black-box" which very few people, including the traders, can fully understand.

The simplest models have one stochastic factor and model either the evolution of one chosen forward rate (as in Black's model) or model the process of the *spot rate* (the "short maturity" rate) and describe the movement of the rest of the yield curve in a quasi parallel manner (see Fig. 6.1). Examples of the latter include the Vasicek model and its extensions, including Ho–Lee, Cox–Ingersol Ross (CIR), Black–Karasinski and the popular Hull–White model that we shall detail here.

Models which try to "correctly" describe the movement of the yield curve in an *arbitrage free* framework are generally termed *yield curve models*. In yield curve models either the spot rate or forward rates are stochastically modelled and conditions are applied so that all future movements of the yield curve are *non-arbitrage* – that is we cannot have a strategy of buying and selling liquid instruments along the yield curve to produce a risk free profit or arbitrage. For the more complex models the mathematical proof of consistency with no arbitrage can be quite involved.

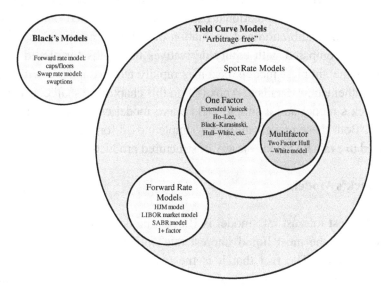

Figure 6.1: Different interest rate models.

Most models also assume that the movement of spot rates or forward rates are either normal or lognormally probability distributed. Normally distributed models, although they can often be more analytically tractable, can unfortunately produce negative rates. Although this happens with relatively low probability and does not seem to influence the pricing of the majority of products, it is obviously considered to be slightly unrealistic. Some models have been developed which use a lognormal or lognormal chi-squared distributions, which avoid these problems.

The various interest rate models possess different base equations or equation of state which describe the basic stochastic process governing the evolution of interest rates (Appx E.1). All the models have either a stochastic equation that define the evolution of a single forward rate or swap rate (Black's models) or full yield curve models that model the entire yield curve and have as their stochastic variable the spot rate $r(t)$ (Vasicek models) or the forward rate (HJM or LIBOR market models). The models are also characterised by the number of stochastic factors and are generally limited to one or two. Interest rate quantitative analysts or "quants" can talk for hours (maybe even days) about their preferred type of model.

Simple interest rate models allow closed forms for European options. This allows quick computational calculations to be carried out, which is handy for fast calibration and evaluation of risk parameters. It should be noted that compared with equity derivatives the maths for closed forms even for the simplest models becomes rapidly tedious and we will leave most mathematical details to Appx (E). In this chapter we shall concentrate on Black's model and a simple yield curve model called the Hull–White model. Both these models allow for simple closed form solutions and can be used to evaluate a wide variety of structured products.

6.3 Black's Model

The simplest interest rate model is Black's model and this is the market standard for the most liquid interest rate options including caps, floors and swaptions. The fact that it is the market standard for vanilla and simple options is important since any other model developed must calibrate to Black's model.

Caps and floors are simply European call and put options on forward rates. Swaptions are options to enter into interest rate swaps with strike equal to the swap rate and we shall discuss these in detail later.

Black's model is market standard to such an extent that the implied volatility is quoted by brokers and the OTC market instead of the premium or price. Thus, it is assumed that all market participants use the same model and indeed, in a couple of minutes on a Bloomberg terminal you will find the pricing model.

The implied volatilities of these vanilla interest rate options are used to calibrate the models used to price more exotic options. This is the case even if the final model used to price the exotic option is not Black's model.

6.3.1 *Black's model for forward rates*

Black's model assumes that simple forward rates are lognormally distributed. It is only applicable for European options since it models one particular underlying forward rate rather than modelling the whole yield curve. All other rates used for discounting and not explicitly involved in the final option payoff are assumed constant and non-stochastic.

If $f_t = f(t,T,T+h)$ is the forward rate between T and $(T+h)$ at time t the evolution of the forward rate is given by

$$\frac{df_t}{f_t} = -\sigma_T \; dz, \qquad (6.1)$$

where $\sigma_T = \sigma(T,T+h)$ is the volatility of the forward rate fixing at time T for period h and dz is a normally distributed random variable. Equation (6.1) is very similar to the Black–Scholes equation for equities but there is no effective drift term since we are simulating the actual forward. The forward rate is thus lognormally distributed (Fig. 6.2). Since this is similar to the Black–Scholes equation for equities and we can use a similar methodology to derive closed forms for cap/floors and swaptions (Appx E.2).

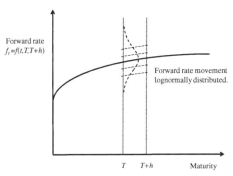

Figure 6.2: Black's forward rate model.

6.3.2 *Black's cap*

The most simple interest rate options are the *cap* and *floor*. Anybody who has entered into a capped mortgage will be familiar with an interest rate cap. A cap is composed of a series of *caplets* for different interest rate periods which are essentially call options on a floating rate or LIBOR on different dates in the future at say 3 month intervals. The market convention is that a caplet fixes at the start of each floating rate period and pays at the end. Thus a buyer of a cap will receive at the end of each floating rate period a payment of the floating rate minus the cap strike if the floating rate fixed at the beginning of the period was above the strike.

A buyer of a cap will benefit if the interest rate rises. Somebody exposed to floating rate payments can purchase a cap to effectively hedge against a rise of rates. The payoff of a single period caplet (Fig. 6.3(a)) is written

$$Payoff_{caplet} = Max\,(f_T - K, 0)\,. \qquad (6.2)$$

A floor is effectively the inverse of a cap and is composed of a series of floating rate put options or *floorlets* (Fig. 6.3(b)). A buyer of a floorlet will be protected should rates fall.

$$Payoff_{floorlet} = Max\,(K - f_T, 0)\,. \qquad (6.3)$$

In a similar fashion to put/call parity there is no arbitrage cap/floor relation for a given strike given by *Cap Price = Floor Price + Swap Price*.

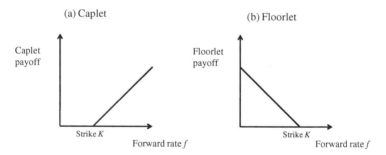

Figure 6.3: Caplet and floorlet payoff profiles.

The total payoff of an *N* period cap over its life is given by the sum of the payoff of *N* caplets.

$$Payoff_{cap} = \sum_{i}^{N} h_i Max(f_i - K, 0), \qquad (6.4)$$

where we have denoted floating rates $f_i = f(t_i, t_i, t_i + h_i)$ with interest fixing times t_i and accrual periods h_i.

The entire cap is priced as a series of caplets and the $Max(f_i - K, 0)$ term is analogous to the $Max(S(T) - K, 0)$ term of an equity call option. The closed form caplet can therefore be derived by replacing the equity price with the forward rate in the Black–Scholes call option equation and assuming zero drift. The closed forms are presented in Appx (E.3). The interest rate for discounting is assumed to uncorrelated with respect to the forward rate so the discounting factors in Black–Scholes equation can be retained. This last assumption is obviously unrealistic and is remedied in more complex models such as the Hull–White model.

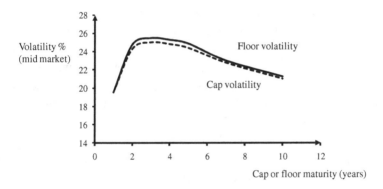

Figure 6.4: Example market cap and floor volatilities.

6.4 Market Volatility of Caps and Floors

Rather than quoting the price of caps and floors in the interbank market often the implied volatility is quoted. From this dealers can calculate the actual price using Black's model. A different volatility is quoted for each spot starting cap of different maturity and strike. This volatility $\sigma_{cap}(T, K)$ is effectively the flat volatility or average volatility used for all caplets within the cap to recover the market price of the cap. Usually the market (see Fig. 6.4) exhibits a humped structure with higher cap volatilities for intermediate maturities. This average volatility is not in general equal to the true forward volatility $\sigma(t_i, t_i + h)$ of each caplet or forward rate period.

The actual volatility of each forward rate or the forward-forward volatility as it is known must be established by "bootstrapping" using caps of different maturities. Starting with the cap with the shortest maturity (where the forward volatility is equal to the average cap maturity) the forward volatilities for the other caplets of different maturities can be determined and this is a standard procedure.

6.5 The Hull–White Model

The widely used *Hull–White interest rate model* is probably the simplest one factor term-structure model that can be successfully applied to modelling a wide range of products. It is essentially an arbitrage free adaptation of an earlier model called the Vasicek model and is sometimes referred to as an *extended Vasicek* model.

The Hull–White framework models the *spot rate* $r(t)$ as a random normal process. The spot rate $r(t)$ is the short rate or the zero rate as the maturity tends to zero. A *mean reversion* parameter a is included which avoids very high and very low rates being produced by the model. When rates are too high or too low they are forced back towards the expected forward rate curve (see Fig. 6.5).

The high level of analytical tractability offered by the model allows many types of European structures to be evaluated as closed form solutions which provide increased speed of computation. Structures with Bermudan and American exercise features can be priced with recombining trees and finite difference techniques.

One criticism of the model is that the normal spot rate process allows the possibility of negative interest rates. In reality these effects are very small for most structures when the current term-structure is positive, forward rates are not too low and reasonable levels of mean reversion are used although this can produce a problem for low rates usually for example in Japanese Yen.

The Hull–White model is an arbitrage free whole yield curve model. It provides an exact fit to today's observed term-structure and movements of the yield curve are modelled as approximately parallel shifts for low mean reversion parameters (Fig. 6.6). The model is thus good for pricing products dependent on the level of floating rates or LIBOR but not really suitable for certain products where the payout is strongly dependent on changes in shape of the yield curve.

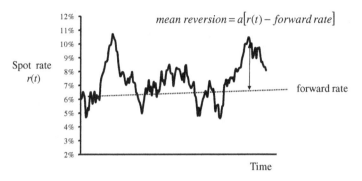

Figure 6.5: Mean reversion effect on the spot rate.

The basic process for the spot rate *r(t)* in the Hull–White model is given by

$$dr(t) = [\theta(t) - a\,r(t)]dt + \sigma\,dz(t). \tag{6.5}$$

As mentioned here, the spot rate *r(t)* is essentially the instantaneous forward rate or zero rate for zero maturity and can be visualised as the shortest maturity interest rate of the yield curve at time *t*. It differs from the Black–Scholes type equation in that it is a normal rather than lognormal process with *dr* being directly proportional to the random process (Appx E.4).

Importantly, the drift term in Eq. (6.5) with time interval *dt* is more complex than for Black's model. The function $\theta(t)$ allows a fitting to the zero curve. The parameter *a* determines the *mean reversion* effect within the model and the spot rate *r(t)* will revert to $\theta(t)/a$ at a rate *a*. A simpler model with no mean reversion and *a* = 0 is known as the *Ho–Lee model*. The drift of the spot rate *r* follows the slope of the instantaneous forward rate curve and reverts back at a rate *a* when it moves away from the forward rate curve. This is demonstrated in Fig. 6.5.

The spot rate volatility σ within the model is constant with time and maturity. Thus once the initial term-structure has been determined to provide $\theta(t)$ the only two parameters to calibrate within the model are σ and mean reversion a. The effect of mean reversion is to produce a declining forward rate volatility (Fig. 6.7).

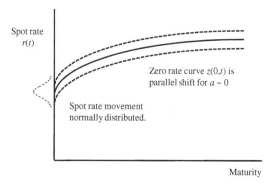

Figure 6.6: Spot rate movement in the Hull–White model.

In Eq. (6.5) the $\theta(t)$ function can be calculated from the initial interest rate term structure and in limit of low mean reversion ($a \sim 0$) is equal to the *slope* of the instantaneous forward curve. For this reason it is important when using the Hull–White model to use smooth zero curve interpolation with no steps or discontinuities so the slope is continuous.

In the model the spot rate value r follows a normal process so the discount bond or discount factor value has a lognormal process with a closed form that is used in establishing the closed forms for caps/floors and swaptions.

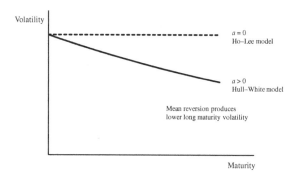

Figure 6.7: Effect of mean reversion on volatility.

6.5.1 *The Hull–White caplet*

In Black's formula for pricing a caplet the discounting of the payoff from maturity uses the initial zero curve to calculate the discount factor $D(0,T+h)$ for a caplet payoff at time $T+h$. However, the Hull–White model provides a complete framework for interest rate movements so instead we can use a stochastic discount factor as the rates move between today $t=0$ and $(T+h)$. Obviously in such a model the level of the spot rate $r(t)$ at a future time t determines the level of the forward rate $f(t,T,T+h)$ so we must integrate the movement of rates across this time period to provide the discount factor. Since in Hull–White there is a closed form for discount factors we use these to evaluate closed form solutions for caps and floors (Appx E.5).

In fact, Hull–White can be used to provide numerous closed form solutions for more complex structured notes as in Chapter 7. Unfortunately, since the complexity rapidly increases even for simple structures numerical methods are usually preferred.

6.6 Swaptions

After caps and floors, swaptions are the most commonly traded form of OTC interest rate derivative. A large liquid market exists in the major currencies for a wide range of maturities. Swaptions are used to hedge future liabilities and fixed rate payments from possible changes in interest rates.

A European swaption provides the holder with the option to enter into an interest rate swap at a predefined date in the future. A holder of a *payer's* swaption with strike K maturing at time T has the right to enter the payer's forward swap at time T with maturity date T_M. This is illustrated in Fig. 6.8. If exercised at time T the holder will pay a fixed rate K and receive the floating rate until maturity T_M. Thus, the holder of a payer's swaption will exercise if floating rates across the interest rate curve rise so that the effective swap rate at time T is greater than strike K. The opposite is a *receiver's* swaption with strike K, which allows the holder to receive fixed rate K and pay floating rate until maturity.

A swaption with an option maturity T and swap maturity T_M is known as a "$T \times (T-T_M)$" swaption. Thus a "1×7 strike 6% payer's swaption" is an option exercisable in 1 year to enter a 7 year swap on that date and pay the fixed rate of 6%.

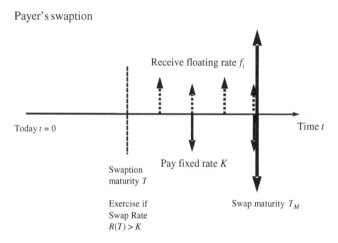

Figure 6.8: Payer's swaption cash-flows.

6.7 Black's Model for Swap Rates

In a similar fashion to Black's model for forward rates used to price caps it is market practice to use a lognormal one-factor model for the evolution of forward swap rates. Thus

$$\frac{dR_t}{R_t} = -\sigma_R \, dz \, , \qquad (6.6)$$

where $R_t = R(t,T,T_M)$ is the swap rate at time t for a swap starting at time T and maturing at time T_M. The volatility for the particular forward swap rate is given as $\sigma_R = \sigma_R(T,T_M)$. The forward swap rate for the swap starting at time T is defined as in Chapter 2 as Eq. (2.10).

$$R(0,T,T_M) = \frac{D(0,T) - D(0,T_M)}{\sum_{t_i > T}^{T_M} D(0,t_i) l_i} \, . \qquad (6.7)$$

Obviously, such a model is inconsistent with Black's forward rate model and forward and swap rates cannot both be lognormal in a consistent framework at the same time. It is not a true yield curve model but a simplification that represents the market standard for European swaptions. Since everybody in the OTC market uses Black's model for European swaptions a volatility surface of option maturity versus swap length is quoted for different strikes $\sigma_R = \sigma_R(T, T_M, K)$ (see Fig. 6.9).

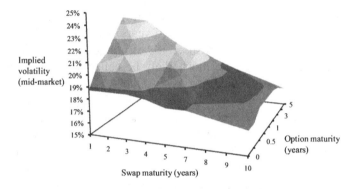

Figure 6.9: Typical broker swaption volatility surface.

6.7.1 *Black's model for European swaptions*

Consider the valuation of a payer's swaption. If exercised the holder will enter at time $t = T$ the forward swap if it has positive value by paying the fixed rate K and receiving the floating rate. Thus, on date T the swaption will be exercised if the swap rate on that date R lies above the strike K. The swaption payoff at time T can then be written as

$$Payoff_{swaption} = Max(R_T - K, 0) \sum_{t_i > T}^{T_M} D(T, t_i) h_i. \qquad (6.8)$$

This is analogous to the usual Black–Scholes call payoff where instead the underlying is the forward swap rate R_T multiplied by the annuity or *PV01* of the forward starting swap. The *PV01* factor must be included since the holder if exercising the option enters a swap of maturity $(T-T_M)$ at time T. We can use the Black–Scholes methodology to calculate the expectation of this payoff and discount back from time T to today to give a simple closed form (Appx E.6).

Wrong Bermudans?

Months had been spent building and perfecting our Hull–White model and the calibration looked pretty good. Flavour of the month amongst investors were 15, 20 and 30 year Bermudan callables traded in large size. They paid the investor a large fixed coupon but after a non call ("NC") period (NC2, NC3 or NC5 years) you had the right to cancel the swap. Most investors realised it was not going to be a 30yr trade at all and that they would most likely be called soon after the NC period. Most of the demand for these came out of Germany and were structured as zero coupons which showed very high IRRs (internal rates of return) if optimistic call times were presented. We were put in "comp" on these deals and managed to get a few and apparently booked decent profits since not many banks had finished their models. Then the "vampire squid" bank – not an end investor – finished their Bermudan model and rang us up to trade direct with us and they liked our price so we traded. Soon afterwards we started to worry and doubts surfaced as to whether we had the wrong price or the wrong model or calibration. Everyday thereafter they called us again to try and trade. It was pretty suspicious and so we tried to avoid picking up the phone. Who knows who had the right price? In retrospect it turns out that to correctly price Bermudan callables one-factor is good but two-factors is better but nobody really realised that in those days.

6.8 Hull–White Swaptions

In contrast to Black's model, since the Hull–White model is a whole yield curve model both caps, floors and swaptions are priced on a consistent basis within the same framework and we don't artificially have to use separate models as with Black's model.

A fairly simple closed form pricing formula for swaptions can be obtained in the Hull–White model (Appx E.7). Having a closed form solution is important since it allows for fast volatility and model calibration.

Within the Hull–White model the swaption price is given as the expected payoff as Eq. (6.8) discounted using stochastic discount factors rather than the non-stochastic discount factor as in Black's model. For a European swaption exercise this occurs for a particular normal variate value Z^* which provides a particular forward swap rate R_T .We determine the value of Z^* by iteration or root solving. By integrating the payoff using the stochastic discount factor we can show that the European swaption value is given for this particular value of Z^*. Thus, although a closed form exists it is more complicated to solve than for Black's model.

6.9 Hull–White Model Calibration

The Hull–White model possesses several parameters that must be estimated before market prices can be evaluated for exotic interest rate derivatives. The parameter $\theta(t)$ which allows fitting to the interest rate term structure is derived from the current zero coupon curve $z(0,t)$. The volatility σ and mean reversion parameter a are, however, more difficult to estimate and must be determined from the market value of liquid cap/floor contracts and swaptions observable in the OTC market.

Caps and floors are quoted in the market as forward rate based Black's volatilities and swaptions are quoted as forward swap rate volatilities. This is obviously a completely different definition from the spot rate volatilities in the Hull–White model and the different models are essentially incompatible from a theoretical perspective. The calibration procedure for the Hull–White model (and any similar model) generally follows the following route:

1. Determine the relevant, most liquid cap/floor or swaption volatilities.

2. Calculate, using the Black's formula the cap/floor or swaption prices.

3. Solve simultaneously for the mean reversion a and volatility σ parameters by minimising the price error (absolute or mean squared error) between the prices calculated using Hull–White cap/floor and swaption pricing formulae and the Black's market prices.

Various alternative fitting schemes can be used, for example, where the relative error between prices is taken or where different fitting weights are applied to different instruments.

Unfortunately, it turns out for the simple Hull–White model that the volatility term structures described by two parameters (a and σ) are not sufficient to perfectly fit the large range of volatility surfaces demonstrated by a wide range of maturities of caps/floors and swaptions. This is particularly true when rates are very low as with JPY currency and when the volatility surface is deformed away from its "usual" shape.

To fully fit the volatility surface requires a more complex model with more fitting parameters. Generally, as a compromise market traders will calibrate the model to just a few caps/floors or swaptions that most closely match the instrument being priced in terms of overall maturity, option maturity and whether it is cap or swaption "like".

Another problem, as with equity options, is that caps/floors and swaptions demonstrate slight *skew* with strike K. Different volatilities are shown in the market for OTM, ATM and ITM strikes. The Hull–White model cannot accommodate a volatility skew and traders again modify a and σ slightly to account for this.

Thus, although the calibration problems encountered by the simple one-factor Hull–White model can be "fixed" by assuming different fixed a and σ for different trades it is rather unsatisfactory. This is particularly true when trading large portfolios of different positions. However, the same situation exists in most equity derivative exotics books; you cannot have uniform volatility parameters across the entire book within a simple stochastic one factor modelling framework. An alternative is to implement a more complex framework (HJM, two-factor Hull–White or multifactor LIBOR market models) which includes more factors and allows fitting of a wider range of volatility surfaces although as with equities none of these models is completely "perfect".

6.10 Numerical Methods

Once one ventures much beyond caps, floors and swaptions closed forms become very complicated for even one factor interest rate models. Many closed forms start to have integrals that are slow and technically difficult to compute (see for example the *chooser note* in Appx (F.9)). Also products often have Bermudan callable and path dependent features which cannot be solved by closed form. Instead, it is easier to use a discrete numerical calculation to effectively solve the Hull–White equation directly. Here we shall briefly detail two common methods: a trinomial tree (a form of finite difference approach) and Monte Carlo simulation.

6.10.1 *Hull–White model trinomial trees*

A great advantage of a one-factor Markovian interest rate model is the ability to build recombining lattices and trees for valuation. These allow pricing of interest rate derivatives with American and Bermudan early exercise features which have become more common over the last few years. The Hull–White trinomial tree has been widely documented by Hull and White themselves and here we shall merely detail the major features. Certain important details of its implementation are often neglected and are described in Appx (E.8). It is equivalent to solving a partial differential equation (PDE) for the Hull–White interest rate process Eq. (6.5) on a discrete finite difference grid.

If we discretise the Hull–White equation Eq. (6.5) we replace dt with Δt the time step size in our lattice

$$\Delta r(t) = \big[\theta(t) - a\,r(t)\big]\Delta t + \sigma\,\Delta z(t). \qquad (6.9)$$

From this equation we can build a discrete lattice in Δr and Δt by following a simple recipe shown in Fig. 6.10.

First build a trinomial lattice for the spot rate r by ignoring the interest rate term-structure for the process and setting $\theta(t) = 0$ in Eq.(6.9).

Secondly, assign branching probabilities to each node on the lattice. To account for the drift term $-ar(t)$ different branching probabilities for up, middle and down (p_u, p_m, p_d) must be applied for movements forward in time through the lattice. These probabilities are dependent on the vertical displacement of the node in the lattice (Eq. A.100).

Finally include the interest rate term-structure $\theta(t)$ by displacing all the nodes on the tree by a factor $\alpha(t)$ so that the market term-structure is satisfied. This can be done for most purposes when the term-structure is

Financial Derivative Investments

well defined with an analytical formula Eq. (A.101) for the displacement or by fitting the tree to the discount factors from the market zero curve.

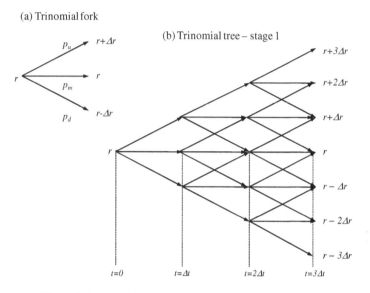

Figure 6.10 (a) and (b): Building a Hull–White trinomial tree.

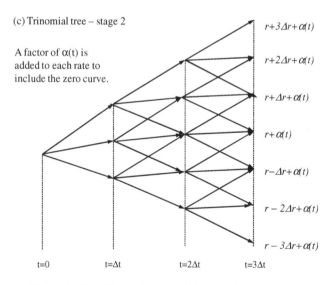

Figure 6.10(c): Fitting the trinomial tree to the term-structure.

Building the tree in the spot rate r is relatively simple but actually pricing a derivative instrument on the lattice requires knowledge of a few implementation issues. These include how to include fixed and floating payments on the net, how to "roll-back" through the net to achieve present values, including Hull–White closed forms at each node where relevant and pricing of options with features such as discrete barriers, path dependence approximations etc. We outline a few of these issues in the Appx (E.8) for those who are interested.

6.10.2 *Hull–White Monte Carlo*

For path dependent options a tree is not well adapted. An alternative for European style path-dependent options is to use a Monte Carlo simulation. In the most generic form in Hull–White model we can just simulate the spot rate using the discrete process Eq. (6.9) and adding to the previous spot rate at each time step Δt.

$$
\begin{aligned}
r(t_{i+1}) &= r(t_i) + \Delta r(t_i) \\
&= r(t_i) + \left[\theta(t_i) - a\,r(t_i)\right]\Delta t + \sigma\sqrt{\Delta t}\,Z_i
\end{aligned}
\tag{6.10}
$$

$$
t_i = i\,\Delta t \quad i = 0,1,2,\ldots,N \quad and \quad Z \sim \phi(0,1).
$$

The initial point $r(0)$ is an estimate of the initial spot rate. Using the various Hull–White closed forms we can calculate discount factors, forward rates and hence the value of swaps, bonds etc. at any simulation point. Another possibility is to "jump" to arbitrary times using a closed form equation to simulate the discount factor (see Eq. A.92) in a similar fashion to Black–Scholes Monte Carlo with equities.

As with any Monte Carlo various speed enhancement techniques can be used including antithetic variables, quasi random number sequences etc. Another valid option is also to perform Monte Carlo directly on a Hull–White trinomial tree or lattice since we have already calculated the branching probabilities at every node it is fast and easy to move from node to node and it is easy to store path dependent information (averages, maxima, etc.) at each node.

6.11 Other Interest Rate Models

There is a huge amount of literature on different interest rate pricing models of varying complexity and practical usefulness. Although simple models such as Hull–White have their limitations (primarily volatility calibration and simple yield curve movements) they are easy to understand and relatively robust. Here we outline a few of the more popular models although they are mathematically a lot more difficult and we shall leave the details to Appx (E).

The *Hull–White two factor model* is an obvious extension and allows a wider range of volatility and term-structure movements. The Hull–White drift term includes a second stochastic factor (Appx E.1). It can be implemented on a three-dimensional lattice.

The *Heath Jarrow Morton model* (HJM model) for forward rates was for a long time viewed as an alternative (Appx E.9). It can be readily extended to 2–3 factors (which seems all that is required to model most historic yield curve movements) but is *non-Markovian*. This non-Markovian property means that each interest rate path in the model is path dependent and thus pricing cannot be performed on lattices and non-recombining "bushy" trees are produced. Monte Carlo pricing must used in pricing which is a disadvantage for pricing American and Bermudan options with early exercise dates.

Another alternative in the *LIBOR market model* (LMM), which is highly favoured since it builds a model for discrete forward rates that are actually traded in the market (Appx E.10). The model is lognormal (so no negative interest rates) and can fit the volatility term structure quite well. Through numerical approximations closed form solutions can be provided for caps, floor and swaptions. In general, however, the model is not very analytically tractable and Monte Carlo simulation must be applied for pricing exotic options. The *SABR model* is a variant of Black's model but with a second stochastic volatility process (Appx B.16.2). This model is good for describing volatility smiles of short-dated options and can be extended within the LMM framework to price longer-dated structured equity products.

6.12 Hedging an Interest Rate Derivatives Book

Whereas hedging an equity derivatives book may involve continuously monitoring and re-hedging a large number of equities, trading an interest rate derivatives book presents different problems. These days with the Euro there are relatively few major currencies to trade (USD, JPY, EUR, GBP, CHF etc.) although there are plenty of other more exotic currencies with smaller derivatives markets. The major problem lies in hedging the entire term structure of risk with liquid instruments. Static replication of the portfolio risk is not generally possible and a dynamic hedging approach must be taken.

The principal risk is delta risk and gamma risk across the curve. By maturity bucketing the risk we can perturbate or shift the interest rate curve slightly "bucket by bucket" and re-evaluate all the derivatives (and vanilla instruments) to provide a *delta map* of the portfolio as a function of maturity. By choosing the maturity buckets to correspond to particular liquid futures and swap contracts we can work out what vanilla instruments must be bought/sold to delta hedge the book. In a similar manner by a double perturbation we can evaluate the bucketed gamma risk.

Hedging the vega is a bit more complicated but it can be done with a series of caps/floors or swaptions depending on the nature of the instrument. A bit of common sense must be used here to pick contracts that possess similar maturities/exercise dates to the contracts in the book.

Thus by selecting a series of futures, swaps, caps/floors and swaptions the risk of delta, gamma and vega can be minimised across the trading book. As with equity derivatives generating the risk parameters of all the exotic trades in the book can be very time consuming and requires algorithm optimisation and computing power to build numerous pricing lattices and perform simulations.

Chapter 7

Interest Rate Products

7.1 Introduction

In this chapter we shall present the more common interest rate products which have been marketed to institutional and high net worth individuals. Most interest rate products are structured so as not to place capital at risk and instead to enhance yields the coupons become dependent on the level of floating rates with such features as caps/floors, barriers, ranges and ratchets (Fig. 7.1).

Simpler products can be priced using closed form solutions in a one-factor framework such as the Hull–White model. Bermudan callables, where the issuer has the right to redeem the notes on certain coupon dates, are also popular as a method of increasing yields and generally require tree or lattice techniques.

Although most products are structured to depend on the level of rates some are related to the shape of the yield curve (CMS, spread trades, etc.) and also sometimes FX risk is embedded (dual currency notes, FX barriers etc.). These more complex products are either priced using an *ad-hoc* simplified Black–Scholes approach or in a more complete multifactor framework with for example correlated rate and FX processes.

7.2 Capped/Floored Notes

The majority of interest rate structured notes have traditionally been based around incorporating various forms of caps and floors to enhance coupon or provide a market view such as the notorious *inverse floaters* which provide bearish views on rates.

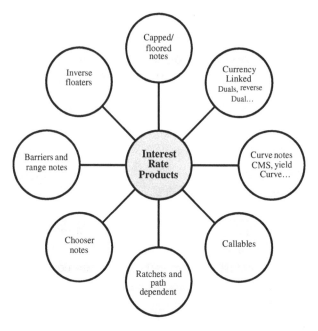

Figure 7.1: Different interest rate products.

7.2.1 *Capped floating rate note*

A capped floating rate note pays a slightly higher spread than a straight floating rate note (FRN) since the investor effectively sells a cap on the floating rate. In the example a coupon of LIBOR+50bp is paid but the coupon cannot exceed 7% even if rates rise.

The floating rates are fixed at the start of the ith coupon period at time t_i and paid at the end of the period t_i+h_i. Thus for each coupon period the note pays a floating coupon of $f_i = f(t_i,t_i,t_i+h_i)$ plus a fixed spread q. If the market floating rate (LIBOR) rises the total coupon cannot exceed the cap level K. The capped payoff for the ith coupon period can therefore be written as

$$Payoff_{capped \atop FRN} = f_i + q - Max(f_i - (K-q),0). \qquad (7.1)$$

This profile is shown in Fig. 7.2. The value of the complete capped FRN considering all the coupon periods is just that of an FRN, paying a spread q, minus a cap with effective strike $(K-q)$ (Appx F.1) The cap can be evaluated using a closed form under Black's model or the Hull–White model described in Chapter 6.

Example 7.1

EUR CAPPED FLOATING RATE NOTE		
ISSUER	:	AA rated Issuer
CURRENCY	:	EUR
MATURITY	:	5 year
ISSUE PRICE	:	100%
COUPON	:	6 month EURIBOR + 0.50%
COUPON CAP	:	Coupon cannot exceed 7%
PAYMENT DATES	:	Semi-annual Act/365
REDEMPTION	:	The Notes are redeemed on the Maturity Date at 100%.

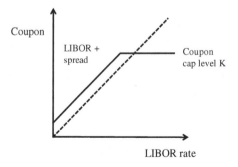

Figure 7.2: Capped floating rate note payoff.

7.2.2 Reverse floating rate note

A *reverse floating rate note* or *inverse floater* pays a floating coupon that increases as interest rates decrease (and vice versa). It is a very common form of structure and allows a bearish view on rates to be taken by investors. In Example 7.2 (from a few years ago when rates were high enough to make inverse floaters seem like a sensible strategy) the notes pay a fixed coupon for the first two years and then are inverse floating for the next 8 years.

Example 7.2

EUR REVERSE FLOATING RATE NOTE	
ISSUER	: AA rated Issuer
CURRENCY	: EUR
MATURITY	: 10 year
ISSUE PRICE	: 100%
COUPON	: Year 1: 9.0%
	Year 2: 8.0%
	Years 3–10: 12.5% <u>minus</u> 6 month EURIBOR
PAYMENT DATES	: Annual 30360 basis
REDEMPTION	: The Notes are redeemed on the Maturity Date at 100%

For reverse FRN paying a fixed coupon C minus the floating rate the payoff for the ith coupon period is shown in Fig. 7.3 and can therefore be written as a floorlet

$$Payoff_{reverse \atop FRN} = Max(C - f_i, 0). \qquad (7.2)$$

The entire reverse FRN can be priced as a floor with strike C plus the discounted principal at maturity (Appx F.2). Thus, a reverse FRN is simply a deeply in-the-money floor plus principal.

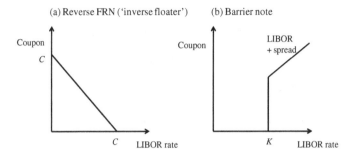

Figure 7.3: Inverse floater and digital barrier notes.

7.3 Barrier Notes

7.3.1 *Digital barrier note*

In a *digital barrier note* an enhanced coupon is paid, provided the interest rate fixing lies above (or below) the barrier level. In Example 7.3 a coupon of LIBOR + 70bp is paid when LIBOR sets above a 5.5% barrier level at the start of each 3 month period.

This payoff is shown in Fig. 7.3 (b) and can be written as (i) buying an FRN paying a spread q, (ii) buying a floor strike K and (iii) selling a digital floor strike K with payout $(q+K)$ (Appx F.3). The digital floor can be priced using closed forms (Appx F.5) although describing a digital as a *floor spread* is more practical for hedging purposes. This is analogous to using *call and put spreads* when pricing equity digitals as described in Section 3.8.

7.3.2 *Minimum payoff range note*

A *minimum payoff range note* pays an increased floating range coupon if LIBOR fixes within a predefined range. If LIBOR falls outside the range the investor receives a minimum fixed coupon. An example payoff profile is shown in Fig. 7.4. This structure is suited to investors who

Example 7.3

GBP BARRIER NOTE	
ISSUER	:	AA rated Issuer
CURRENCY	:	GBP
MATURITY	:	2 year
ISSUE PRICE	:	100%
COUPON	:	3 month LIBOR + 0.70% but no coupon is paid for periods when 3 month LIBOR set below Barrier Level.
BARRIER LEVEL	:	5.5%
PAYMENT DATES	:	Quarterly Act/365
REDEMPTION	:	The Notes are redeemed on the Maturity Date at 100%.

have a neutral view on rates and feel that LIBOR will not move significantly from its current level over the life of the notes.

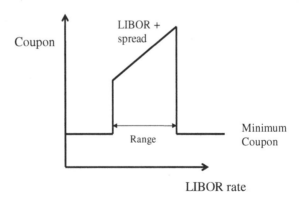

Figure 7.4: Minimum payoff range note.

If the range is defined by a lower barrier of strike L and an upper barrier of strike U the structure can be priced as: (i) buying an FRN with spread q, (ii) selling a cap with strike U, (iii) buying a floor with strike L and (iv) buying a digital cap and floor with strikes U and L and payoffs $(C-U-q)$ and $(C-L-q)$ respectively (Appx F.4). Decomposing it in this way allows closed forms to be used.

Example 7.4

EUR MINIMUM PAYOFF RANGE NOTE	
ISSUER	: AAA rated Issuer
CURRENCY	: EUR
MATURITY	: 2 year
ISSUE PRICE	: 100%
COUPON	: If 3 month EURIBOR sets within RANGE 3 month EURIBOR + 0.60% otherwise 2.0% fixed
RANGE	: 6.0–6.5%
PAYMENT DATES	: Quarterly Act/365
REDEMPTION	: The Notes are redeemed on the Maturity Date at 100%.

7.4 Accrual Notes

Accrual notes are similar to barrier and digital notes but instead there are daily observations and fixings to determine the coupon payout. Although investors seem to like daily fixings, it renders them significantly more tedious to price and trade since we must price (or approximate) a daily digital option and record the daily LIBOR fixings.

7.4.1 *Digital accrual note*

A fixed coupon C is accrued daily if the daily LIBOR fixing remains below a barrier of strike K. If the coupon is defined as a fraction Annual Coupon × (Number of days below strike)/ (Number of days in year) then we can price as a series of daily digital floorlets. This is shown schematically in Fig. 7.5.

Example 7.5

GBP DIGITAL ACCRUAL NOTE	
ISSUER	: AA rated Issuer
CURRENCY	: GBP
MATURITY	: 2 year
ISSUE PRICE	: 100%
COUPON	: 6.5% but accruing only on days when daily closing 6 month LIBOR falls below or equal to Barrier Level.
BARRIER LEVEL	: 7.0%
PAYMENT DATES	: Semi-annual
REDEMPTION	: The Notes are redeemed on the Maturity Date at 100%.

If we approximate daily observations by a continuous observation we can solve to give a closed form solution using the Hull–White model (Appx F.6). This product generally favours shorter maturities since the range is not automatically re-struck but determined at issuance.

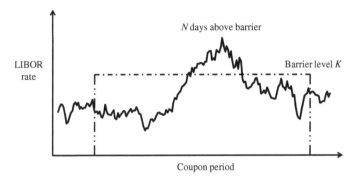

Figure 7.5: Digital accrual note.

7.4.2 *Barrier accrual floating rate note*

Similar to the fixed rate barrier accrual notes but instead a floating rate (fixed at the beginning of the period) plus spread q accrues if the daily fixing of LIBOR is below the barrier. This is illustrated in Example 7.6. The closed form solution is discussed in Appx (F.7).

7.4.3 *Minimum payoff range accrual notes*

A variant on the above two structures is one which pays a floating rate accrual coupon within a specified range and smaller fixed coupon when it lies outside the range (see Fig. 7.6).

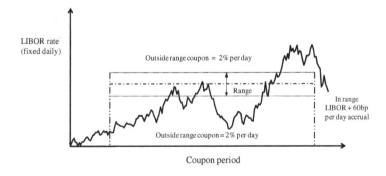

Figure 7.6: Minimum payoff range accrual note.

Example 7.6

<table>
<tr><td colspan="3">**GBP BARRIER ACCRUAL FLOATING RATE NOTE**</td></tr>
<tr><td>ISSUER</td><td>:</td><td>AAA rated Issuer</td></tr>
<tr><td>CURRENCY</td><td>:</td><td>GBP</td></tr>
<tr><td>MATURITY</td><td>:</td><td>2 year</td></tr>
<tr><td>ISSUE PRICE</td><td>:</td><td>100%</td></tr>
<tr><td>COUPON</td><td>:</td><td>3 month LIBOR + 0.65% but accruing only on days when daily closing 3 month LIBOR falls below or equal to Barrier Level.</td></tr>
<tr><td>BARRIER LEVEL</td><td>:</td><td>7.0%</td></tr>
<tr><td>PAYMENT DATES</td><td>:</td><td>Quarterly Act/365</td></tr>
<tr><td>REDEMPTION</td><td>:</td><td>The Notes are redeemed on the Maturity Date at 100%.</td></tr>
</table>

This can be priced using the same principles as the previous couple of examples and a continuous time approximation is usually made to give a closed form solution (Appx F.8). For each coupon period t_i to t_i+h we must integrate over time t and if the instantaneous forward rate $f(t,t,t+h)$ is within the range the coupon period LIBOR fixing $f(t_i,t_i,t_i+h)$ plus a spread is accrued. If the daily LIBOR lies outside the range a fixed coupon C is payable. At the end of the coupon period the total accrued coupon is paid.

7.5 Chooser Notes

Chooser notes allow the investor to set a range at the start of each coupon period and if the floating rate sets within the range at the end of the period the floating rate plus spread is paid (see Example 7.8).

Example 7.7

EUR MINIMUM PAYOFF RANGE ACCRUAL NOTE		
ISSUER	:	AAA rated Issuer
CURRENCY	:	EUR
MATURITY	:	2 year
ISSUE PRICE	:	100%
COUPON	:	If the daily close of 3 month EURIBOR sets within RANGE then coupon accrues on a daily basis at 3 month EURIBOR + 0.60%. Otherwise coupon accrues on a daily basis at a 1.5% fixed rate.
RANGE	:	5.0–6.5%
PAYMENT DATES	:	Quarterly Act/365
REDEMPTION	:	The Notes are redeemed on the Maturity Date at 100%.

To value chooser options requires us to assume the investor is rational and he will set the range to optimise his expected payout at the start of each period. This requires us to calculate the expected payout and maximise with respect to where the barrier is placed. This requires a payout calculation for each coupon period and a differentiation of the expected payout with respect to the barrier level. Performing a differentiation and setting it to zero is a standard approach to obtaining the turning point and maxima and minima of a function (Appx F.9).

A *range chooser accrual note* in Example 7.9 is a variant in which the investor decides a range at the start of each period and coupon accrues on a daily basis if it remains within the range (Fig. 7.7).

Example 7.8

<table>
<tr><td colspan="3">**USD RANGE CHOOSER NOTE**</td></tr>
<tr><td>ISSUER</td><td>:</td><td>AA rated Issuer</td></tr>
<tr><td>CURRENCY</td><td>:</td><td>USD</td></tr>
<tr><td>MATURITY</td><td>:</td><td>3 year</td></tr>
<tr><td>ISSUE PRICE</td><td>:</td><td>100%</td></tr>
<tr><td>COUPON</td><td>:</td><td>1 month USD LIBOR + 0.70% if 1 month USD LIBOR sets within RANGE otherwise no Coupon is payable.</td></tr>
<tr><td>RANGE</td><td>:</td><td>Investor sets monthly 2 business days prior to each 1 month period an interest rate range of 1%. If 1 month USD LIBOR sets within RANGE, otherwise no interest rate payment will be made.</td></tr>
<tr><td>PAYMENT DATES</td><td>:</td><td>Monthly Act/360</td></tr>
<tr><td>REDEMPTION</td><td>:</td><td>The Notes are redeemed on the Maturity Date at 100%.</td></tr>
</table>

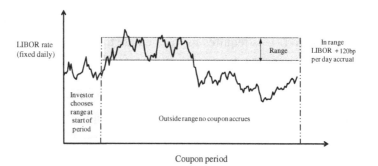

Figure 7.7: Range chooser accrual note.

7.6 Range Reset Notes

A range reset note is where the range is reset automatically (no investor choice) at the start of each coupon period on the basis of the current LIBOR. In the Example 7.10 a range of ±50bp around LIBOR is set every 3 months.

Example 7.9

USD RANGE CHOOSER ACCRUAL NOTE		
ISSUER	:	AA rated Issuer
CURRENCY	:	USD
MATURITY	:	2 year
ISSUE PRICE	:	100%
COUPON	:	3 month USD LIBOR fixing at the beginning of each period + 1.20% multiplied by an Accrual Factor for each period as determined below.
ACCRUAL FACTOR	:	Number of days 3 month USD daily LIBOR sets in interest rate RANGE divided by the number of days in each period.
RANGE	:	Maximum and minimum interest rate range determined by investor 5 business days before start of each coupon period. For all coupon periods the range of maximum and minimum levels will be 0.75%
PAYMENT DATES	:	Quarterly Act/360
REDEMPTION	:	The Notes are redeemed on the Maturity Date at 100%.

Example 7.10

GBP RANGE RESET NOTE		
ISSUER	:	AA rated Issuer
CURRENCY	:	GBP
MATURITY	:	18 months
ISSUE PRICE	:	100%
COUPON	:	If 3 month LIBOR at end of coupon period is within the interest rate RANGE then a Coupon of 3 month LIBOR + 0.40% is payable otherwise no coupon is paid.
RANGE	:	Upper limit of range is set at 3 month LIBOR fixing at beginning of coupon period + 0.5%. Lower limit of range is set at 3 month LIBOR fixing at beginning of coupon period − 0.5%.
PAYMENT DATES	:	Quarterly on Act/365
REDEMPTION	:	The Notes are redeemed on the Maturity Date at 100%.

7.7 Ratchet Notes

A *ratchet note* is where the coupon is based on the floating rate but its movement is limited at each period. The Example 7.11 shows a ratchet note that can only "ratchet up" the coupon by a maximum 25bp at each coupon period and can never go down if rates decline. It might seem great that you get paid a spread for this, but if rates rise rapidly then the investor misses out on the benefit. This ratcheting process is shown in Fig. 7.8. Obviously, if there is a rapidly rising forward the curve the market is expecting rates to rise rapidly and the investor is effectively selling potential upside to provide downside coupon protection plus an enhanced spread.

Example 7.11

EUR RATCHET NOTE		
ISSUER	:	AA rated Issuer
CURRENCY	:	EUR
MATURITY	:	5 year
ISSUE PRICE	:	100%
COUPON	:	3 month EURIBOR + 0.40% subject to interest rate Ratchet.
RATCHET	:	Coupon can increase by 0.25% per period but cannot decrease from one period to another.
PAYMENT DATES	:	Quarterly on Act/360
REDEMPTION	:	The Notes are redeemed on the Maturity Date at 100%.

Pricing ratchets is rather more difficult than the previous products since they are path dependent and thus ideally require a Monte Carlo simulation. Another alternative is if there are early exercise features is to use a tree and store a range of information for different paths at each node this can in simple cases provide a reasonable approximation to the price.

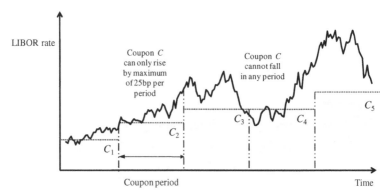

Figure 7.8: Ratchet note.

7.8 Callable Notes

Callable notes where the issuer has the right to redeem the notes early are very common and come in many forms. Usually an enhanced coupon is paid for a certain *non call period* (NC) and then steps up to a higher level as in Example 7.12 with the issuer being able to redeem the notes at 100% on any future coupon date. Essentially, this amounts to the issuer buying an embedded Bermudan swaption since if future swap rates rise above the step up coupon level it is preferable for the issuer not to call the notes. Obviously, if rates fall or probably don't materially rise the issuer will call the notes soon after the NC period.

The subjective nature of the early redemption at the issuers choice (rather than a hard call) makes these products too complicated for most retail investors but callables are very popular with institutional investors and are a very common form of yield enhancement.

Pricing Bermudan callables requires a lattice technique but unfortunately accurate pricing of Bermudan swaptions requires two or more factors to model the yield curve and this requires a 3+ dimensional lattice or tree. Another technique that various investment banks have experimented with (but is infrequently used) is specialised Monte Carlo for the multifactor interest rate process where various approximations can be made to determine the swaption *exercise boundary* (actually a surface) (see Section 3.7.2).

Example 7.12

USD CALLABLE FIXED/FLOATING NOTE	
ISSUER	: AA rated Issuer
CURRENCY	: USD
MATURITY	: 10 year
ISSUE PRICE	: 100%
COUPON	: Year 1,2: 6 month USD LIBOR+0.50% semi-annually on Act/360 basis.
	Year 3–10: 9% pa annually on Act/360 basis.
ISSUER CALL OPTION	: The issuer has the right to redeem the Notes at 100% at the end of year 2 or on any interest rate payment date thereafter subject to a notice of 10 calendar days.

7.9 Constant Maturity Notes

Rather than reference a floating rate such as 3 month LIBOR many structures reference the swap rate of constant maturity or a *constant maturity swap* rate (CMS). In Example 7.13 the coupon is based on observing the 5 year swap rate at each coupon date. Many structures can be devised using the 5 year swap rate such as caps, barriers, ranges etc. which are analogous to LIBOR based structures. Often CMS trades are marketed as *yield curve* trades in the sense that the CMS provides information on the whole level of rates and shape of the yield curve rather than just the short maturity LIBOR. Perhaps, however, the main attraction seems to be that since yield curves are generally positively sloped short maturity forward rates often lie below the swap rate so investors perhaps fall for the illusion that CMS structures somehow yield more.

Example 7.13

EUR CONSTANT MATURITY NOTE	
ISSUER	: AA rated Issuer
CURRENCY	: EUR
MATURITY	: 5 year
ISSUE PRICE	: 100%
COUPON	: The "5 Year Swap Rate" minus 1.0% pa reset annually. First coupon 5.8%.
PAYMENT DATES	: Annually on 30/360 basis
5 YEAR SWAP RATE	: The average 5 year bid swap rate, as quoted by 5 reference banks 2 days prior to any interest rate period.
REDEMPTION	: The Notes are redeemed on the Maturity Date at 100%.

Pricing of some CMS trades can rather clumsily be performed with closed forms. We can use Black's swap model to model the forward CMS rates or the Hull–White model for pricing since we can derive a stochastic closed form for the forward swap rate. In reality, however, both models incorrectly price the correlation between the different forward swap rates if many coupons which reference the CMS rate are involved in the structure. Ideally 2+ factors should be used to model CMS products or at least check the validity of using a simpler model.

7.10 Yield Curve Notes

Yield curve notes can take many forms but generally involve a payoff (for each coupon or at maturity if short dated) that is based on the difference between two reference rates on the yield curve. Example 7.14 is a non-capital guaranteed note that redeems an amount linked to the difference between the 7 year swap rate and 6 month EURIBOR. The product is essentially a leveraged forward contract directly linked to the shape of the yield curve and will make/lose money should the curve steepen/flatten.

Example 7.14

EUR YIELD CURVE NOTE		
ISSUER	:	AA rated Issuer
CURRENCY	:	EUR
MATURITY	:	5 year
ISSUE PRICE	:	100%
COUPON	:	7%.
PAYMENT DATES	:	Annually on 30/360 basis
REDEMPTION	:	The Notes are redeemed on the Maturity Date at:
		100%×(1+5×(SWAP RATE–LIBOR RATE–0.70%)
SWAP RATE	:	7 Year EUR bid Swap rate fixed 2 days prior to Maturity Date.
LIBOR RATE	:	6 month EURIBOR fixed 2 days prior to Maturity Date.

Options on yield curves are usually priced using a simple Black–Scholes model for two assets (each asset representing the relevant rate). Each asset has a volatility and a joint correlation that is usually estimated from historical data. Closed forms or a three-dimensional variant of the binomial tree technique can be used (Appx B.11). A one-factor Hull–White model only really describes a parallel movement of the yield curve and is useless for pricing products that involve a change in slope or gradient. Multifactor yield curve models must be used but care must be taken to examine what the calibrated model actually implies for the actual process of yield curve flattening and steepening. Usually the second factor in an interest rate model, such as the HJM model, principally governs this process.

7.11 FX Linked Notes

FX linked interest rate products are really hybrid products and are described in Chapter 10. However, since mixing rates and FX is historically so common in the world of interest rate structured products we will discuss them briefly here.

Example 7.15

JPY/AUD DUAL CURRENCY NOTE	
ISSUER	: AA rated Issuer
CURRENCY	: JPY
MATURITY	: 10 year
ISSUE PRICE	: 100%
COUPON	: AUD 4.9%.
PAYMENT DATES	: Annually on 30/360 basis
REDEMPTION	: The Notes are redeemed on the Maturity Date at 100%.

The most common form of FX linked interest rate product is the *dual currency note* based on cross currency swaps. An investor can invest is say USD but receive floating (or fixed) coupons in another higher yielding currency (say AUD (Australian dollar)) and have the principal repaid in USD. Thus, the investor receives higher interest coupons than he would have if he had invested in USD but takes FX risk on the future coupons. The AUD coupons are present valued using a AUD zero curve and a cross currency basis swap applied (Appx A.3). Example 7.15 shows a JPY/AUD dual currency note.

Example 7.16

USD/JPY BARRIER NOTE	
ISSUER	: AA rated Issuer
CURRENCY	: USD
MATURITY	: 18 Months
ISSUE PRICE	: 100%
COUPON	: 6 month USD LIBOR +0.95%, subject to FX Barrier.
PAYMENT DATES	: Semi-annually on Act/360 basis
FX BARRIER	: Interest is only accruing on days where USD/JPY exchange rate is closing above 80 JPY per USD.
REDEMPTION	: The Notes are redeemed on the Maturity Date at 100%.

Other structures involve payouts linked to FX options. These can for example involve coupons or principal linked to FX barriers and ladders or features such as floating coupons accruing only when FX is above a certain level. Example 7.16 is a floating rate note where interest only accrues if daily USD/JPY fixes above a barrier level. Example 7.17 shows a fixed rate USD/GBP note with the coupon linked to an FX ladder based on a series of FX barriers options (Appx B.19). For these examples to a first approximation, since they are short dated maturities and the FX volatility dominates (since it is so high relative to the rate volatility), we could probably use one stochastic factor FX model. However, this is not always an accurate pricing approach for the numerous product possibilities that exist and modelling of more complex hybrid structures is discussed in Chapter 10.

Example 7.17

USD/GBP LADDER NOTE	
ISSUER	: AAA rated Issuer
CURRENCY	: USD
MATURITY	: 1 year
ISSUE PRICE	: 100%
COUPON	: 7.5% provided the USD/GBP exchange rate remains above 1.50 during the life of the note. Otherwise the coupon is set according to the following schedule based on the lowest level that the USD/GBP rate reached during the life of the note:

<table>
<tr><td>USD/GBP</td><td>Coupon</td></tr>
<tr><td>1.48</td><td>7%</td></tr>
<tr><td>1.47</td><td>6%</td></tr>
<tr><td>1.46</td><td>5%</td></tr>
<tr><td>1.45</td><td>4%</td></tr>
<tr><td>1.44</td><td>3%</td></tr>
<tr><td>1.43</td><td>2%</td></tr>
<tr><td>1.42</td><td>1%</td></tr>
<tr><td>1.41</td><td>0%</td></tr>
</table>

REDEMPTION	: The Notes are redeemed on the Maturity Date at 100%.

Chapter 8

Pricing Credit Derivatives

8.1 Introduction

The advent of the *credit derivative* over the last 10–15 years led to a rapid development of products where the investment is in pure synthetic credit risk. Although credit is usually an asset class for institutional investors the appeal of these products has led to distribution amongst high net worth and even occasionally retail investors.

The precursor to the new structured credit market was the traditional *asset swap* market where fixed rate bonds were swapped to floating rates plus a *credit spread*. Also important to the evolution of the *collateralised debt obligation* market (CDO) were cash debt securitisations to give *asset backed securities* (ABS) and credit enhancement of assets by specialised credit insurers called *monolines*. Development of the *credit default swap* (CDS) by JP Morgan and others led to standardised ISDA documented contracts traded bilaterally between financial institutions. These have provided investments credit linked to a wide range of major corporates, financials, sovereigns and even residential and commercial mortgage ABS. Figure 8.1 shows typical credit curves for corporates expressed in terms of their credit spread or CDS *premium* where more credit worthy companies exhibit tighter credit spreads.

In this and the following chapter we will discuss the new range of structured credit products that have been recently successfully marketed and various modelling pricing and hedging techniques that have been developed.

8.2 Market Credit Curves

A quick survey of the bond markets show that bonds of different issuers demonstrate different yield curves. The major variations are primarily due to market credit risk perceptions. Although liquidity effects are important, in a relatively efficient market the spread of the yield curve above the "risk free" government curve is seen as a measure of credit risk or risk of default by an issuer on a debt obligation. The shape and level of a corporate yield curve is related to (i) the underlying interest rate curve and (ii) the shape of the credit curve. The credit spread is roughly seen as a measure of the market expected loss on a bond or loan and as we shall see later is approximately equal to the probability of default multiplied by the expected loss on a default.

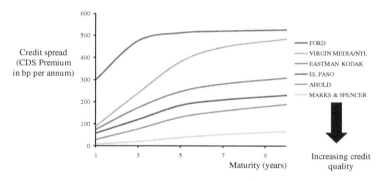

Figure 8.1: Example corporate credit curves.

In practice the market swap or LIBOR curve is taken as the "riskless" curve. This market convention is a hangover from the asset swap market. The interbank swap curve is approximately traditionally an AA rated bank curve and is not totally risk free since as we have seen recently the banks themselves are not riskless and have themselves credit spread curves. The spread above LIBOR for most debt issuers is approximately equal to the credit default swap premium. Thus, if a debt obligation, for example a 5 year USD Xerox bond, is said to yield US Treasuries + 180bp (or "T+180") the 180bp is a measure of the credit risk. However, the swap curve might lie 60bp above the Treasury curve and thus the obligation might be quoted as LIBOR +120bp (or "L+120"). We will discuss the specific definitions of credit spreads later.

The credit curve or yield spread is also a function of maturity and seniority of the debt. Typically, investors will require higher credit premiums to hold a bond for longer. This is not always the case, however, particularly for bonds which are speculative and have a high probability of default in the near future and demonstrate a downwards sloping or "inverted" yield curve since if the company survives near term problems it probably is improving in credit quality.

8.3 Capital Structure and Leverage

As a preliminary it is interesting to consider what determines corporate credit quality and the underlying nature of credit risk. The *firm value* or *enterprise value* of a company is given as the sum of the equity and the debt value of a company. Roughly speaking this should of course equal the assets of the company but this may include intangible assets and such factors such as goodwill. The typical seniority of company debt is illustrated in Fig. 8.2. The company's *capital structure* is composed of equity at the bottom and then tiers of debt of increasing seniority such as subordinated debt, senior unsecured debt (most bonds fall into this category) and secured debt in the form of bank loans (and sometimes secured bonds).

High quality companies are virtually unlevered and may have no debt but *high yield* companies could have very little equity *cushion* (10–20%) in the overall capital structure. During the *leveraged buyout* (LBO) "madness" of 2006–2007 some aggressive refinancing took true equity down to a few percent and replaced equity with super-subordinated debt such as zero coupon *payment-in-kind* (PIK) notes and even direct subordinated loans to equity holders. Such low "true" equity amounts do not provide an alignment of interest between debt-holders and equity holders. In these cases the equity holders really just hold a form of call option of the future value or performance of the company. Which high yield company would you rather lend money to for virtually equivalent credit spread in Fig. 8.3? Answer: (c) my cable company since it has lower leverage, hard assets and the equity is listed with a visible market value. Listed equity is an important consideration when the other two companies have little true equity and equity valuations are estimated by accountants paid for by the company and/or private equity sponsor.

Just looking at leverage as the ratio *equity/debt* of the overall capital structure can be slightly meaningless if a company has high earnings to cover its actual interest payments and pay down debt. Often leverage is often described as *debt/EBITDA* (Earnings-Before-Interest-Tax-Depreciation-Amortisation). A very highly leveraged company might have over 4–5× leverage. However, one should examine published leverage figures carefully to consider to which level of debt they really correspond and do they exclude forms of highly subordinated debt. Also has the EBITDA been "massaged" to include one-off financial events such as asset sales or even extrapolated future cost savings etc. Many other credit metrics, such as interest coverage and debt refinancing dates are important and credit analysis is a complex art requiring investors to see through the debt marketing material and highlights of company accounts.

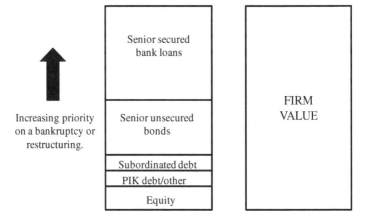

Figure 8.2: Typical corporate capital structure.

8.4 What Happens in a Bankruptcy?

Seniority of debt is very important in a bankruptcy situation. On bankruptcy or default of an issuer, holders of obligations and loans will be paid out in order of seniority. Debt holders will always rank above equity holders who take the first loss and losses are then applied from the equity upwards in the capital structure as in Fig. 8.2. Typically senior debt holders will rank above subordinated debt holders. Correspondingly this is reflected in the level of credit spreads with senior debt trading at tighter spreads than junior debt.

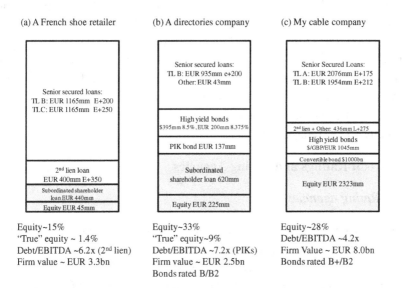

(a) A French shoe retailer

Senior secured loans:
TL B: EUR 1165mm E+200
TLC: EUR 1165mm E+250

2nd lien loan
EUR 400mm E+350

Subordinated shareholder
loan EUR 440mm

Equity EUR 45mm

Equity~15%
"True" equity ~ 1.4%
Debt/EBITDA ~6.2x (2nd lien)
Firm value ~ EUR 3.3bn

(b) A directories company

Senior secured loans:
TL B: EUR 935mm e+200
Other: EUR 43mm

High yield bonds
$395mm 8.5%, EUR 200mm 8.375%

PIK bond EUR 137mm

Subordinated
shareholder loan 620mm

Equity EUR 225mm

Equity~33%
"True" equity~9%
Debt/EBITDA ~7.2x (PIKs)
Firm value ~ EUR 2.5bn
Bonds rated B/B2

(c) My cable company

Senior Secured Loans:
TL A: EUR 2076mm E+175
TL B: EUR 1954mm E+212

2nd lien + Other: 436mm L+275

High yield bonds
$/GBP/EUR 1045mm

Convertible bond $1000bn

Equity EUR 2323mm

Equity~28%
Debt/EBITDA ~4.2x
Firm Value ~ EUR 8.0bn
Bonds rated B+/B2

Figure 8.3: Example capital structures for different companies.

Having been caught up in a few bankruptcies, it is rare in my experience that a company goes bust overnight with no warning. Generally debt *covenants* (such as maximum debt/EBITDA, interest coverage etc.), which are written into the debt documentation to protect the lenders, are triggered as a company gradually goes wrong. Obvious major recent exceptions have usually involved fraudulent accounts such as Parmalat, Enron, Worldcom or unusual events such as Lehman Brothers that went from investment grade to bust virtually instantaneously. If, however, a covenant is breached there is time for a company to re-negotiate with loan and bond-holders. Depending on the jurisdiction there could be a *covenant wavier* or reset for a fee paid to the lenders or a restructuring of the company. It could be a "friendly" recapitalisation where by new equity is injected into the company by a private equity sponsor. An "unfriendly" restructuring may consist of loan holders dictating terms, wiping out existing equity holders, changing terms on existing debt (lower coupon, longer maturity etc. to make it less onerous) and doing a *debt for equity* exchange where they assume equity control of the company. There are lots of possible options and bankruptcy, appointment of a receiver, and an asset sale to attempt to redeem loan holders is really a last resort. In several jurisdictions (for example in the US where there is the well-known Chapter 11) the company itself can perform a restructuring under the control of a judge or government administrator to re-negotiate contracts with all parties involved such as workers, suppliers and not just debt holders. This means that some jurisdictions are considered friendlier than others for debt-holders, which implies that in some sense the UK and Germany are preferable to France.

8.5. Credit Ratings and Rating Agencies

8.5.1. *Rating agencies*

Several rating agencies (S&P, Moody's, Fitch etc.) provide issuers and their debt various credit ratings. Recently during the credit crisis they have been somewhat discredited primarily as a result of aggressive structured finance credit ratings (particularly of real estate CDOs) and a total failure to identify the leverage problems associated with the major financial companies from Lehman and Bear Stearns to AIG (which was rated AAA). However, they were and still are a major driver of the credit markets with investors relying on their expertise to neutrally assess companies and credit based structures and funds. Generally, their assessment of corporate credits is pretty good although it is acknowledged that they are often behind the curve if events are fast moving. Market credit spreads are often a better indicator of a rapidly deteriorating credit. For example, the agencies were caught out unexpectedly on several recent occasions which involved bankruptcy following major company fraud of investment grade companies (e.g. Parmalat, Enron, Worldcom) although, arguably, they are just victims of the same fraudulent set of accounts as other investors.

Each agency has a separate long term debt ratings scale ranging from very high quality (S&P AAA maximum) to *investment grade* (S&P BBB rating) to sub-investment grade (S&P BB/B rating) and ratings for credits close to default (CCC) (see Table 8.1). Sub-investment grade corporates are often called *high yield* (HY) due to the large bond yields they provide. These ratings provide a good guide to investors as to the quality of a particular debt issue and the inherent credit risk. For many investors the credit rating is the major determinant on the excess return or credit spread they wish to receive on a debt issue. For example, a fund might be allowed have restrictions to purchase AAA/AA debt or investment grade and above.

Table 8.1: Equivalence of S&P, Moody's and Fitch long term rating categories.

S&P	Moody's	Fitch	
AAA	Aaa	AAA	Prime
AA+	Aa1	AA+	
AA	Aa2	AA	High grade
AA-	Aa3	AA-	
A+	A1	A+	
A	A2	A	Upper medium grade
A-	A3	A-	
BBB+	Baa1	BBB+	
BBB	Baa2	BBB	Lower medium grade
BBB-	Baa3	BBB-	
BB+	Ba1	BB+	
BB	Ba2	BB	Non-investment grade speculative
BB-	Ba3	BB-	
B+	B1	B+	
B	B2	B	Highly speculative
B-	B3	B-	
CCC+	Caa1	CCC	Substantial risks
CCC	Caa2	CCC	Extremely speculative
CCC-	Caa3	CCC	
CC	Ca	CCC	In default with little prospect for recovery
C	Ca	CCC	
D	C	DDD/DD	In default

Ratings are not of course static and can go up and down. Rating agencies can also place ratings on upgrade/downgrade notice and on ratings watch where they are more closely and frequently monitored. Unfortunately, ratings are not perfect and as mentioned above the major problem is that they are a "lagging" indicator of credit quality and reflect the opinion of a small group of analysts. Although ratings are supposedly continually updated the actual review frequency is lower. A better measure of credit quality for liquidly traded bonds is the actual market credit spread.

Recently, a major and long overdue realisation amongst investors is that rating agencies rate on the basis of ultimate credit worthiness to maturity and not on the basis of illiquidity and price volatility before maturity (a fact most investors who pre-credit crisis bought AAA rated ABS and who always marked them at par forgot). Obviously, an investment grade bond of a large company with lots of debt is more liquid than that of a smaller company and much more liquid than a equivalently rated structured product such as ABS or a CDO – which in extreme cases could potentially have only a handful of other buyers in the entire world making it very sensitive to potential liquidity events and price fluctuations.

This "blindness" of many investors to any other important investment criteria apart from rating and yield has led to a massive *ratings arbitrage* over the last 15 years for the investment banks to exploit. Ratings arbitrage is a major driver of the credit markets and can work in many ways. Historically, investment managers who are constrained to buy for example investment grade bonds might attempt to achieve higher returns by purchasing investment grade bonds that trade with an abnormally wide credit spread. Through ratings arbitrage, however, investment bankers might repackage high spread, lower rated bonds either through a collateralised debt obligation (CDO) or *credit enhancement* by an AAA/AA rated monoline insurer. By obtaining a higher rating for the bonds at low cost the credit risk can be placed at a tighter spread with investors and an arbitrage achieved.

The methodologies used by the ratings agencies to assign ratings differ and although this does not often cause major differences with bond issues for structured credit ratings, particularly of intermediate or *mezzanine* debt, this is often noticeable. S&P rates on the probability of suffering a loss (even if it is only $1) whereas Moody's rates on the basis of expected loss (the sum of probability multiplied by loss amount). This second approach always seemed more logical to me.

8.5.2 Historical default probabilities

Through a vast accumulation of historical default data the ratings agencies have been able to compile tables of historical default probabilities for different ratings. These can be summarised as (i) *cumulative default probabilities* (for a given rating the probability that a default occurs over a given period of time) or (ii) *marginal default probabilities* (the probability for a given rating a default will occur over a given future period). The marginal default probability, for example between years 1 and 2, is analogous to a forward default probability. The overall cumulative default data up to 2007 are shown in Fig. 8.4.

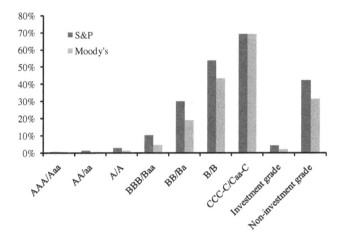

Figure 8.4: S&P and Moody's cumulative default probabilities.

Figures 8.5 and 8.6 show Moody's cumulative and marginal default data more clearly on logarithmic scales. They show that very high quality AAA/AA/A rated credits nearly riskless in the short term. For lower quality credits default probability is high even for short maturities and an inversion is exhibited in the marginal distribution. This inversion arises from the fact that if default does not occur early on with a low quality credit then the company usually survives and the credit quality improves. Interestingly, this is what is observed in market credit spreads for credits close to bankruptcy.

Care should be taken in using this historic data since it has been compiled from the rating agencies experience with US corporate credits and defaults are obviously cyclical with the state of economy. In a recession the default rate will rise (see Fig. 8.7). Also, for high rated entities there have never been many defaults (there are only about four AAA rated US companies at present) and the statistics are not that good so the margin of error on establishing averages is high.

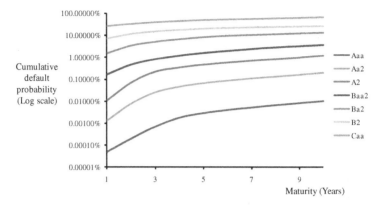

Figure 8.5: Moody's cumulative default probabilities (log scale).

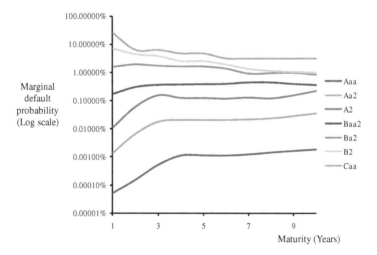

Figure 8.6: Moody's marginal default probabilities (log scale).

Figure 8.7: Historical variation of high yield bond default rate (1982–2010).

8.5.3 *Recovery rates*

The value of a bond after a default is often called the *recovery rate* and the rating agencies have complied average recovery rates for defaulted debt. The recovery rate is higher if the seniority of debt is higher with senior secured debt being about 65–75% compared with 35–45% on senior unsecured debt.

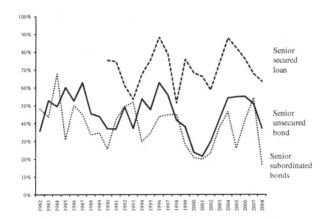

Figure 8.8: Historical variation of recovery rate for bonds and loans.

Averages can be misleading though, and in recessionary periods recovery rates can be lower. Figure 8.8 shows historical variation of recovery rates compiled from various sources for 30 days after a default event. Recovery rates are slightly dependent on the time observed after the official default time and credit derivatives settle soon after a default date. In the credit crisis 2008–2010 many companies that had aggressively leveraged themselves in 2006–2007 that ran into trouble seem to have lower than expected recoveries. In addition recovery rates depend strongly on the industrial sector and whether a company has hard assets.

8.6 Asset Swaps

The origins of the credit derivatives market lie in the *asset swap* market that existed several years before. Many of today's (older) credit default swap traders developed their expertise trading asset swaps. Asset swaps initially provided the benchmark for pricing in the CDS market. As liquidity has increased CDS market trading now dominates credit pricing and drives cash prices.

An asset swap allows an investor to swap a fixed rate bond into a floating rate instrument removing the interest rate risk and creating a LIBOR plus spread instrument that is essentially pure credit risk. Typically, the underlying bond plus the swap are sold as an asset swap *package* either at 100% for a *par asset swap* or at the market price of the bond for a *market value asset swap.*

The spread over LIBOR is essentially the credit risk premium. The evolution of the asset swap allowed investors to arbitrage different credit perceptions between different markets. For example an illiquid bond of a particular issuer trading in Euro might be cheaper when swapped into USD than any regular USD denominated asset of the issuer available. This created more efficiency and liquidity for assets and allowed spread to truly become the proxy for credit risk.

In a par asset swap the buyer purchases a fixed rate bond at an effective price of par (100%) and swaps it into a floating rate coupon. Thus the *asset swap buyer* pays 100% and receives a bond plus a swap contract. Under the swap the buyer pays the fixed bond coupon C (plus principal at maturity) and receives a floating rate plus a spread s from the seller (see Fig. 8.9). When this swap plus bond is priced at fair value the *asset swap spread* can be determined (Appx G.1).

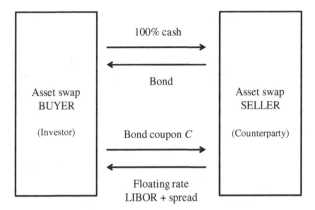

Figure 8.9: Par asset swap cash-flows.

When the bond price is significantly above par there is an effective upfront payment by the seller as is the case in a low rate environment when the bond was previously issued with a higher coupon. This then becomes a funding transaction and must be priced at the relevant funding level for the asset swap seller. An alternative is to price the asset swap at the actual bond price rather than par and this is called a *market value asset swap* (Appx G.2). Cross currency asset swaps exist and these allow cheap bonds in one currency to be effectively converted into the investors preferred currency.

Market participants are often very careless about talking about which bond spreads they are actually talking about when you want to do a trade. Unfortunately, spread definitions are mathematically very different and produce different bond prices. For example saying "L+200bp" could mean an asset swap spread (par or market?) or alternatively the bond yield minus the underlying interpolated rate of the swap's curve (sometimes known as the *I-spread*). Another common definition is *Z-spread* which is the amount of spread that must be added to the zero curve to correctly price the bond (Appx G.3). The only spread you can easily economically lock-in though is the asset swap spread.

For floating rate notes with credit risk the notion of *discount margin* is often used. Discount margin is the effective spread that would need to be added to the floating rate coupons for the FRN to price at par (100%).

8.7 Credit Default Swaps (CDS)

In a market standard or vanilla *credit default swap* (CDS), one counterparty (the protection *buyer*) pays a spread or *premium* to the other counterparty (the protection *seller*) for credit protection on a particular credit (the *reference entity*). In a sense a CDS is similar to buying insurance on a bond of the reference entity.

In the event of a default or *credit event* associated with the reference entity the protection seller will pay 100% to the buyer who will deliver a par nominal amount of the defaulted underlying asset to the seller. The premium payments will then cease and the swap will terminate. In this settlement process the buyer, assuming he originally purchased the asset at close to par 100%, will be compensated for any drop in value of the asset on a credit event. This process is outlined in Fig. 8.10.

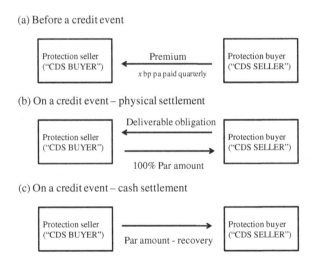

Figure 8.10: How a credit default swap works.

The type of asset that can be delivered is closely controlled and it is important that the CDS references senior unsecured debt. Mostly senior unsecured bonds of any maturity in any major currency can be delivered. A *reference obligation* is usually specified in the documentation which serves as a guide to the type and seniority of the debt that can be delivered. A CDS that references senior secured debt is termed a *loan credit default swap* (LCDS) and has secured loans as a deliverable. They trade at tighter spreads since the recovery rate is lower although briefly during the credit crisis they traded at the same level as CDS due to issues of lower liquidity.

A credit event as currently traded by the market is actually more widely ranging than a pure default by the reference entity and currently includes various ISDA defined events: *bankruptcy, failure to pay, restructuring, repudiation/moratorium, obligation default and obligation acceleration.* Bankruptcy, failure to pay and restructuring are the key credit events used in CDS (see Table 8.2). Restructuring is the most sensitive due to numerous disagreements since the development of the original restructuring definition and following the problematic Conseco restructuring is currently the most controversial. The current ISDA offers four types of restructuring options Old-R (Full Restructuring), No-R (No Restructuring – used for US high yield), Mod R (Modified Restructuring – standard for US investment grade names) and Mod-Mod-R (Modified-Modified Restructuring – used in Europe). The major difference between these definitions concerns the maturity of deliverable obligations. In the US a study of HY defaults by Fitch gave approximately 52.8% Chapter 11, 41.4% missed coupon or principal payment, 5.1% distressed bond exchange and 0.6% other. Thus approximately 40% of credit events will be encompassed by a failure to Pay. Really the rating agencies in their default data only really cover bankruptcy and failure to pay and it is debatable how many restructuring credit events their statistics actually include. There is always some debate on whether a company restructuring constitutes a credit event. Some companies (like GMAC with subsidiary Rescap) prove very cunning and manage to "strong-arm" investors into voluntarily accepting a bond tender or exchange and thus modifying the terms of the bonds without triggering a Restructuring credit event.

Instead of physically delivering a reference obligation on a credit event, *cash settlement* is also very common (see Fig. 8.10). The seller will pay to the buyer 100% minus the recovery rate or *final price* of the relevant reference obligation or similar asset. The price is determined by a post credit event poll of a group of well known dealers of the relevant reference obligation using an ISDA specified process. Many of these price determination polls are carried out these days by Markit, a financial data company owned by several dealers. Economically, a cash-settled transaction is equivalent to a physically settled transaction. The reason physically settled transactions can defer to cash settlement, is to avoid squeezes on the bonds if there is a problem with delivering the assets (I remember with the Indonesia default in the Asia crisis the bonds actually traded up on a credit event since only physical settlement was possible in those days). In recent years I have only ever cash settled on contracts.

The most liquid contract traded is the 5 year although 3, 7 and 10 year are also fairly liquid and other maturities can be quoted although the bid/offer will be bigger. Typical market sizes are USD or Euro 20–50mm for investment grade credits and 5–10mm for high yield. As with futures contracts market CDS contracts roll every 3 months (generally the 20th) of March, June, September and December.

Table 8.2: The six IDSA CDS credit events (simplified).

Credit Event	Description
Bankruptcy	Bankruptcy or insolvency of the reference entity. It is widely drafted so as to be triggered by a variety of events associated with bankruptcy or insolvency proceedings under English law and New York law, as well as analogous events under other insolvency laws.
Failure to Pay	Failure of the reference entity to make, when and where due, any payments under one or more obligations. Grace periods for payment and thresholds are taken into account.
Restructuring	Restructuring covers events as a result of which the terms, as agreed by the reference entity and the holders of the relevant obligation, governing the relevant obligation have become less favourable to the holders that they would otherwise have been. These events include a reduction in the principal amount or interest payable under the obligation, a postponement of payment, a change in ranking in priority of payment or any other composition of payment.
Repudiation/Moratorium	The reference entity disaffirms, disclaims or otherwise challenges the validity of the relevant obligation. Usually applicable to sovereigns.
Obligation Acceleration	The relevant obligation becomes due and payable as a result of a default by the reference entity before the time when such obligation would otherwise have been due and payable.
Obligation Default	A relevant obligation becomes capable of being declared due and payable as a result of a default by the reference entity before the time when such obligation would otherwise have been capable of being so declared.

CDS can be offered on other underlying credit assets, other than bonds and loans, for example ABS and CDOs. The sovereign CDS market where government bonds are deliverables (usually denominated in major currency and not local currency) has been around since the days of the Asia crisis but recently surfaced in the press when the Greek economy hit problems. Also CDS credit index products are now popular and the two major ones in Europe are the iTraxx Europe Main (composed of investment grade names) and the XOVER (more volatile high yield/spread names). Their US equivalents are the CDX NA IG and the CDX NA HY/XO. Also indices exist for Asia, Japan, emerging markets, industrial sub-sectors and even ABS (the ABX). Importantly every time these contracts roll the constituents change slightly (based on discussions between dealers) and so contracts are not directly fungible and only the couple of near term contracts retain liquidity (which is annoying when you want to have a long term hedge).

8.8 Basis Packages

As we can see from the above discussion a CDS is a credit hedge for a cash bond (or "cash"). If the bond credit spread is greater than the CDS spread then we have a possible *negative basis trade* – we can buy the bond and buy credit protection via CDS on the same notional. If it is a fixed rate bond we can further hedge out the interest rate risk using an individual interest rate swap or on a portfolio basis for a portfolio of basis trades. This trade allows the investor to lock in a positive interest or *positive carry* if held to maturity of

$$Carry = Bond\ Spread\ - CDS\ Spread.$$

This carry is not all profit though since the effective investor funding cost of holding a cash bond must be taken into account. For a highly rated bank that can fund close to LIBOR the funding cost is negligible (it might even be slightly negative) but for most other investors it is positive and governed by the interbank repo market. Generally a typical negative basis might be around -15 to -45bp per annum for investment grade bonds however this went to -250bp during the credit crisis when the repo funding market shut down.

Capital Structure Arbitrage and Mr K.

There was a time when "capital structure arbitrage" seemed a good trade. The CDS/equity correlation was good so selling protection on a high yield corporate using CDS and shorting a delta of its stock to hedge seemed to make money 90% of the time. Plus it was positive carry – if the trade went against you just sat in it and over a period of time the carry got you out flat. Unfortunately, 10% of the time things could go wrong and sometimes horribly wrong. The General Motors trade was the prime example of this. We thought it was a great original idea since the GMAC CDS was already wide, indicating imminent bankruptcy, and the GM equity was very, very overpriced and still full of optimism for the company's prospects. In our view it was a trade that could only go one way as GM was sure to slide into inevitable bankruptcy in the long term. Unfortunately in 2005 Mr K. an 80 something billionaire investor thought differently about GM's prospects and decided to tender for the stock. The stock price rallied massively against us and we incurred a big loss. Then we realised that every other "hedgie" had thought it was originally a good trade too and was in the same trade. They mostly capitulated and bailed out with large losses causing bigger movement in the CDS, forcing the trade to move even further against everybody. Despite being down heavily on the trade we remained convinced about the fundamentals so stubbornly sat in it. It was positive carry so we ran the trade. Eventually, after 12 months the trade had crept back and we had made a meagre profit before getting out. Mr K. bailed out at a later date and the rest is GM history as GM eventually filed Chapter 11. Unfortunately that was pretty much the end of the cap structure arb trade for most people especially as a new LBO craze was in town making the trade extremely toxic. Any hint of an LBO and the stock would be up 10% and the spread out 400 bp and nobody liked to do the opposite trade (buy protection/buy stock) since that was negative carry.

Here I have been deliberately vague with the notion of credit spread of the bond. From our discussion of asset swap spreads we should really consider it to be the asset swap spread, but many people use the *Z-spread* which gives a slightly different result (Appx G.3). A more advanced technique uses default curve adjusted spread where the *reduced form model* is used to price the bond (Appx G.8). Although theoretically correct the problem with the latter technique is that it makes negative basis trades look optically better than they really are and in some cases they are not even truly positive carry.

If the bond spread is tighter than the CDS spread then the reverse trade is possible – sell (or short) the cash bond and sell credit protection via CDS. This is called *positive basis* and does not (in my experience) occur that often as a potentially profitable trade once all the real costs of shorting the bond have been taken accurately into account.

8.9 Credit Pricing Models

To price credit derivatives requires a market based approach to pricing. Any credit derivative model must take the current market level of credit spreads as an input and imply default probabilities. These implied default probabilities can then be used to value CDS and other credit instruments. This is similar to valuing equity exotic options using the volatilities implied from simple, vanilla options.

There are currently two main approaches to pricing default based derivative products. The first is based on stochastic processes describing the evolution of the value of a company (*stochastic firm value models* or *structural models*) and the second approach is where default occurs suddenly and catastrophically through a simple random process (*reduced form models or catastrophe models*). The reduced form model is more widely used for market trading and the structural model is used these days only for risk management, academic purposes and as a guide in capital structure trading (trading company equity versus its debt).

8.9.1 *Stochastic firm value models*

In the *stochastic firm value* approach the asset value of the company is modelled by a random variable using a process similar to the Black–Scholes process. If $A(t)$ is the firm value or enterprise value at time t then

$$\frac{dA(t)}{A(t)} = \mu_A dt + \sigma_A \, dz, \tag{8.1}$$

where μ_A is the drift and σ_A is the firm value volatility. A default occurs when the firm value $A(t)$ falls below some defined level $X(t)$ which can be viewed as the level of the company debt. In the stochastic firm value model default can then be viewed as a form of barrier option as in Fig. 8.11. A problem with such a model is specification of the parameters such as drift, volatility and the barrier level. Many different theoretical variants of the model have been published and various closed form solutions exist. The simplest model consists of replacing the barrier with a put option which is equivalent to a put option on the firm value (Appx G.4.1). If the debt is treated as a zero coupon bond with a defined maturity then default occurs if the firm value falls below this debt level at maturity.

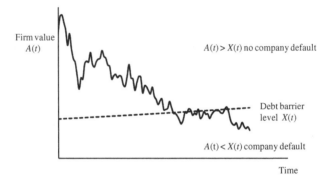

Figure 8.11: The Stochastic Firm Value model.

More complex models assume varying barrier levels and term structure of debt. An implication of such a model is that $A(t)$ evolves over time it becomes "known" when a default will occur. In a sense default is not an unexpected event. For a company of high credit quality then $A(0)>>X(0)$ and default is impossible over a reasonably short time horizon. This does not correspond to the rating agency data where there is a small but finite probability that highly rated companies can unexpectedly default over short time periods and this small possibility of default over short time horizons is also reflected in short-dated market spreads. A pure diffusion process cannot accommodate this unless other factors are included, for example a jump diffusion process or a stochastically varying barrier as in the widely documented JP Morgan CreditGrades model

(Appx G.4.2). Several commercially available risk management products have been developed that use refinements of this approach.

8.9.2 Reduced form models

In a *reduced form* model or *catastrophe* model, default is suddenly triggered by a random process and hence a sudden catastrophe. The time of default is modelled by using a Poisson probability distribution that is good at describing the random occurrences of events. Thus, typically, a credit event is modelled by the *first arrival time t* of an event in a random Poisson process with intensity, $\lambda(t)$. For a Poisson default process the probability of default in the interval of time t to $t+\Delta t$ (assuming no default has previously occurred) is given by $\lambda(t)\Delta t$. $\lambda(t)$ is known as the hazard rate or default intensity. All the information specifying the probability of a credit event and the process involved is encapsulated in one variable, the hazard rate, and this is why it is called a reduced form model.

An advantage of such a model is the relatively few parameters required to calibrate the model. Generally, the post default value of an obligation, the recovery rate R, is estimated from historical and fundamental analysis and the default intensity $\lambda(t)$ as a function of maturity determined from market asset swap or credit default swap curves. The recovery rate can also be implied from the market as the value other dealers using to calculate CDS unwinds and from the price of digital CDS. Here we shall focus on the *par recovery* version of the model where loss on a bond is measured as a fraction of par (100%) plus accrued interest since it most correctly describes the recovery process on a defaulted bond. This model is pretty much the market standard for pricing of credit derivatives (Appx G.5).

Other assumptions in the model are that the default process is locally independent of the random evolution of the bond price or interest rates. Although we could include random or stochastic process for the default intensity, interest rates and recovery rate, in the basic model no attempt is made to model the spread movement and the effect of other market variables and their effect on the default process is ignored. The probability of default and the final price or recovery rate of the defaulted obligation are completely independent. When these other parameters are seen as important they must be correctly modelled using framework described for hybrids in Chapter 10.

From the properties of the Poisson distribution we can calculate the *cumulative probability of default* up to a time t that is

$$Q(0,t) = \Pr[\tau \le t],$$

where τ is the actual time of default. Figure 8.12 shows example cumulative probability curves as a function of time for two different constant hazard rates. We can see that even with flat default intensities these curves bear a superficial resemblance to real spread curves (Fig. 8.1). Also very useful is the *survival probability* which is the probability of no default occurring by time t and is defined as

$$L(0,t) = \Pr[\tau > t] = 1 - Q(0,t).$$

The survival probability is an exponentially decaying function with time and can be viewed as analogous to a discount factor in swaps pricing. By discounting a credit risky cash-flow or coupon using the survival probability we can calculate the expected value that this coupon will be paid in the future (Appx G.5). Thus if a coupon C will be paid at time t, except if there is a credit event before that date, then the expected coupon is C multiplied by the survival probability $L(0,t)$.

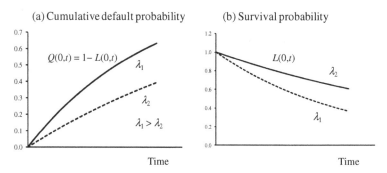

Figure 8.12: The Reduced Form model: cumulative default and survival probabilities.

Also we can use the survival probability and the definition of the hazard rate to calculate the probability of default in a future time interval t to $t + \Delta t$ as

$$\Pr[t < \tau \le t + \Delta t] = \Pr[\tau > t]\lambda(t)\Delta t \quad. \tag{8.2}$$

This can be viewed as a marginal or forward default probability. Using these results we can value credit default swaps.

8.10 Pricing Credit Default Swaps

Using the reduced form model outlined above a valuation formula for a typical vanilla CDS can be derived. A CDS can be considered as (i) a premium flow, typically paid quarterly, that terminates on a credit event and (ii) a payment of (100% − recovery rate R) on a credit event. This is shown schematically in Fig. 8.13.

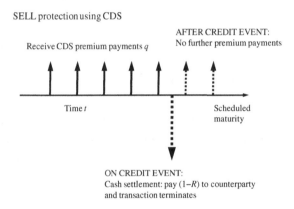

Figure 8.13: Pricing CDS credit contingent cash-flows.

Assume that the default intensity and interest rates are non-stochastic. The effect of introducing these as stochastic processes can be shown to be very small. Also, including correlation between rates and default intensity has negligible effect for reasonable correlation levels.

We can value the CDS of maturity T as the present value of the expected premium flows, which can terminate at default time τ if $\tau < T$, minus the credit event payment which only occurs if default occurs before maturity. Thus

$$V_{CDS}(0,T) = PV\ premium\ payments\ until\ \tau$$
$$- PV\ payment(1-R)\ at\ \tau. \tag{8.3}$$

If we simplify and assume that default can only occur at the end of each coupon period t_i ($i=1,...,N$) we can write this as (i) the sum of the premium payments q discounted using a discount factor times a survival probability minus (ii) the sum of the discounted contingent payments $(1-R)$ times the probability of a credit event in each coupon period:

$$V_{CDS}(0,T) = q \sum_{i}^{N} D(0,t_i) \Pr[\tau > t_i] h_i$$
$$- (1-R) \sum_{i}^{N} D(0,t_i) \Pr[t_{i-1} < \tau \leq t_i]. \tag{8.4}$$

Using the definition of these probabilities we can write in terms of the survival probability and the hazard rate

$$V_{CDS}(0,T) = q \sum_{i}^{N} D(0,t_i) L(0,t_i) h_i$$
$$- (1-R) \sum_{i}^{N} D(0,t_i) L(0,t_i) \lambda(t_i) h_i. \tag{8.5}$$

We know that a market value CDS is initially valued at zero. If we assume hazard rates, interest rates and the recovery rate are constants we can obtain a very simple relation for the market CDS premium

$$q = \lambda(1 - R). \tag{8.6}$$

This shows that the CDS premium for a flat curve is equal to the default intensity times the loss amount $(1-R)$. This is intuitively what we might expect since it represents the expected loss per annum. At a later time t the market spread (or hazard rate) may have moved and the swap is valued as the risky-annuity or risky *PV01* or *RPV01* times the difference between the original traded spread $q(0,T)$ and the current market spread $q(t,T)$. The *RPV01* can be determined as the sum over the discount factors times survival probabilities.

$$V_{CDS}(t,T) = (q(t,T) - q(0,T)) RPV01$$
$$= (q(t,T) - q(0,T)) \sum_{i}^{N} D(0,t_i) L(0,t_i) h_i. \tag{8.7}$$

The above calculation assumed that credit events occurred, on coupon dates and in reality credit events can occur any time. Also, on a credit event all accrued premium is normally owed. The calculation above must be modified to include an integral over time rather than a discrete sum but we leave this for Appx (G.6).

It is worth noting that in attempt to harmonise models ISDA provides a freely available market standard model with proposed market standard settings. I guess this agrees with the Bloomberg model that virtually everybody uses these days. The normal process on a CDS unwind if you disagree with the exact amount is that your salesman emails a snapshot of the Bloomberg screen after the trade.

8.11 Building Hazard Rate Curves

For a given credit a series of market CDS levels of different maturities can be used to build a default intensity curve $\lambda(t)$. A market default intensity curve provides the market default probability expectations and can be used to price a trading book of CDS of different maturities. This also allows pricing and hedging of a wide variety of structured credit products.

From Eq. (8.5) we can see that building a default intensity curve requires a "bootstrapping" technique similar to that used in constructing a zero curve (Appx G.7). Usually a single recovery rate assumption R is made for all maturities and the default intensity curve is built starting with the shortest maturities. Thus if 1 year is the shortest CDS quoted with premium $q(0,1)$ we can find the 1 year hazard rate $\lambda(1)$ using Eq. (8.6) then using both the 2 year CDS premium $q(0,2)$ and the 1 year hazard rate we can find from Eq. (8.5) the 2 year hazard rate $\lambda(2)$. By continuing this process using all available CDS maturities we can build a hazard rate curve. This simple approach builds effectively a "step" curve with flat sections. Intermediate points on the $\lambda(t)$ curve can be determined using an interpolation technique or fitting a polynomial curve to all maturities.

The wide bid/offer on the CDS must be taken into account when building the curve. Banks use a bid and offered curve for initial pricing and a mid curve for book valuation. The lack of liquidity across curves can lead to discontinuities and curve building problems. CDS points which are unknown are usually interpolated by traders by eye although for many credits Markit provides daily credit curves from dealer contributions.

8.11.1 *Recovery rates in credit curve building*

The recovery rate assumption demands careful attention and is effectively a trading parameter. A starting point used in determining the recovery rate is often the historical recovery values determined by the rating agencies for similar debt modified by some quick fundamental analysis plus or minus a margin to reflect a bid/offer. Generally, since the main dealers can observe what recovery rate each are using for market unwinds the market settles around a standard market level. Markit also does a daily recovery rate survey and these are published for all to see.

ISDA provides a market standard model parameters for the US and Western Europe of 40% for senior unsecured debt, 20% for subordinated and 70% for senior secured debt (for LCDS). These values are lower for Japan (35% for senior unsecured) and emerging markets (25% for senior unsecured). Otherwise, values for senior unsecured corporate debt might range from 30–55%, financial groups slightly lower at 15–45% and emerging market corporates and sovereigns anything from 0–40%. Recovery rates on subordinated debt will be lower at 0–15%. Actual values used are dependent on market conditions and are often inconsistent between dealers in less liquid names (funny that it always seems to be in their favour when you do an unwind and the CDS is in the money in your favour!). Actually, vanilla CDS valuation is not that sensitive to recovery rate when close to the money since it is first order in the difference in market and traded spreads in Eq. (8.7). However, certain structured products (for example digitals) are extremely sensitive and a wide bid/offer in recovery of 35–65% will often be used.

8.12 Modelling "Risky" Bonds

Bonds subject to credit risk or "risky" bonds can be priced in a similar manner to CDS using the reduced form model. However, we must realise that on a default a bond holder is legally owed par (100%) plus accrued interest by the issuer. Also most bonds trade at a negative basis to CDS so to allow both cash and CDS to be priced consistently with the same hazard rate curve the basis effect can be accommodated by the use of a *market financing* or *effective repo* curve (Appx G.8).

8.13 Digital CDS

Digital CDS are cash settled credit default swaps that pay 100% rather than (100% − recovery rate) as in a vanilla CDS. Digital CDS are now more frequently traded and the premium paid is slightly higher due to the higher payout on default (Appx G.9). The market value digital CDS premium is given from Eq. (8.6) simply by the hazard rate:

$$q_{\underset{CDS}{digital}} = \lambda = \frac{q_{CDS}}{(1-R)}. \tag{8.8}$$

However, the actual digital CDS premium paid is highly dependent on the actual recovery rate assumption R. As this is an uncertain value and difficult to hedge a wide bid/offer on the recovery rate R is used.

8.14 Loan Credit Default Swaps (LCDS)

As previously mentioned a CDS referencing a secured loan is called a *loan credit default swap* or LCDS. This is a recent innovation and now contracts are ISDA standardised and traded by many investment banks and hedge funds. Usually these are loans of high yield companies and reference the most senior loans (A or B/C tranches) unless otherwise specified. The recovery rate on a default should be higher for a for a LCDS than a CDS so consequently the market spread should be lower. Since cross default usually exists in loan and bond documentation and the nature of credit events specifies non-payment on bonds or loans or a debt restructuring we could expect that LCDS and CDS should be triggered at the same time. In this sense we can assume the default probability to be the same. So from Eq. (8.6) the ratio of LCDS spread to CDS spread should be approximately

$$\frac{q_{LCDS}}{q_{CDS}} = \frac{(1-R_{LCDS})}{(1-R_{CDS})}, \tag{8.9}$$

where R_{LCDS} is the expected loan recovery with $R_{LCDS} > R_{CDS}$ (see Section 8.5.3). There exists an LCDS index product called the LevX in Europe and LCDX in the US which is composed of HY corporate names.

8.15 Counterparty Default Correlation

All of the above analysis assumes that credit protection is bought and sold from counterparties that are uncorrelated with the reference entity and default correlation can be assumed to be a negligible effect. Default correlation is a measure of the likelihood that both counterparty and reference entity will default within a given time period. Default correlation can be expected to be higher for companies within related industries, sectors and geographical regions. For example the default correlation between a two Japanese banks could be expected to be higher than the correlation between a US retailer and a European bank.

Obviously, if we sell protection to a correlated counterparty this correlation effect poses no real problem. However, a more serious problem is apparent if we buy protection from a correlated counterparty. In general if a counterparty defaults the buyer must repurchase credit protection from another market counterparty. If correlation is high the spread replacement cost may be prohibitively high or indeed the credit may have become illiquid. More worrisome still is if the default of the reference entity provokes a direct default of the counterparty (or vice versa). In general, common sense dictates that one should attempt to purchase protection from uncorrelated counterparties, however, this is not always possible and indeed more and more traded structures include correlation effects. The premium for buying protection from a correlated counterparty should be theoretically lower than for the uncorrelated case (Appx G.10).

In reality there is only the one market spread for a corporate CDS and attempts are made through *credit lines*, *netting* of trades and *margining* to reduce risk between counterparties. Consider the case where a highly rated bank buys protection off an unrated counterparty such as a hedge fund. Under the credit agreement between them the hedge fund will provide an *upfront* margin amount (5%, say) and a mark-to-market *variation margin* on a daily basis. The amount of upfront margin is usually based on a grid (produced by the banks credit risk department) based on spread or rating of the underlying CDS. More sophisticated banks look across at the portfolio of trades they have with a counterparty and apply diversification and *netting* of long/shorts across names, sectors and maturities to give an effective overall margin. Currently moves are in progress to establish a CDS clearing system through exchanges to reduce counterparty risk.

Many investment products are based on default correlation and these include correlated CDS, first-to-default baskets and synthetic CDOs and we shall describe the pricing of these in the next section.

8.16 Modelling and Trading Default Correlation

There has recently been large growth in default correlation products such as baskets and CDOs. This has led to significant research and development into techniques for modelling default correlation processes. Most of these models involve *copula functions* to transform independent random variables into correlated random variables that then produce correlated defaults. The most common implementation which has become the market standard is the *normal copula* model due to its easy analytic tractability and implementation.

In the normal copula model uncorrelated normally distributed random numbers are transformed using a correlation matrix into correlated random variables from a multivariate normal distribution. These correlated variables are then mapped into default times based on implied cumulative default probabilities derived from market CDS spreads. Figure 8.14 shows how a correlated normal variate Z provides a probability that is mapped onto the cumulative default distribution of the reduced form model to give a default time. These correlated default times then can be used to derive a portfolio loss distribution as a function of time. A knowledge of default times for each individual credit allows for precise valuation of any basket or portfolio structured credit product (Appx G.12).

Usually, the model is implemented using a Monte Carlo simulation which for calculating hedging greeks for large portfolios, can be computationally intensive. Quite accurate closed form approximations for pricing can be achieved for simplified cases of homogenous correlations, spreads, loss on default, etc. (Appx G.13). However, when you really want to determine the greeks accurately is usually in a period of stress when a few names in the portfolio have deteriorated in quality from the mean of the portfolio. These de-correlated credits begin to dominate the product's behaviour and for this inhomogeneous case a tedious Monte Carlo is often the only route.

The normal copula model is attractive due to its simplicity and computational efficiency. Other models are sometimes used, however, with the preferred candidate being based on the Student t distribution. Also models can be constructed which use correlation structure implied from tranched market indices (see Section 9.6.4).

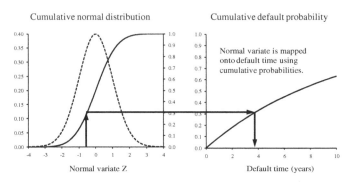

Figure 8.14: The normal copula model: mapping a normal random variable to a default time.

Also it is worth noting that the normal copula is essentially a structural model at its heart with default occurring when a stochastic normal variable falls below a barrier level determined by the market implied hazard rate. This is similar in concept to the stochastic firm value model discussed in Section 8.9.1. We thus have a slight contradiction in that we use inputs from a *reduced form* CDS model into a correlated *structural model* for pricing structured correlation products. The output is then re-mapped to a reduced form model to give a default time as Fig. 8.14.

Development of accurate correlation models allowed the development of delta hedging of CDO tranches by trading desks (Appx G.12). The models can be used to evaluate credit spread deltas (CS01s) and *jump-to-default* (JTD) risk for each underlying credit in the portfolio and correlation risk. Typically, after a few CDO tranched trades a *structured credit trading book* starts to have hundreds of names (each with a credit curve of sensitivities) that must be monitored and hedged. Often just with CDS it is impossible to hedge simultaneously CS01 and JTD in each name so small JTD (positive or negative) risk must be run in many names. Trading a structured credit book is decidedly non-trivial especially when market correlation starts to swing around.

Chapter 9

Structured Credit Products

9.1 Introduction

The development of *credit default swaps* (CDS) has allowed a wide range of investment products with embedded synthetic credit risk to be developed and sold to traditional institutional credit investors and more recently to high net worth individuals and retail investors. Figure 9.1 provides an overview of the major products.

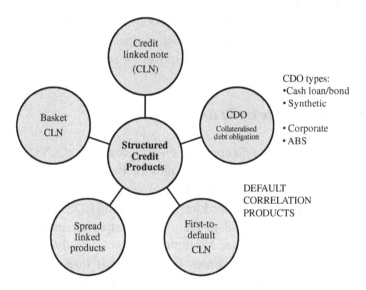

Figure 9.1: Different structured credit products.

Credit linked notes (CLNs) allow the structuring of customised bonds as alternatives to the usual cash corporate, financial and sovereign bonds available in the secondary market. Basket CLNs provide diversification of risk and default correlation products such as *first-to-default baskets* (FTDs) and *collateralised debt obligations* (CDOs) enable varying leverage and increased yields. For "risky" credits it is possible to structure capital protected notes analogous to equity products. Credit spread options also exist, but despite their use by more sophisticated counterparties such as hedge funds they are used extremely infrequently in investment products to end investors and we will ignore them here although they can be modelled using framework in Appx (I.2).

9.2 Credit Linked Notes

A *credit linked note* (CLN) issued by a financial issuer is composed simply from a standard note issue with an embedded CDS. This provides several benefits for investors, for example it can allow creation of a cash bond for tailored maturity or be denominated in a currency where no actual corporate cash bond exists. It also can allow the note to pay a higher spread than an existing cash bond since often the spread in the CDS market can be slightly higher (positive basis). Finally, by combining with a positive funding spread for certain issuers the spread of the notes can be boosted further.

9.2.1 *Floating rate credit linked note*

The simplest case is a *floating rate credit linked note* (CLN). The coupon is enhanced by the CDS premium q plus the issuer funding level x. This is shown schematically in Fig. 9.2. On a *credit event* the notes redeem early at the *final price R* determined for the underlying CDS contract. Thus, an amount $(100\%-R)$ is paid to the swap counterparty and an amount R redeemed to the note-holder. No further coupon is usually paid. In general, the issuer will demand a lower funding spread than usual due to the possibility of early termination. The note documentation mirrors the hedge CDS in terms of credit events and other related definitions.

Example 9.1 shows a CLN linked to Greece in USD currency. Usually for a corporate credit linked note we would have as credit events: bankruptcy, failure to pay and restructuring (although not for

US high yield). Since we cannot really have bankruptcy for a sovereign the credit event *repudiation/moratorium* is included, which covers the event that Greece may simply conveniently choose to forget the fact that it issued any debt.

1. Credit linked note (CLN) cash-flows

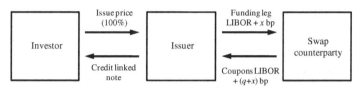

2. Early redemption on a credit event (cash settlement)

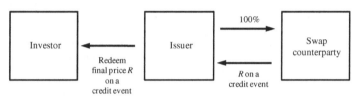

Figure 9.2: Floating rate credit linked note.

9.2.2 *Fixed rate credit linked note*

A credit linked note that pays a fixed rate will include a fixed/floating interest rate swap which will be terminated early on a credit event. Depending how the note is documented it is the investor or the swap counterparty who will "take" the *swap unwind risk*. If the investor takes the swap unwind risk then the early termination redemption amount will be the *final price* (determined under the CDS contract) minus the interest rate swap unwind cost (if any). Since the investor cannot lose more than 100% of his capital the swap counterparty may be exposed to loss if the recovery rate or final price is very low or the swap unwind costs very high (for example with a cross-currency swap). This is generally not a problem for corporate credits but for financials where recovery might be lower care must be taken. An alternative is if the CDS position is combined in the same trading book as the interest rate swap and the position can then be re-hedged as the interest rate exposure changes. This is equivalent to having a funding leg that is contingent on no default (Appx H.1).

Example 9.1

USD GREECE CREDIT LINKED NOTE		
ISSUER	:	AA rated Issuer
CURRENCY	:	USD
MATURITY	:	5 year
ISSUE PRICE	:	100%
COUPON	:	6 month USD Libor + 1.2%
REFERENCE ENTITY	:	Hellenic Republic
REFERENCE OBLIGATION	:	Any senior, unsecured debt obligation of the Reference Entity.
CREDIT EVENT	:	Failure to Pay Restructuring Repudiation/Moratorium
REDEMPTION	:	If the Notes, unless previously redeemed, will be redeemed at 100% on the Maturity Date.
EARLY REDEMPTION	:	If a Credit Event occurs on or before 25 Business Days prior to the Maturity Date the Notes will be redeemed early at an amount equal to 100% × Defaulted Reference Obligation Final Price.

9.2.3 *SPV issued credit linked note*

Many CLNs are issued by special purpose vehicles (SPVs) (Section 1.8.2) where the SPV will buy underlying collateral securities (other bonds or short dated securities) with the note proceeds. The SPV then simultaneously enters into a CDS contract with the swap counterparty. The underlying collateral will be typically be of AAA/AA quality and will be uncorrelated with the reference entity of the CDS.

The SPV note works in a similar fashion to a CLN issued by a financial issuer but the redemption amount on a credit event will be different. The CDS counterparty is documented as senior to the note-holder on a CDS credit event. On a credit event at time τ the underlying collateral is sold at market value $V_{collateral}$, any interest rate swap unwound at market value V_{swap} and the redemption is dependent on the proceeds of the sale of the underlying collateral. In this way it is note-holder that takes the market spread risk on the collateral on a credit event. The redemption amount for the notes is thus given by

$$Max[V_{collateral}(\tau) - (1-R) - V_{swap}(\tau), 0]. \tag{9.1}$$

Many variations exist, for example the collateral can have a different maturity from the maturity of the CLN (longer or shorter) or the collateral can be denominated in a different currency from the notes and a cross currency swap included.

The major advantage of a SPV issued CLN is that a much higher yield can often be provided due to the extra spread of the underlying collateral. The extra spread paid to the note-holders is the CDS premium plus the spread of the underlying collateral securities rather than the negative funding usually required by most financial issuers. Pre-credit crisis it was typical to use underlying AAA ABS securities paying, say +50bp, rather than, say −20bp, for the equivalent AAA rated financial issuer. More recently actual government securities are used as collateral. The disadvantage of an SPV is that it is not a true financial issuer such as a bank and is sometimes misunderstood by investors.

9.2.4 *Leveraged credit linked note*

Leveraged CLNs have been extremely popular but have sometimes proven to be very toxic. Before the Russia crisis (1998) many emerging market investors loved these structures in which the issuing bank effectively lent you 100–200% to purchase more cash emerging market bonds. These days the products are constructed synthetically using CDS. The spread is enhanced by taking 2–3 times exposure to the same underlying credit. For example rather than an investor buying Euro 10mm of notes backed by Euro 10mm of CDS he might buy a leveraged CLN with Euro 20–30mm CDS exposure. These products have a spread trigger level where if the spread of the underlying CDS goes above a certain level (or based on a price fall) the structure is unwound and the investor is redeemed 100% minus the CDS unwind cost. This is pretty toxic since credit spreads are notorious for "spiking up" and lacking liquidity when there is a crisis which means that investors are forced to liquidate at the worst point even if there is no actual credit event. For the credit swap counterparty the risk is "gap risk" that there is a rapid default with no chance to unwind the structure.

Example 9.2

USD DIGITAL BASKET CREDIT LINKED NOTE		
ISSUER	:	AA rated Issuer
CURRENCY	:	USD
MATURITY	:	5 year
ISSUE PRICE	:	100%
COUPON	:	8.25%
REFERENCE ENTITY	:	DaimlerChrysler STM Micro Gap France Telecom
REFERENCE OBLIGATION	:	Any senior, unsecured debt obligation of the Reference Entities.
CREDIT EVENT	:	Bankruptcy Failure to Pay Restructuring
REDEMPTION	:	The Notes, unless previously redeemed, will be redeemed at 100% on the Maturity Date.
NOMINAL REDUCTION	:	If a Credit Event occurs with any Reference Entity the Nominal of the Notes will be reduced by 25%.

9.3 Basket Credit Linked Note

Different types of *basket credit linked note* exist and they allow investors to obtain diversification of credit risk in the same investment. Example 9.2 shows a four-name digital basket CLN, where the nominal and coupon steps down by 25% after each credit event. Essentially this product is composed of a series of digital CDS in which the investor receives the average spread of the four CDS (Appx H.2).

9.4 Principal Protected Credit Linked Note

In a *principal protected note* (PPN) the investor is guaranteed to receive the initial investment amount on the scheduled maturity date. Only the coupons are "risky" and subject to significant credit risk. These notes allow investors to gain exposure to emerging market and high yield sectors whilst limiting their overall risk.

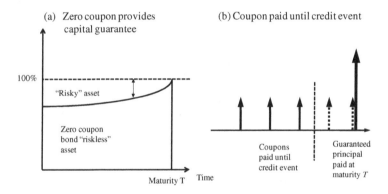

Figure 9.3: Principal protected credit linked note.

Typically on a credit event no further coupon is paid although accrued interest may be paid. Usually, the principal is guaranteed by a very highly rated counterparty (AAA or AA) and is redeemed at the scheduled maturity date. This is equivalent to a purchasing a highly rated zero coupon bond to protect the capital and approximately 100% minus the price of the zero coupon bond invested in "risky" asset. This is shown schematically in Fig. 9.3.

The structure can be priced as an issuer, guaranteeing the principal and paying a funding leg until the maturity date and the swap counterparty paying a risky fixed coupon until a credit event. The issuer swap is thus the present value of the funding leg minus the sum of the fixed coupons each multiplied by the relevant discount factor and survival probability (Appx H.3)

Example 9.3

USD ARGENTINA PRINCIPAL PROTECTED NOTE		
ISSUER	:	AA rated Issuer
CURRENCY	:	USD
MATURITY	:	8 year
ISSUE PRICE	:	100%
COUPON	:	If no Credit Event has occurred 8.0% per annum.
		If a Credit Event has occurred the Notes will pay no further coupon and will pay no accrued interest from the previous coupon payment date.
REFERENCE ENTITY	:	Republic of Argentina
REFERENCE OBLIGATION	:	Any senior, unsecured debt obligation of the Reference Entity.
CREDIT EVENT	:	Failure to Pay Restructuring Repudiation/Moratorium
REDEMPTION	:	The Notes will be redeemed at 100% on the Maturity Date.

Example 9.4

USD EASTERN EUROPEAN BASKET PRINCIPAL PROTECTED NOTE	
ISSUER	: AA rated Issuer
CURRENCY	: USD
MATURITY	: 10 year
ISSUE PRICE	: 100%
COUPON	: If no Credit Event has occurred: 7.60% per annum
	The fixed rate Coupon is reduced by 1/3 (= 7.60%/3) on a Credit Event of any of the Reference Entities. In the event of such a Credit Event all accrued interest is paid to the investor. In the event that all 3 names suffer a Credit Event no further coupon will be paid.
REFERENCE ENTITY	: Croatia Hungary Turkey
REFERENCE OBLIGATION	: Any senior, unsecured debt obligation of each Reference Entity.
CREDIT EVENT	: Failure to Pay Restructuring Repudiation/Moratorium
REDEMPTION	: The Notes will be redeemed at 100% on the Maturity Date.

Since a relatively small amount of credit risk is embedded in the notes to attain a reasonable coupon enhancement the notes must be of reasonably long maturity (> 5 years) and high yielding credits must be used. Also a high interest currency is favoured to reduce the cost of the zero coupon bond.

As an interesting example consider the USD 8 year Argentina principal protected credit linked note shown below paying an 8.0% coupon (Example 9.3). This note was sold prior to the Argentina credit event covered by repudiation/moratorium in 2001 (where incidentally the recovery rate was just below 30%). This demonstrates clearly the benefit of having a capital guarantee.

Usually, the protected notes are structured to provide income in the form of an annual coupon but also popular is to structure the product as a zero coupon note where the accrued coupon is paid at maturity providing a capital gain.

A less common method of increasing the coupon is by forcing the note to extend in maturity on a credit event. For example, a 5 year principal protected note where the coupon disappears or falls to a very low level on a credit event and the capital is redeemed in 15 years.

9.4.1 *Basket principal protected note*

Further diversification and risk reduction can be obtained by including several high yielding credits and a coupon that steps down after each credit event. For Example 9.4 with three eastern European credits in the basket the coupon steps down by one-third on each credit event (Appx H.4). The example was traded with a German private bank that placed it with some of its clients with a view to Euro and hence credit convergence.

9.5 First-to-Default Notes

First-to-default (FTD) products have become very popular with investors seeking increased yields. They are a *default correlation* product and allow investors to gain leverage on a basket of names with limited exposure. In a *first-to-default CDS* the credit risk is taken on the first name to default in a basket of N credits (typically 4–5 credits).

If any credit in the basket defaults the investor (the protection seller) is redeemed early and cash settled at $(100\% - R)$ based on the recovery rate R of the defaulted asset. If physically settled, the investor will be redeemed in a par amount of the defaulted reference asset. No further coupon nor premium is paid and the transaction terminates. The investor is thus not exposed to other possible defaults within the basket (see Fig. 9.4).

Due to the increased probability of suffering a credit loss, an enhanced premium or coupon is paid. However, simply stating that the investor assumes leverage in the conventional sense is a bit misleading since the investor is only exposed to the first default in the basket and not subsequent defaults.

Example 9.5

EUR FIRST-TO-DEFAULT BASKET CREDIT LINKED NOTE		
ISSUER	:	AA rated Issuer
CURRENCY	:	USD
MATURITY	:	3 year
ISSUE PRICE	:	100%
COUPON	:	7.5%
REFERENCE ENTITIES	:	Ford Toys R Us Sears Worldcom
REFERENCE OBLIGATION	:	Any senior, unsecured debt obligation of the Reference Entities.
CREDIT EVENT	:	Bankruptcy Failure to Pay Restructuring
REDEMPTION	:	The Notes, unless previously redeemed, will be redeemed at 100% on the Maturity Date.
EARLY REDEMPTION	:	If a Credit Event occurs with any Reference Entity, the Notes will be redeemed early with Principal Amount of Reference Obligations.

The extra spread paid to the investor depends on the correlation within the basket. If the correlation is very low the first-to-default premium is approximately the sum of the N underlying CDS spreads. If, however, the correlation is high the premium rapidly decreases until all the credits are perfectly correlated and the FTD premium is equal to the highest underlying CDS premium in the basket. Figure 9.5 illustrates this for a typical basket and also shows the *second-to-default* product, where the investor is only exposed to the second default in the basket. This latter product due to its different correlation profile is sometimes sold by trading desks at interesting levels for investors since it can reduce and hedge correlation risk incurred from other correlation trades.

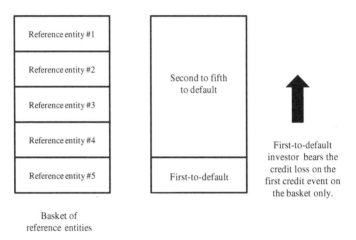

Figure 9.4: First-to-default basket.

Typically, for a diversified basket of 4–10 corporates the asset correlation ranges from 60–75% and this leads to investment grade FTD premiums of around 55–70% of the sum of the spreads in the basket. For highly correlated same sector baskets correlations of 80–90% can be used and premiums paid are much lower.

Pricing FTD baskets is usually carried out using the normal copula model for default correlation described in Section 8.16. Using a correlated multivariate normal distribution correlated default times are obtained using the implied default probabilities obtained from vanilla CDS contracts. Simulating this process many times we can obtain the basket loss distribution as a function of time. From this we can find the *joint survival probability* and *joint first* hazard rate for calculating the expected value and hence fair premium of the FTD CDS contract (Appx H.5).

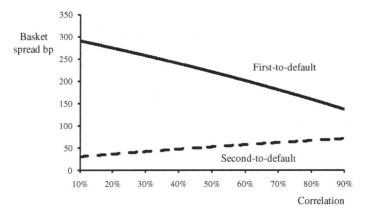

Figure 9.5: First-to-default basket correlation sensitivity.

Example 9.5 shows an investment grade example with physical settlement. The basket was pretty unusual because it really was a bad choice of credits since after it was traded Worldcom went bust and Toys R Us did a restructuring several years later (although after the notes had matured).

A Quality Swiss First-to-Default Basket

As a contrast to Example 9.5, lying around somewhere, I have a tombstone paperweight of a deal we did years ago which has long since matured. Notable because at the time it was innovative, was one of the first first-to-default credit-linked notes ever done and it was traded in size CHF 50mm to a very conservative clientele of a group of top Swiss private banks. The note had an AAA issuer and the names were also top quality UBS, Credit Suisse, Novartis, Roche, Swiss Re. No chance of any of them really going bust unless Switzerland does. Since at the time there existed a decent market bid for CDS in these names with low CHF interest rates it provided a reasonable spread pick up for investors.

Example 9.6

EUR FIRST-TO-DEFAULT BASKET PROTECTED CREDIT LINKED NOTE	
ISSUER	: AA rated Issuer
CURRENCY	: EUR
MATURITY	: 7 year
ISSUE PRICE	: 100%
COUPON	: 7.7% annual coupon subject to no Credit Event with any Reference Entity. No accrued coupon is paid on a Credit Event.
REFERENCE ENTITIES	: Alcatel Compaq Corus Gap Rhodia Bear Stearns Standard Chartered (Subordinated) BSCH (Subordinated)
REFERENCE OBLIGATION	: Any senior, unsecured debt obligation of the Reference Entities.
CREDIT EVENT	: Bankruptcy Failure to Pay Restructuring
REDEMPTION	: If the Notes will be redeemed at 100% on the Maturity Date.

9.5.1 *Principal protected first-to-default notes*

First-to-default notes can also be easily structured in a principal protected format and these have sometimes been sold to European retail investors. Interestingly, I traded Example 9.6 below in very large size with an Italian bank for itself and clients. It matured late in 2008 but had Bear Stearns in the portfolio which was luckily rescued by JP Morgan earlier in 2008 when it got into trouble. This did not constitute a credit event so the investors would have received their last coupon

9.6 Collateralised Debt Obligations

Collateral debt obligations (CDOs) have been a major influence in the development of the credit markets allowing investors to buy *tranches* (tranche = "slice" in French) of diversified portfolios of credit risk (the collateral) with enhanced yields. The rating agencies have been the critical driver in creating the "CDO arbitrage" since the credit rating primarily determines the spread at which the tranche is placed with investors. The arbitrage arises because the rating of CDO tranches is based on historical default probabilities whereas the underlying collateral is purchased at market spreads which may imply a much higher default probability. This arbitrage constituted a very profitable arbitrage for investment banks for many years. The market for CDOs has pretty much collapsed since the credit crisis and only is now slowly recovering. In 2006 supposedly around $550bn of CDOs were issued and in 2009 only around $4–5bn were sold.

There are many types of CDO with various underlying collateral (see Fig. 9.6):

- CLOs (collateralised loan obligations – loan collateral)
- CBOs (collateralised bond obligations – HY bond collateral)
- CSOs or synthetic CDOs (CDOs with CDS collateral)
- CDOs of ABS (CDOs of asset backed securities)
- "CDO–squared" or CDO^2 (CDOs of CDOs)

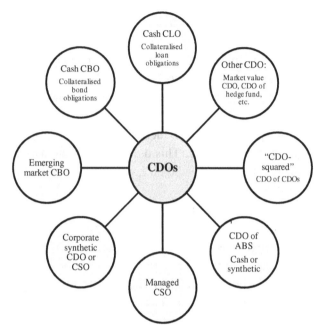

Figure 9.6: Different types of CDO.

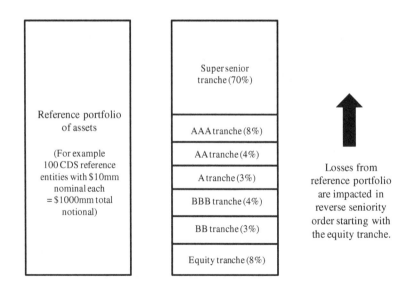

Figure 9.7: Capital structure of a typical synthetic CDO.

CDOs can be static portfolios or managed (usually by third party managers but also sometimes by the investors themselves). Usually, the underlying collateral is not mark-to-market but sometimes *market value CDOs* which have market triggers to provide credit enhancement for senior note-holders are fashionable. The underlying concept remains the same in all these structures. In a similar fashion to a company's capital structure an investor buys a tranche of risk in the CDO capital structure. Different tranches have different seniority, different ratings and spreads. In the simplest form each tranche pays a floating coupon plus spread and credit losses are attributed as they occur upwards from the first loss *equity tranche* and then progressively eating through the mezzanine and then the senior tranches (see Fig. 9.7). Obviously if the underlying collateral pool of assets is diversified, then the probability of the senior tranches suffering a credit loss is very low (hence a high rating), although some losses might occur and these will impact first the equity tranche which is usually unrated. Despite the risky nature of the "equity" the income paid is very high (12%+ per annum) and can be an attractive investment for many investors on the basis of the expected return or yield under different possible default scenarios or *credit loss rates*.

9.6.1 *Cash CDOs*

The first CDOs appeared in the mid 1990s and were based on underlying cash collateral of either mid-market corporate loans (CLOs), high yield bonds (CBOs) or also popular emerging market sovereign and corporate debt. CDOs consisted of two main types – *balance sheet* and *arbitrage*. Balance sheet referred to financial institutions and banks shifting debt off their balance sheet and placing the risk with other investors. The sponsoring bank usually retains some equity or first loss in the trade to ensure an alignment of mutual interest with the investors. These balance sheet deals freed up the balance sheet for fresh lending and released capital. Arbitrage deals, which gradually became the norm, relied on purchasing a cheap portfolio of debt securities relative to the cost of financing through the CDO structure. The *CDO arbitrage premium* is difference between the price of the portfolio minus the cost of the liabilities (the total spread on the tranches of notes) issued to investors minus all fees (administration, rating, management, structuring, etc.) leaving enough excess interest to pay a high yield to the equity investors (see Fig. 9.8).

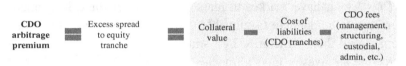

Figure 9.8: The CDO arbitrage premium.

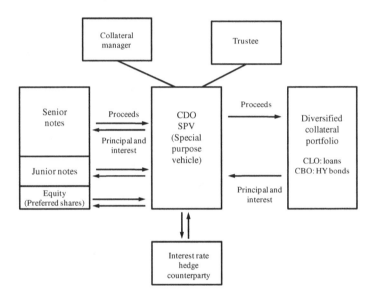

Figure 9.9: A typical cash CDO (CLO or CBO).

The majority of these deals were managed by the sponsor but a new breed of specialised CLO *collateral managers* appeared (Babson, Ares, Stanfield...) who would select and buy the collateral during a "ramp up" phase and then trade and maintain the portfolio to optimise the performance and reduce credit losses. The managers are usually paid a senior management fee and a subordinated fee as an incentive and typically purchase some equity in the transaction. Initially most of this business was based in the US but in recent years specialist European managers have been established (Alcentra, Avoca, Harbormaster...). Less popular are static portfolios where an initial portfolio is purchased and then the structure amortises as the underlying collateral matures. Static portfolios are cheaper due to reduced management fees and it is argued by some that since all CLOs of a particular vintage contain pretty similar pools of loans having a manager makes little difference.

Figure 9.9 shows a typical cash CDO transaction. The CDO special purpose vehicle (SPV) issues notes (senior, mezzanine and equity or junior notes) and purchases a diversified collateral portfolio of loans and/or bonds under the direction of the collateral manager. Various interest rate hedges may be entered into to modify and smooth the cashflows on the notes from the raw interest payments on the collateral

Rating agencies initially rate the different tranches using various statistical models which use stressed historical default probabilities for each of the underlying loans or bonds based on rating. The diversity of and correlation of the collateral pool is taken into account and seniority and maturity of the underlying debt. The rating agencies then periodically review the ratings on a regular basis and can *downgrade* the tranches of notes if there is portfolio credit deterioration. The investors in the CLO have complete transparency and receive on a regular basis *trustee* reports detailing the underlying collateral and its performance.

The main structural factor in determining rating is subordination but to enhance the rating of the CDO tranches various structural features are usually included. A *cash-flow waterfall* is typical for both interest and principal payments based on a series of *overcollateralisation* (O/C) and coverage tests. Figure 9.10 shows a typical interest waterfall for a cash CDO and a similar process exists for the principal payment waterfall. If tests are breached due to credit losses or credit deterioration then cashflow is diverted from the junior tranches to redeem early the senior notes. Typically there will be senior and junior O/C tests and also interest coverage tests with trigger levels set in the deal documentation and they will be of the form of the following ratios:

Senior Tranche = (Par Value of Performing Assets +
Par Coverage Test   Adjusted Par Value of Defaulted Assets)/
                  (Par Amount of the Senior Notes)

Senior Tranche   = (Interest Collected on Assets)/
Interest Coverage Test   (Interest due on Senior Notes)

Also there are common collateral quality tests such as *minimum diversity* and *weighted average rating factor* (WARF) which restrict portfolio trading if breached.

Example 9.7 summarises the terms of a $500mm cash CLO transaction from a well known US collateral manager. It comprises senior notes (classes A-1, A-2), mezzanine notes (classes B, C, D) and unrated equity in the form of *subordinated notes*. The legal final maturity of the structure is 14 years but the structure may be called (for example if the collateral has risen significantly in value) at the request of 2/3 of subordinated note holders. The collateral is expected to be 95% senior secured loans and has significant rating, seniority, spread and diversification constraints placed upon it in order to obtain the CLO note ratings. The subordinated notes are expected to provide a 1200bp spread on the basis of a 2% annual credit loss rate to the collateral pool.

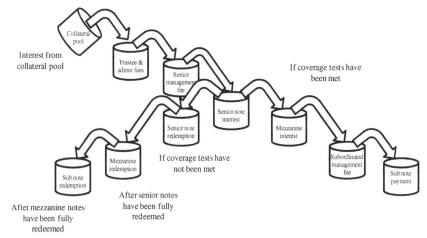

Figure 9.10: Example interest waterfall for a typical cash CDO.

9.6.2 *Synthetic CDOs*

The first synthetic CDOs or CSOs were traded around 1998 and have since become the most popular type of CDOs despite being severely tested in 2002 with numerous *fallen angels* (investment grade names falling to high yield) in portfolios. Using CDS technology rather than cash instruments it is possible to create a large underlying portfolio of 50–200 reference entities from the CDS market. Mainly the names in a typical portfolio are investment grade corporate names, for example 100 diversified credits at $10mm nominal each giving a $1000bn portfolio.

Although some balance sheet deals have been done the vast majority of deals are pure *credit arbitrage trades* as the structuring banks source the high spread names with the highest ratings with a suitable large diversity across industrial sectors. By optimising this allows the highest possible ratings for the highest collateral spread. Once I even built a program incorporating our internal CDO model, the rating agencies models and market spread feeds to automatically optimise the portfolio rating/names/spreads/profit and other market participants developed

Example 9.7

USD COLLATERALISED LOAN OBLIGATION (CLO)	
PORTFOLIO MANAGER	: Independent US based Investment Manager with $22bn of assets under management.
NOTIONAL	: USD 500mm
MATURITY	: Legal/Final Maturity: 14 years Re-Investment Period: 6 years Non-Call Period: 4 years
PORTFOLIO	: *Target Composition* Senior Secured Loans: 95% Non-Senior Sec Assets: 5% *Portfolio Constraints* Min Senior Secured Loans: 90% Max Second Lien Loans: 5% Max High Yield Bonds: 5% Single Issuer Concentration 1.5% Min Moody's Diversity Score: 65 Min Moody's Recovery Rate: 44% Max Moody's Rating Factor: 2350 B1/B2 Min Avg Collateral Coupon: 7.2% Min Avg Collateral Spread: 2.5% Max Non-US Obligors: 25% Max Industry Concentration: 8% Max Floating Rate: 95% Max Structured Finance: 2.5% Max Caa1/CCC+ or below: 7.5% ....

TRANSACTION STRUCTURE	:	Tranche	Amount	%	Rating	WAL	Spread
		A-1	380mm	76.0	AAA/Aaa	7.8yrs	40bp
		A-2	15	3.00	AA/Aa2	9.9	70
		B	26.25	5.25	A/A2	10.0	12-
		C	26.5	5.30	BBB/Baa2	10.0	220
		D	13.5	2.70	BB/Ba2	10.0	400
		Sub Note	38.75	7.75	NR		1200*

WAL= Weighted Average Life (years)
*Based on 2% annual default rate scenario.

RAMP-UP : At least 60% of assets expected to be purchased or committed to purchase by the closing date. The fund will have 6 months after closing to acquire the remainder of its portfolio.

MANAGEMENT FEES : Senior Management Fee: 0.15%. Subordinate Management Fee: 0.35%. Incentive Management Fee: 0.125% payable once Subordinated Notes achieve IRR of 11%. Closing Fees and Expenses: 2.2%.

COLLATERAL TESTS	:	Class	Par Coverage Test	Interest Coverage Test
		A	109.1%	125%
		B	103.5%	120%
		C	103.1%	115%
		D	101.9%	110%

OPTIONAL REDEMPTION : After the Non-Call Period, Notes may be redeemed in whole at the direction of 2/3 of Subordinated Noteholders.

DISCRETIONARY TRADING : Subject to certain conditions upto 20% of the portfolio may be traded per year during the Reinvestment Period at Investment Managers discretion.

ISSUED NOTES : Floating Rate Notes issued from a SPV Issuer based in Cayman Islands and a co-issuing Delaware corporation. Notes listed on Irish Stock Exchange.

similar arbitrage tricks. The use of investment grade corporates as underlyings, due to their low default probabilities, provides highly leveraged structures with equity tranches down to (1–2%) and only (5–7%) beneath the AAA tranche. Investors primarily bought the CDO paper on the basis of rating and compared with similarly rated structured paper the spreads offered were very generous. Despite these generous investor spreads and the high rating costs, the clean structure and the high collateral spreads achievable using CDS made significant profits for the investment banks. It was relatively easy to capture excess arbitrage spread of 10–25bp per annum depending on the portfolio – so around $5–10mm profit on a typical $1bn notional 5 year maturity trade.

Example 9.8

INVESTMENT GRADE CORPORATE SYNTHETIC CDO

NOTIONAL	:	USD 1000mm

MATURITY	:	5 year

PORTFOLIO	:

Static Portfolio	
Number of Obligors:	100
Exposure per Obligor:	$10mm
Moody's Diversity Score:	60
Weighted Average Rating:	A3
Type of Obligations:	Bonds or Loans
Seniority of Obligations:	Senior and Unsecured

TRANSACTION STRUCTURE :

Tranche	Amount	%	Rating	Spread
A	916mm	91.6	NR	10 bp
B	30	3.0	Aaa	60
C	23	2.3	Aa3	110
D	12	1.4	Baa2	320
E	22	2.2	NR	1600

CREDIT EVENTS	:	Bankruptcy, Failure to Pay, Restructuring

ISSUED NOTES	:	Floating Rate Notes for B,C,D,E Tranches issued from a SPV Issuer based in Cayman Islands with AAA ABS underlying collateral with AA rated swap counterparty.

Most synthetic CDOs are static pools with the investors (particularly the equity investors) having a hand in picking (or more usually rejecting) the names in the portfolio. Managed synthetic CDOs have also appeared from time to time with ability for the manager to even short credits within the structure.

The physical tranches of the synthetic CDO can be packaged in different forms. In a cash-flow CDO notes are usually issued by an SPV but since the structuring bank faces the market on the CDS hedges it is just as easy to transfer tranched risk in a synthetic CDO using either a MTN (medium term note) program of any financial issuer, a structured CDS or even a specialised insurance contract.

An innovation in the synthetic CDO market was the so called *super-senior* tranches. Rather than all the most senior part of the capital structure being AAA rated it was possible to tranche the AAA in two parts: a regular AAA tranche and a super-senior tranche with a theoretical rating of much higher than AAA (even though rating agencies don't rate higher than AAA). This type of risk, which paid typically 5–15bp per annum depending on the portfolio and tranching appealed to certain types of counterparty such as insurers and monoline insurers who viewed the risk as negligible on an actuarial basis. In Example 9.8 the A tranche was placed with an AAA rated insurer. These super-senior tranches caused problems for AIG and others when predominately actuarial accounting was unwisely replaced with mark-to-market accounting and the credit crisis provoked a collapse of this market.

Initially, with synthetic CDOs the entire capital structure had to be placed with investors, which could prove difficult. If enough profit could be made on the trade unsold pieces of the CDO could be retained by the structuring bank. However, around 2001 single tranche "delta hedging" technology was developed by several banks. This allowed the banks to increase their arbitrage profits by creating only the "worst value" or most heavily mispriced parts of the capital structure (usually the mezzanine notes) for sale and dynamically delta hedging them using liquid single name CDS. In delta hedging no complete underlying portfolio is purchased and only the delta amount of the tranches actually sold. The best value parts of the capital structure (on a theoretical basis) are generally the equity and senior notes. The single tranche technology could also provide bespoke tranches for different investors.

For several years the synthetic CDO proved extremely profitable for all the investment banks but then the introduction of tranched index products (such as the market iTraxx tranches) led to increased market transparency for investors and markedly reduced the arbitrage.

> **Being an Equity Investor – The Unpredictable Nature of Defaults**
> We structured a bespoke equity tranche for possibly the most sophisticated French non-bank financial institution. They spent ages performing relative value and fundamental credit analysis on all 40–50 names in the portfolio. Finally after many frustrating iterations they decided on their ideal portfolio and the trade executed. Unfortunately within 18 months the trade went sour and had to be restructured ... Enron, Worldcom and British Energy were all in the portfolio and suffered credit events with very low recoveries. This demonstrates how difficult it can be even as an expert to select a CDO portfolio and the very random nature of defaults.

9.6.3 CDOs of ABS and "CDO-squared"

Asset backed securities (ABS) are securitisations of portfolios of "raw" underlying assets and cash-flows that allows the risk of the portfolios to be tranched into notes, rated and sold to investors. Although the most common securitisations consist of credit cards, real estate (commercial and residential), car financing, film finance, etc. some are a bit unusual such as David Bowie virtually securitising all his music (Bowie bonds for $55mm secured on the rights of 25 albums). Unlike with CDOs the underlying assets of ABS are usually in their most basic, raw form – small loans, cash-flows, rents from buildings, royalties from music sales etc. The ratings agencies do their research and credit risk analysis, build a cash-flow scenario model and manage to provide ratings to these structures. Instead of banks clogging up their balance sheets with all these loans, the idea is to sell them into the capital markets at a decent overall funding level using tranched ABS securitisation.

Although we only describe ABS briefly here the amazing size of the ABS market should not be underestimated since global asset securitisation stood at over $8000bn in 2007. Issuance of ABS peaked in Europe before the credit crisis at over (600bn per annum but has at time of writing pretty much dried up (to less than 10% in 2009/10). During the credit crisis many specialist ABS buyers from *structured investment vehicles* (SIVs), off balance sheet bank vehicles (called *conduits*) and credit funds exploded as short term funding dried up (as with Northern

Rock in the UK). Now poor cash strapped governments are filling the financing gap to provide the economy with credit.

In a CDO of ABS the underlying diversified ABS collateral is purchased and re-tranched to form a new CDO. The assets are either placed in an SPV (if mezzanine ABS tranches) as a cash CDO or held on the sponsoring banks balance sheet (a principal finance activity) and tranches of risk rated and sold to different investor groups

---

The CDO Delta Hedge Arbitrage

We obtained risk approval for our CDO delta hedging model before virtually anybody else in the market. Even the great Goldman and Morgan didn't have the delta hedging model and the single tranche technology. We knew a "window" of just 6–12 months existed before it became market standard and "old hat". By risk managing and dynamically delta hedging the individual names in CDOs using vanilla CDS at a trading book level individual tranches of CDOs could be synthetically created for individual investors on demand. There was no requirement to place the senior and equity tranches, which was a tedious and uncertain key to previous synthetic CDO deals and reduced profitability on trades. We had several orders for mezzanine tranches from clients and could provide enhanced spreads for rating compared with existing deals (20–30% or higher). Certain credits could be even omitted from each tranche if investors wished. Spreads had widened and it was possible on the first $1000mm portfolio to achieve at a very conservative correlation level an amazing 2% margin (around $20mm) for just $80mm of notes placed with investors. Due to the uncertainties that remained in re-hedging the deal a large reserve was taken for future hedging risks. Within a year the technique was widespread amongst several investment banks and the arbitrage gradually closed. To maintain margins a new product had to be developed – the synthetic CDO^2.

Two main sorts of CDOs of ABS have proven popular. The first with highly rated AAA/AA collateral and the second with higher yielding A/BBB/BB rated mezzanine tranches. Example 9.9 shows a synthetic CDO of highly rated AAA rated collateral (mainly CLO paper). Notice that there are relatively few obligors (minimum of 20 credits) but relatively high recovery rates (>80%) are assumed by the rating agencies. Special credit events definitions more suitable for ABS securities are used and valuation of defaulted securities takes place 2 years after a credit event to maximise recovery rates.

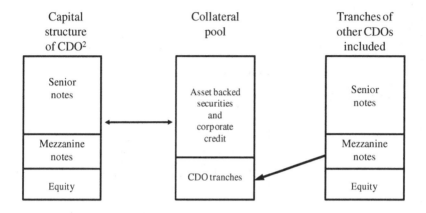

Figure 9.11: Typical "CDO-Squared" or CDO^2.

The single tranche delta hedging technology was then applied to the CDO of ABS market to produce something truly horrible called the "CDO-Squared" or CDO^2 which sold incredibly well to a wide range of investors (see Fig. 9.11). The marketing idea that appealed to investors was that buying a CDO composed of other CDOs and ABS would obviously reduce idiosyncratic risk and be a risk reduction exercise and therefore a great investment. But behind the scenes the CDO single tranche technology was applied by the investment banks. Using this delta hedging technology they could create special single tranches of synthetic CDOs which they would then mix with a bit of ABS and place into new single CDO tranches of the CDO^2. It sounds complicated but from a derivatives modelling and trading point of view quite easy; just another obvious step in the evolution of credit derivatives trading technology. The overall effect was to magnify the arbitrage and increase profits enormously for the investment banks. In many cases it was not even necessary to purchase all the underlying ABS collateral and the reference entities could just be put on the term-sheet to increase diversity and create a "free" short position for the hedger. The idea turned sour when all sorts of subprime ABS were stupidly thrown into the cocktail.

Example 9.9

EURO SYNTHETIC CDO OF AAA RATED ABS

NOTIONAL	:	EUR 1000mm
MATURITY	:	5 year

PORTFOLIO :

Static Portfolio	
Number of Obligors:	20
Exposure per Obligor:	$35–65mm
Moody's Diversity Score:	>15
Weighted Average Rating:	Aaa
Type of Obligations:	ABS
Moodys Average Recovery:	>80%
Seniority of Obligations:	Aaa senior tranches

TRANSACTION STRUCTURE :

Tranche	Amount	%	Rating	Spread
A	900mm	90	NR	8bp
B	70	7	Aaa	50
C	20	2	Aa2	120
D	10	1	A1	450

CREDIT EVENTS : ABS Failure to Pay Principal
ABS Failure to Pay Interest
Principal Writedown
Valuation dates up to 2 years after Credit Events to maximise valuations

ISSUED NOTES : Floating Rate Notes for B,C,D Tranches issued from a SPV Issuer based in Cayman Islands with AAA ABS underlying collateral with AA rated asset swap counterparty.

9.6.4 *Pricing synthetic CDOs*

A typical synthetic CDO can be modelled using a massive normal copula model for the correlated default times similar to that described for the first-to-default basket in Section 8.16. The market CDS spread curves of the underlying portfolio (50–200 names) are used to build the corresponding implied hazard rate or default probability curves. A full matrix of correlations can be used but usually a single correlation factor is preferred for simplicity. The default times are simulated using a Monte Carlo simulation and a credit loss distribution is calculated for each time step until maturity. The present value of the expected loss per tranche is then calculated to provide the fair value premium of the tranche. Usually constant recovery rates are assumed and the spreads are not taken as stochastic (Appx G.12).

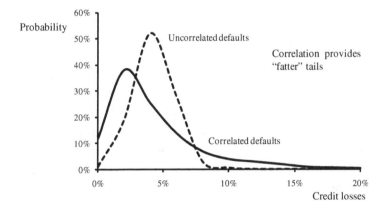

Figure 9.12: Effect of correlation on CDO loss distribution.

From this model it can be seen that the effect of increasing correlation is to widen the loss distribution across the entire capital structure (Fig. 9.12). Correlation provides fatter tails to the loss distribution which decreases the value (or increases the fair value spread or premium) of higher rated tranches. Thus, increasing correlation decreases the value of senior tranches and increases the value of junior tranches. Some mezzanine tranches can be seen to be virtually insensitive to correlation at the crossover between these two regimes (Fig. 9.13).

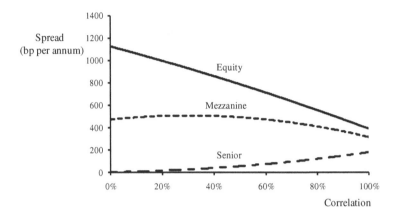

Figure 9.13: CDO tranche correlation sensitivity.

Using the model, it is possible to use the liquid market prices for tranched indices to compute implied correlations. These are visibly never flat across the entire capital structure and a correlation "smile" is evident. This indicates that either supply/demand effects for different rated tranches is important or the simple normal copula model everybody uses has the wrong distribution. This problem is analogous to the volatility smile problem in equity options. Figure 9.14 shows a typical correlation smile and the correlation that must be applied to each tranche (the *compound correlation*) to replicate market values.

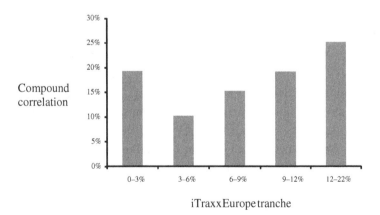

Figure 9.14: Correlation "smile" in CDOs.

9.6.5 *The rationale for investing in CDOs*

For most CDO products one might think that perhaps the only rationale for investing in them is to help the collateral managers earn fees and investment bankers structuring them earn bigger bonuses. However, there are some good reasons to invest in certain CDOs.

Managed CLOs, particularly mid-market cap loans, have generally historically performed well. Mid-market loans are illiquid, hard to source, difficult to analyse and have very high recoveries. Although you pay the managers a fee for their expertise, investing in these, particularly in the equity or the senior tranches at the right part of the credit cycle is probably a good investment.

Synthetic CDOs are not all bad. Avoid mezzanine tranches if you are not being paid a decent coupon and take the equity tranche if you are able to do credit analysis on the names (although this is hard on a lot of names). Sometimes mezzanine tranches can be interesting if they have a participation in the equity included (for example in the form of equity warrants). Avoid distressed or troubled industrial sectors and if a name has a high spread for its rating or its equity is tumbling ask yourself why – is it fundamental or purely technical? Enron and Parmalat were notorious among traders for their high spread/rating ratio years before they went bust but investors did not seem to care and they were included in many baskets and CDOs.

SIV-Lite and Chips

I met a friend in Sweetings for lunch one day (it does the best but possibly most overpriced fish and chips in the City) and he explained that they were now doing CDOs of ABS with pure US subprime collateral. I did not really believe him at first since only a year or so before I had been involved in structuring and getting CDOs of ABS rated with him and the rating agencies (despite being paid couple of hundred thousand or more a deal) insisted that all underlying collateral must be diversified ABS (for example credit cards, mortgages, CLOs, dealer floor plans, etc.) and importantly not just mortgages. CLO as collateral was seen as different because the loans in the CLOs themselves were assumed to be diversified (another crazy notion but anyway). But pure subprime mortgages as collateral surely that was impossible or idiocy. Which investment bank had persuaded the rating agencies to do that? Surely, subprime was almost 100% correlated? Ah... but apparently not since the clever rating agencies assumed that property could never simultaneously go down in value across all the states in the US at the same time. Geographical US diversity was good enough and they had historical data to back up their insane assumption. Anyway, after lunch some of my "favourite" investment bankers came to see me and try to persuade me to manage and invest in a new special structured investment vehicle called a SIV-Lite. "Lite" since it was light on admin (and a liquidity facility in case of a credit crisis it later turned out!). It looked a good concept with plenty of fees for them and us but when I enquired what the collateral was required to pay all those huge fees the answer was "100% US subprime". We passed on the trade since something bad was going to happen pretty soon.

Chapter 10

Fund Options and Hybrids

10.1 Introduction

Most structured products fall within the scope of equities, rates or credit but other products can be linked to other types of underlying asset such as funds, commodities, FX and even volatility. By combining different types of assets *hybrid products* with different risk profiles can be constructed, for example notes with payoffs linked to equities and FX rates. In this chapter we shall provide an overview of fund options and the now common CPPI strategy and a brief introduction to popular hybrids. Other structured products linked to other underlying assets such as commodities (crude oil linked notes for example) are less common but can be treated using Black–Scholes model with the relevant underlying asset or futures contract as the underlying.

10.2 Fund Linked Notes

Fund linked investment products, where the underlying is a managed fund rather than an equity index, have become very common over the last 10 years. Usually the underlying fund will be a large fund which is actively managed by a major third party investment manager (Fidelity, Gartmore, SGAM, etc.). The products are particularly attractive to investors since they are able to invest in a well known fund with a successful track record and have the benefit of capital guarantee and other product features that can be structured using derivatives. The fund linked investment provides increased diversification over a basket or index. Also these products are attractive for the fund managers since it allows them an alternative route to increasing assets under management.

To produce capital guaranteed and other structures requires creation of options contracts on the value of the fund (or the price per unit). Luckily, by essentially treating the fund as an equity index, the Black–Scholes technology can be used for pricing and hedging. Most funds typically can be viewed as highly diversified equity baskets in which the constituents change. Since there are no implied volatility available for a fund a conservative historical volatility must be used in pricing. Typically fund volatilities are very low (even lower than indices) due to the diversification effect, active management but also strangely the way in which the NAV (net asset value) is periodically calculated. Example 10.1 shows a 3 year capital guaranteed note on a diversified basket of 6 funds from different managers.

For a fund to be suitable for writing an option *due-diligence* of the fund and fund manager must be carried out and several criteria must ideally be met. The fund must be large, liquid with several years of "smooth" track record with no undue discontinuities in the price. There must be clear investment guidelines and the same trading strategies must be persistently followed with no strategy "drift". An agreement with the fund manager must be established so the units of the underlying fund can be traded at insignificant cost on the most frequent basis (ideally intraday or daily) as possible to enable delta and gamma hedging. Portfolio transparency is also desirable since it reduces hedging risk to have the composition of the portfolio to allow identification of any large or undiversified positions. Also, the methodology and periodicity of calculating the fund's NAV (daily, weekly or monthly) is an important consideration.

By trading fund units it is possible to delta hedge and gamma hedge simple (and sometimes more complex) options on the fund. However, perfect volatility hedging is impossible and the option must be priced using a conservative volatility and the hedger (generally selling volatility) will make money if the actual volatility falls below this value. Generally long only equity funds are the easiest since by correlation analysis with underlying market equity indices (S&P, FTSE, etc.) it is possible to estimate index deltas for re-hedging when it is not possible to trade fund units intraday. Also the vega of index options can be used to hedge the option volatility to a certain extent.

Fund options can be created on hedge funds and absolute return funds but generally CPPI strategies (see below) are preferred to create high participation capital guaranteed structures.

Example 10.1

USD PROTECTED WORLD EQUITY FUNDS BASKET		
ISSUER	:	AA rated Issuer
CURRENCY	:	USD
MATURITY	:	3 year
ISSUE PRICE	:	100%
UNDERLYING BASKET	:	An basket composed of the following equity funds with associated weightings: 35% GT Europe 25% GAM Gamco 10% Fidelity Latam 10% Fidelity Hong Kong & China 10% Baring Eastern Europe 5% Fidelity Nordic
COUPON	:	Zero coupon
REDEMPTION	:	Each Note will be redeemed at maturity at an amount equal to $R = 100\% + 50\% \; Max(BASKET_{final} - 100\%, 0),$ where $BASKET_{final} = \sum_{i=1}^{N} \omega_i \dfrac{S_i(T)}{S_i(0)}$ with ω_i is the indicated weighting of the ith Fund ($i=1,...,6$) in the Basket. $S_i(T)$ is the arithmetic average of the NAV of the ith Fund taken monthly on the 12 months before the Maturity Date. $S_i(0)$ opening NAV of the ith Fund on the Issue Date.

10.3 CPPI Investments

Constant proportion portfolio insurance (CPPI) is a popular alternative to true fund options and allows a high initial participation in the performance of the underlying with a capital guarantee. CPPI structures can be structured on a wide range of tradable underlying assets including commodities, equities, funds, hedge funds and even CDO and ABS tranches. Many tens of billions of dollars of such products have been sold to high net worth investors, particularly with hedge fund of funds as the underlying but investors are generally blinded by the high initial participation of the product compared with conventional options with no comprehension of the pitfalls.

CPPI is not an option or derivative in the normal sense but rather a trading strategy where a variable exposure to a certain underlying risky asset is maintained whilst guaranteeing a minimum value of the portfolio until maturity. CPPI is a bit of a misnomer since participation is not constant but variable.

The trading strategy is based on an algorithm that the hedger follows to allow rebalancing (usually daily) between the "risky" and "riskless" asset (Appx I.1). The minimum value of the portfolio (the "Floor") is given by a riskless zero coupon bond guaranteed by a highly rated counterparty. The amount of risky asset is given by the difference between the current value of the notes (the value of CPPI investment which is initially 100%) and the Floor value times a gearing or leverage level. Thus initially if the zero coupon of Floor is 80% and the gearing is 4× the investor will buy notes at 100% and have an effective 4×(100%–80%) = 80% participation in the underlying. Example 10.2 details this product based on suitable hedge fund of funds (for example Man Directional Index, GAM Diversified, etc.).

At a later stage if the underlying has risen in value so the total value of the CPPI investment is 110% and the zero coupon Floor is now at 85% then the participation is 4 ×(110%–85%) = 100%. Generally, participation is capped at say 100% but it could be allowed to rise above this in certain structures.

The CPPI structure is unfortunately, however massively path dependent. Consider what happens if the underlying falls in value. For example, if the CPPI value falls to 90% when the Floor is 85% then the participation drops to 4×(95%–85%) = 40%. In the limit where the CPPI falls to the Floor the participation is zero. This clearly demonstrates the major problem with CPPI. If the asset temporarily falls in value then the participation declines quickly reducing the ability of the investment to "bounce back" or recover even if the underlying rises to its original value. After a sharp drop in asset values the investor finds himself "stopped out" and locked into a zero coupon for the rest of the term of his investment. There is no magic to CPPI products just general misunderstanding of their possible behaviour.

(a) Underlying rises – no deleveraging   (b) Temporary deleveraging

(c) Deleveraging and underperformance   (d) Underlying falls – Floor locked in

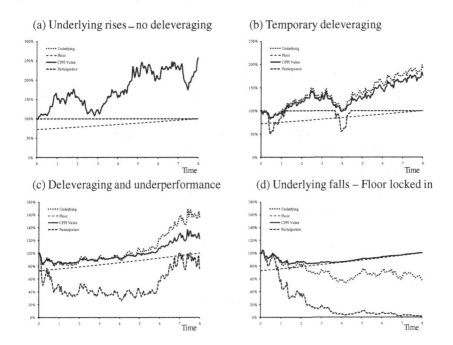

Figure 10.1: Typical CPPI scenarios.

This is clearly illustrated in Fig. 10.1. In scenario (a) the CPPI value rises in value with the underlying and participation is 100%. In scenario (b) the CPPI value dips close to the Floor in year 1 and year 4 causing the participation to be reduced below 100% (it falls to about 50%) and recovers back to 100% as the underlying rises. This causes the CPPI to underperform the underlying at maturity. In (c) the underlying falls and the CPPI falls to a low participation of 20–40% before rallying. This produces a large underperformance of the CPPI strategy compared with the underlying by maturity. In scenario (d) the underlying falls and the CPPI hits the Floor and the investor is locked into a zero coupon bond until maturity.

Many variants of CPPI exist: minimum (and maximum) investment levels can be included, variable leverage levels, minimum coupon, auto-selection of the underlying, diversified portfolios, etc. Generally management fees are structured into the product (say 1% per annum) and these can be "protected" at a minimum asset level for the manager and if necessary high water mark performance fees, similar to hedge funds fee structures, can be accommodated in the products.

The risks for the counterparty which determine the pricing are primarily the execution risk in dynamically re-hedging the underlying portfolio and more precisely the "gap risk" inherent in these products. If the CPPI value falls rapidly below the Floor before the counterparty can rebalance the portfolio then the counterparty takes a loss not the investor (who is always guaranteed the Floor). Obviously, greater gearing and more illiquid underlying risky assets pose a greater gap risk and the worst scenario is where the counterparty cannot rebalance the portfolio in an illiquid market crash. Sometimes counterparties buy gap risk insurance from specialist market insurance counterparties to offset this risk. The real risk management of these products is thus mainly qualitative and requires application of common sense. Although a Monte Carlo simulation of the CPPI product is fairly easy, applying a Black–Scholes continuous process to the underlying does not obviously model the gap risk correctly. A "jump" process must be included, which is difficult to specify exactly and must be based on a historical statistics and scenario analysis.

Example 10.2

EUR HEDGE FUND OF FUNDS PROTECTED CPPI NOTE	
ISSUER	: AA rated Issuer
CURRENCY	: EUR
MATURITY	: 8 year
ISSUE PRICE	: 100%
UNDERLYING	: Diversified Fund of Funds Index
COUPON	: Zero coupon
REDEMPTION	: Each Note will be redeemed at maturity at an amount equal to $$R = 100\% + Max(\frac{CPPI(T)}{CPPI(0)} - 100\%, 0)$$ where: CPPI(T) is the final value of the CPPI valuation based on the CPPI Strategy on the Maturity Date. CPPI(0) is the initial value of the CPPI valuation on the Issue Date.
CPPI Strategy	: On a daily basis an allocation is made to the Underlying and a Reserve Asset in the form of a AA rated zero coupon bond. If the underlying falls in value less is allocated to the Underlying and more Reserve Asset is purchased to provide 100% capital protection at maturity. The initial CPPI value is 100%. At any time the amount invested in the Underlying is the CPPI value minus the value of the Reserve Asset value times a gearing level of 400% subject to a maximum investment in the Underlying of 100% of the CPPI value.

10.4 Hybrid Products

Hybrid asset investment products have been much talked about (and little actually traded) for many years but are now a profitable, slowly growing niche area and becoming part of the mainstream.

Many of the other products we have previously discussed have hybrid aspects but have been simplified to one dominant stochastic factor. For example, in long dated equity options the equity risk is modelled as a random variable but interest rate risk, which is viewed as a secondary uncorrelated risk is held as a constant factor that is dynamically hedged through the life of the option. Similarly for CDS both the interest rate and hazard rate are constants (or curves) and the default process is modelled as the only random factor. In general these approximations work out fine but more problematic examples are convertible bonds which for a complete description must really be modelled at least with stochastic equity and credit spreads which are most definitely correlated.

So by hybrids we mean products whose payout is determined by several different asset classes that are modelled by several stochastic correlated processes. An example could be basket options whose payouts are linked to mixed constituents say equity indices, commodities, FX and even rates.

Example 10.3 shows a capital guaranteed note with a payoff linked to a Russian equity index and the Ruble FX rate. This is a two factor problem and we could use a Black–Scholes closed form for two assets but the monthly averaging lowers the effective volatility of each underlying and will modify the correlation between the two factors. Example 10.4 is a short dated note with 95% capital guarantee and presents a five factor problem with a basket of four BRIC (Brazil, Russia, India and China) currencies and the S&P BRIC equity index. We could simplify the basket to a one factor problem but a more accurate method is to Monte Carlo simulate the five correlated factors. Importantly in both these baskets by including different low correlated assets (FX versus equities) we have decreased the effective basket volatility and hence increased the participation.

Example 10.3

USD PROTECTED NOTE LINKED TO RUSSIAN EQUITY INDEX AND RUBLE/USD EXCHANGE RATE

ISSUER : AA rated Issuer

CURRENCY : USD

MATURITY : 4 year

ISSUE PRICE : 100%

UNDERLYING 1 : The Russian Depositary Index
RDXUSD   Weighting 60%

UNDERLYING 2 : The Russian Ruble and USD cross currency exchange rate
RUBUSD   Weighting 40%

COUPON : Zero coupon

REDEMPTION : Each Note will be redeemed at maturity at an amount equal to

$R = 100\%$

$$+90\% \, Max(60\% \frac{RDXUSD(T)}{RDXUSD(0)} + 40\% \frac{RUBUSD(T)}{RUBUSD(0)} - 100\%, 0)$$

where:
RDXUSD(T) is the arithmetic quarterly average closing price of Underlying 1 until the Maturity Date (16 observations).
RDXUSD(0) opening price of Underlying 1 on the Issue Date.
RUBUSD(T) is the arithmetic quarterly average closing price of Underlying 2 until the Maturity Date (16 observations).
RUBUSD(0) opening price of Underlying 2 on the Issue Date.

In general, to price these hybrid products requires us to combine our various existing frameworks using Black–Scholes models for equity, index, FX and interest rate curve models (such as Hull–White) for rates and credit spreads where applicable (Appx I.2). By including correlations between these random processes obtained from historical data we can perform a Monte Carlo simulation to price most products. However, common sense dictates that our modelling framework is very simple compared with the reality of how markets behave and great care should be taken. The complexity of trading these products requires skilled traders with knowledge of all the underlying asset classes but allows higher margin products to be created.

Enron Correlation

Some very clever structured finance guys (unfortunately later to be the "Natwest 3") worked upstairs from me and were always asking indicative pricing on all sorts of hybrids linked to US energy companies and in particular Enron. Strange options that would hedge residual risks of their complex structured finance transactions, for example put options on EOG (a listed subsidiary of Enron) that would knock-in on an Enron credit event. Needless to say, our opinion on correlation differed and we never really traded. My correlation levels (verging towards 100%) were far too conservative to fit in with the pricing structure on their deals and it was always easier to persuade the bank to absorb the risk naked rather than throw structured finance profits away on expensive, fancy option contracts to hedge the risk of improbable events that would never actually happen....

Example 10.4

USD PROTECTED NOTE LINKED TO BASKET OF BRIC CURRENCIES AND BRIC EQUITY INDEX BASKET		

ISSUER	:	AA rated Issuer
CURRENCY	:	USD
MATURITY	:	3 year
ISSUE PRICE	:	100%
UNDERLYING BASKET	:	An basket with the indicated weightings composed of the following BRIC currencies 10% BRL 10% RUB 10% INR 10% CNY plus 60% S&P BRIC 40 Index
COUPON	:	Zero coupon
REDEMPTION	:	Each Note will be redeemed at maturity at an amount equal to $R = 95\%$ $+ 100\% \ Min(Max(BASKET_{final} - 100\%, 0), 50\%),$ where the basket value is defined as $$BASKET_{final} = \sum_{i=1}^{N} \omega_i \frac{X_i(T)}{X_i(0)}$$ where ω_i is the indicated weighting of the ith underlying $(i=1,...,5)$ in the Basket $X_i(T)$ is the closing price of the ith underlying on the Maturity Date. $X_i(0)$ opening price of the ith underlying on the Issue Date.

Appendix A

Introduction to Swap Finance

A.1 Discount Factors, Zero Rates and Forward Rates

The discount factor for a period from time 0 to time t is given as

$$D(0,t) = \frac{1}{\left(1+z_A(0,t)\right)^t}, \tag{A.1}$$

where $z_A(0,t)$ is the annualised zero rate for maturity t. If $z(0,t)$ is the continuously compounded zero rate we can write the discount factor as

$$D(0,t) = e^{-z(0,t)t}. \tag{A.2}$$

In this book we shall switch freely between the continuously compounded and annualised rates but they are not exactly equivalent and we shall denote both by $z(0,t)$. Now the continuously compounded zero rate is related to the equivalent annual rate by

$$z_A(0,t) = (e^{z(0,t)} - 1).$$

So the difference between the compounded and annualised rate is approximately second order in the rate. The continuously compounded zero rate $z(0,t)$ rate is given from Eq. (A.2) as

$$z(0,t) = -\frac{\ln[D(0,t)]}{t}. \tag{A.3}$$

The simply compounded forward rate at time t between T and $T+h$ is defined as

$$f(t,T,T+h) = \frac{1}{h}\left(\frac{D(t,T)}{D(t,T+h)} - 1\right),$$ (A.4)

and the corresponding continuously compounded relation is

$$f(t,T,T+h) = \frac{\ln[D(t,T)] - \ln[D(t,T+h)]}{h}.$$ (A.5)

In certain interest rate derivative models the notion of the *instantaneous forward* rate is used. This is effectively the limit of the continuously compounded rate as the time interval h tends to 0, making the instantaneous forward rate related to the derivative or slope of the zero curve.

$$f(t,T) = \lim_{h \to 0} f(t,T,T+h) = -\frac{\partial \ln[D(t,T)]}{\partial T}$$ (A.6)
$$= z(t,T) + T\frac{\partial z(t,T)}{\partial T}.$$

This shows that for a positively sloped zero curve the forward curve will always lie above the zero curve.

A.2 Day Count Conventions

The *reference period* usually corresponds to a single coupon period. In practice the interest paid in each coupon period must be adjusted for *day count convention*. To adjust for day count convention the interest earned between two dates is given by

$$Interest\ earned\ = \frac{No.\ of\ days\ between\ dates}{No.\ of\ days\ in\ reference\ period}$$
$$\times\ Interest\ earned\ in\ reference\ period.$$

Each day count convention is expressed as a ratio X/Y where X is the way in which the number of days between dates is calculated and Y is the way in which the number of days in the reference period is calculated. The three most popular conventions used in different markets are Actual/Actual, 30/360 and Actual/360 (or Act/365 for GBP) and are outlined in Table A2.1 below.

Table A2.1: Day count conventions.

Day Count	Methodology	Example Market
Actual/Actual	X is the actual number of days in the interest period and Y is the actual number of days in any given reference period.	US Government bonds.
30/360	X is the number of days in the interest period calculated assuming 30 days per month and Y is calculated assuming 360 days per annum.	Eurobonds and corporate bonds.
Actual/360 Actual/365	X is the actual number of days in the interest period and Y is calculated assuming 360 or 365 days per annum.	Floating rate and money market instruments.

For clarity in this book we will ignore the exact day count convention and use the notion of *accrual periods h*. In performing a real market calculation we must modify accrual periods to account for day count convention as required.

A.3 Other Types of Interest Rate Swap

An interest rate swap is where a series of fixed (or floating rate) payments is exchanged into a series of floating rate (or fixed rate) flows with a market counterparty. Table A2.2 outlines a few common "exotic" swaps. Most follow the methodology described above but some require slight adjustment to the conventional rates used for example *convexity* and *quanto* adjustments for correct valuation.

A.4 Convexity in Futures and Floating Rate Contracts

Due to daily margining and settlement *convexity* effects mean that the forward rate derived from futures contracts is not exactly the true forward rate.

Table A2.2: Different types of swaps.

Common Swaps	Description	Valuation
Step-up swap	Swap notional steps up with a preset schedule	Apply different notional for each coupon period.
Amortising swap	Swap notional steps down with a preset schedule.	Apply different notional for each coupon period.
Basis swap	Transform one cash-flow into another for example 3M floating rate into 6M floating rate.	As fixed/floating swap but different coupon periods and types can be applied to each leg. Basis correction to one leg.
Compounding swap	The interest in either leg of the swap accretes or compounds over the life of the swap and is paid at maturity.	As fixed/floating swap but instead of regular payments on one leg a bullet payment or large coupon is paid at maturity.
CMS swap (Constant maturity swap)	A standard floating rate is exchanged for a swap rate of a specified maturity for example 6M LIBOR versus 10 year swap rate.	The forward swap rate must be calculated at each fixed coupon payment date as the coupon. A convexity adjustment to the forward swap rates must be applied (Appx A.7).
CMT swap (Constant maturity treasury)	A standard floating rate is exchanged for a Treasury rate of a specified maturity for example 6M LIBOR versus 10 year Treasury rate.	The forward Treasury rate must be calculated at each fixed coupon payment date using a yield curve constructed from liquid treasury bonds.
LIBOR-in-arrears swap	For the floating rate leg the rate fixing is made at the end of the interest period and payment at the same time.	As fixed/floating swap but must apply a convexity adjustment to the forward rates used (Appx A.6).
Currency swap	Cash-flows of currency 1 are swapped into currency 2. Fixed/Fixed,Floating/Floating and Fixed/Floating varieties.	For each leg a zero curve constructed for interest rates in each currency and market convention is usually to apply a spread or basis correction to foreign currency discount factors e.g. USD/JPY −15bp. Exchange of principal to reduce counterparty exposure.
Diff or quanto swaps	Cross currency swap where the same currency notional is used for both legs. For example 3M $LIBOR versus 3M EURIBOR on Euro 10mm notional.	A quanto correction must be applied to foreign currency forward rates due to correlation between forward FX rate and forward rate (Appx A.8).

$$f_{fut}(0,T,T+h) \neq f(0,T,T+h).$$

A common correction used is

$$f(0,T,T+h) = f_{fut}(0,T,T+h) - \frac{\sigma^2 T(T+h)}{2}. \qquad (A.7)$$

Here σ is a suitable interest rate volatility factor and typically about 1%.

In general for bonds and other coupon paying instruments the amount by which the expected interest rate exceeds the forward rate is known as convexity. This arises though the non-linearity between bond prices and sensitivity to rates (and yields). For standard swap payments e.g. 3 month LIBOR is fixed and is then paid 3 months later there is fortunately no convexity effect.

A.5 Analytical Convexity Adjustments

A general method for adjusting for this convexity effect is widely known. Consider the forward bond yield y_f for maturity T. The price of the bond B at time T is a function of the yield $y(T)$ which has a volatility σ_y. Using a series expansion we can approximate $B(y)$ as an expansion around the forward yield to second order

$$B(y) \sim B(y_f) + (y - y_f)\frac{\partial B}{\partial y}\bigg|_{y=y_f} + \frac{1}{2}(y-y_f)^2 \frac{\partial^2 B}{\partial y^2}\bigg|_{y=y_f},$$

If we assume stochastic lognormal yields

$$dy = y\sigma dz$$
$$E\left[dy^2\right] \sim y_f\sigma^2 T,$$

the expectation of the bond price is then given as

$$E[B(y)] \sim B(y_f) + (E[y] - y_f)B'(y_f) + \frac{1}{2}y_f^2 \sigma^2 B''(y_f)T.$$

But the expected bond price is by definition the forward bond price

$$E[B(y)] = B(y_f).$$

So we can write the difference between the expected yield and the forward rate as

$$(E[y] - y_f) \sim -\frac{1}{2} y_f^2 \sigma^2 \frac{B''(y_f)}{B'(y_f)} T, \qquad \text{(A.8)}$$

which is the *convexity adjustment*. The above methodology can also be applied to forward swap rates.

A.6 Pricing LIBOR-in-Arrears Swaps

Usually, a swap fixes the floating rate at time t and pays at later time $t+h$. A *LIBOR-in-arrears* swap fixes at time t and pays at the same time t. This requires a convexity adjustment and the forward rate used is

$$f(0,t_i,t_i+h) + f^2(0,t_i,t_i+h) \frac{\sigma_i^2 h t_i}{1 + hf(0,t_i,t_i+h)}, \qquad \text{(A.9)}$$

where are the σ_i is the volatility of the relevant forward swap rate.

A.7 Pricing a CMS Swap

A *constant maturity swap* (CMS) has a swap rate instead of the floating or fixed rate on one payment leg. The swap rates are observed at time t_i and paid at t_i+h. A convexity correction must be applied to the forward swap rates used. If $R_i = R(0,t_i,t_i+T)$ is the CMS forward swap rate for a T maturity swap at time t_i then the swap rate used is

$$R_i - \frac{1}{2} R_i^2 \sigma_{R_i}^2 \frac{B''(R_i)}{B'(R_i)} t_i - \frac{R_i h_i f_i \rho_i \sigma_{f_i} \sigma_{R_i} t_i}{1 + f_i h_i}, \qquad \text{(A.10)}$$

where are the σ_R and σ_f are volatilities of the forward swap rate and forward rate and ρ is the correlation between them.

A.8 Pricing a Diff or Quanto Swap

A *quanto* swap is a cross currency swap where the same currency notional is used for both legs but the floating rates reference floating rates in different currencies. For example, 3M $LIBOR versus 3M EURIBOR with both legs having a Euro 10mm notional. A quanto correction must be applied to foreign currency forward rates due to correlation between the forward FX rate and forward rate. The effective forward rate used in pricing is

$$f(0,t_i,t_i + h)\left(1 + \rho_i \sigma_{f_i} \sigma_{FX} t_i\right), \tag{A.11}$$

where ρ_i is the FX/Forward rate correlation and σ_{FX} the FX rate volatility. Quanto corrections are discussed in more detail in Section 3.9.

Appendix B

Pricing Equity Options

B.1 Modelling Stock Prices

Stock prices are most frequently modelled as geometric Brownian processes. For each small discrete time period Δt the change in stock price ΔS is related to an overall drift μ and a random change Δz

$$\frac{\Delta S(t)}{S(t)} = \mu \Delta t + \sigma \Delta z. \qquad (A.12)$$

Here σ is the volatility per unit time of the stock price $S(t)$ at time t. The random variable Δz is normally distributed with mean 0 and variance Δt. The expected return of ($\Delta S/S$) over time period Δt is equal to

$$E\left[\frac{\Delta S}{S}\right] = \mu \, \Delta t,$$

whilst the variance is

$$Var\left[\frac{\Delta S}{S}\right] = E\left[\left(\frac{\Delta S}{S}\right)^2\right] - \left(E\left[\frac{\Delta S}{S}\right]\right)^2 = \sigma^2 \, \Delta t.$$

Thus, the relative change in $S(t)$ is normally distributed

$$\frac{\Delta S(t)}{S(t)} \sim \phi(\mu \Delta t, \sigma^2 \Delta t). \qquad (A.13)$$

In continuous time the interval Δt approaches zero and the return of the stock price can be written as the differential change

$$\frac{dS(t)}{S(t)} = \mu\, dt + \sigma\, dz. \tag{A.14}$$

The actual drift and volatility of equities can be estimated from historical data. The volatility can be estimated for M daily observations as

$$\sigma^2 = \frac{1}{M-1} \sum_{i=1}^{M} [y_i - \overline{y}]^2,$$

where the daily logarithmic return is given by

$$y_i = \ln\left(\frac{S_i}{S_{i-1}}\right).$$

B.2 Ito's Lemma

Ito's lemma is perhaps the most useful result from the field of *stochastic calculus* that is applied in option pricing. It can be used to evaluate the differential equation governing the evolution of option prices and allows derivation of the famous Black–Scholes option pricing equation. An Ito process for variable x (for example a stochastic equity price) has an equation is given by

$$dx = \alpha(x,t)\, dt + \beta(x,t)\, dz, \tag{A.15}$$

where the random evolution of x depends on a drift α and a variance β both of which are functions of x and time t. Now consider a function $f(x,t)$, for example an option price, dependent on x and t. Ito's lemma shows that $f(x,t)$ follows the stochastic process

$$df = \left(\alpha\, \frac{\partial f}{\partial x} + \frac{\partial f}{\partial t} + \frac{1}{2}\beta^2\, \frac{\partial^2 f}{\partial x^2} \right) dt + \beta\, \frac{\partial f}{\partial x}\, dz. \tag{A.16}$$

We can demonstrate Ito's lemma from a Taylor's series expansion of $f(x,t)$

$$\Delta f = \frac{\partial f}{\partial x}\Delta x + \frac{\partial f}{\partial t}\Delta t + \frac{1}{2}\frac{\partial^2 f}{\partial x^2}\Delta x^2 + \frac{\partial^2 f}{\partial x \partial t}\Delta x \Delta t + \frac{1}{2}\frac{\partial^2 f}{\partial t^2}\Delta t^2 + \ldots$$

Now we can write Eq. (A.15) discretely as

$$\Delta x = \alpha(x,t)\Delta t + \beta(x,t)\sqrt{\Delta t}\, Z, \qquad (A.17)$$

where $Z \sim \phi(0,1)$ is standard normally distributed such that $E[Z]=0$ and $E[Z^2]=1$. So to first order in Δt we can write

$$\Delta x^2 \sim \beta^2(x,t)Z^2\Delta t,$$

which gives in the differential limit of the Taylor's series to first order in dx and dt

$$df = \frac{\partial f}{\partial x}dx + \frac{\partial f}{\partial t}dt + \frac{1}{2}\frac{\partial^2 f}{\partial x^2}\beta^2 dt.$$

Now by substitution we have Ito's lemma

$$df = \left(\alpha\frac{\partial f}{\partial x} + \frac{\partial f}{\partial t} + \frac{1}{2}\beta^2\frac{\partial^2 f}{\partial x^2} \right)dt + \beta\frac{\partial f}{\partial x}dz.$$

Thus, $f(x,t)$ has a drift of

$$\left(\alpha\frac{\partial f}{\partial x} + \frac{\partial f}{\partial t} + \frac{1}{2}\beta^2\frac{\partial^2 f}{\partial x^2} \right),$$

and a variance given by

$$\beta^2\left(\frac{\partial f}{\partial x} \right)^2.$$

B.3 The Black–Scholes Equation

The stock price follows an Ito process

$$dS = S \mu \, dt + S\sigma \, dz,$$

so from Ito's lemma Eq. (A.16) the price $f(S,t)$ of any single stock derivative, such as a call option, is determined by S and t.

$$df = \left(\mu S \, \frac{\partial f}{\partial S} + \frac{\partial f}{\partial t} + \frac{1}{2}\sigma^2 S^2 \frac{\partial^2 f}{\partial S^2} \right) dt + \sigma S \, \frac{\partial f}{\partial S} dz. \qquad \text{(A.18)}$$

Consider a portfolio where we have sold one option and bought $\partial f/\partial S$ shares. The value of the portfolio at any time is given by

$$\Pi = -f + \left(\frac{\partial f}{\partial S} \right) S.$$

The instantaneous change in value of the portfolio in time interval dt is given as

$$d\Pi = -df + \left(\frac{\partial f}{\partial S} \right) dS.$$

Substituting for df from Ito's lemma we have the result

$$d\Pi = \left(-\frac{\partial f}{\partial t} - \frac{1}{2}\sigma^2 S^2 \frac{\partial^2 f}{\partial S^2} \right) dt, \qquad \text{(A.19)}$$

which is independent of dz. The portfolio is thus hedged against price movements and instantaneously riskless over the period dt. Obviously, for a hedged portfolio in an efficient market the investor in the portfolio cannot earn more than the risk free rate r. Thus, we can set the riskless portfolio return to be r. This gives

$$d\Pi = r\,\Pi\,dt$$

$$= \left(\frac{\partial f}{\partial t} + \frac{1}{2}\sigma^2 S^2 \frac{\partial^2 f}{\partial S^2}\right)dt = r\left(f - S\frac{\partial f}{\partial S}\right)dt.$$

Rearranging provides the well known Black–Scholes differential equation

$$\frac{\partial f}{\partial t} + rS\frac{\partial f}{\partial S} + \frac{1}{2}\sigma^2 S^2 \frac{\partial^2 f}{\partial S^2} = r\,f. \tag{A.20}$$

The Black–Scholes *partial differential equation* (PDE) allows evaluation of a wide range of derivatives which are dependent on the underlying variables S and t. Many solutions can be obtained depending on the boundary conditions applied to the two-dimensional PDE. For example, for a European call option of maturity T the boundary condition at time T is simply the payoff

$$f(S(T),T) = Max\,(S(T) - K,0).$$

The PDE can be solved using a variety of techniques including finite difference lattices and "trees" which we shall discuss in detail later. Generally, the boundary condition at the terminal payoff date is known and a solution is obtained as $f(S(0),0)$, the option price today (at $t=0$) at today's spot equity price $S(0)$.

B.4 Some Important Black–Scholes Results

Since the growth rate of the stock can be replaced by the risk free interest rate r, the risk neutral process for the stock price is now given by

$$\frac{dS(t)}{S(t)} = r\,dt + \sigma\,dz.$$

Using Ito's lemma Eq. (A.16) we can consider the process for $f(S,t) = \ln S(t)$.

$$d \ln S = \frac{\partial(\ln S)}{\partial t}dt + \frac{\partial(\ln S)}{\partial S}dS + \frac{1}{2}\frac{\partial^2(\ln S)}{\partial S^2}(dS)^2$$

$$= \frac{dS}{S} - \frac{1}{2}\frac{1}{S^2}\left(\sigma^2 S^2\, dt\right)$$

$$= \left(r - \frac{\sigma^2}{2}\right)dt + \sigma\, dz.$$

This shows that *ln(S(t))* is normally distributed and *S(t)* is lognormally distributed. Integrating we have

$$\ln S(t) = \ln S(0) + \int_0^t d\left(\ln S(t)\right)$$

$$= \ln S(0) + \left(r - \frac{\sigma^2}{2}\right)t + \sigma Z(t),$$

where

$$Z(t) = \int_0^t dz(t) \sim \phi(0,t).$$

This then gives the widely used result for the stock price at any future time

$$S(t) = S(0)\, e^{(r-\frac{\sigma^2}{2})t + \sigma Z(t)}. \tag{A.21}$$

We can show that this gives the correct expected value. To do this requires use of the *moment generating function* result demonstrated in Appx (B.7). The expected value at time *t* of the underlying price is thus given by

$$E[S(t)] = E\left[S(0)\, e^{(r-\frac{\sigma^2}{2})t + \sigma Z(t)}\right] = S(0)\, e^{(r-\frac{\sigma^2}{2})t} E\left[e^{\sigma Z(t)}\right]$$

$$= S(0)\, e^{(r-\frac{\sigma^2}{2})t}\, e^{\frac{\sigma^2 t}{2}} = S(0)e^{rt},$$

which is the initial value of the stock price $S(0)$ compounded at the risk free rate r and thus the forward rate which is what we would intuitively expect for a stock paying no dividend.

B.5 The Black–Scholes Option Pricing Equation

Consider a call option with final payoff $Max(S(T)–K,0)$ at maturity T. The price at time t where $t < T$ can be given by the expectation of the final payout discounted back to time t.

$$P_{Call}(t,T) = E\left[D(t,T)\,Max(S(T) - K,0)\right] \tag{A.22}$$

Here $D(t,T)$ is the discount factor to present value the payoff to time t which is for constant continuously compounded interest rates r is

$$D(t,T) = e^{-r(T-t)}.$$

To simplify things we shall introduce the indicator function

$$\begin{aligned} \chi_{S(T)>K} &= 1 \quad \text{if } S(T) > K \\ &= 0 \quad \text{if } S(T) \leq K. \end{aligned} \tag{A.23}$$

The call price can now be written as

$$\begin{aligned} P_{Call}(t,T) &= e^{-r(T-t)}E\left[(S(T) - K)\,\chi_{S(T)>K}\right] \\ &= e^{-r(T-t)}E\left[S(T)\chi_{S(T)>K}\right] - e^{-r(T-t)}E\left[K\chi_{S(T)>K}\right]. \end{aligned} \tag{A.24}$$

Consider the inequality $S(T) > K$. We can substitute Eq. (A.21)

$$S(T) = S(t)\,e^{(r-\frac{\sigma^2}{2})(T-t)+\sigma Z(T-t)} > K.$$

Now $Z(T-t)$ is normally distributed $\phi(0,(T-t))$ so to simplify we can rescale the variable Z to be standard normal distributed $\phi(0,1)$ by dividing by $(T-t)^{1/2}$ so that

$$\frac{\left\{\ln\left(S(t)/K\right)+\left(r-\sigma^2/2\right)(T-t)\right\}}{\sigma\sqrt{T-t}} > Z \sim \phi(0,1).$$

Initially, consider the second term in Eq. (A.24). The expectation can be evaluated as written as

$$E\left[\chi_{S(T)>K}\right] = E\left[\chi_{\frac{1}{\sigma\sqrt{T-t}}\left\{\ln\left(\frac{S(t)}{K}\right)+\left(r-\frac{\sigma^2}{2}\right)(T-t)\right\} > Z}\right] = N(d_2),$$

where N is the *cumulative normal distribution* and

$$d_2 = \frac{\left\{\ln\left(S(t)/K\right)+\left(r-\sigma^2/2\right)(T-t)\right\}}{\sigma\sqrt{T-t}}.$$

The first term in Eq. (A.24) can be evaluated using *Girsanov's theorem*. Girsanov's theorem (Appx B.7) is a frequently used result from stochastic calculus and allows us to decompose the expectation of an exponential stochastic process multiplied by another function

$$E\left[e^{\lambda X} f(X)\right] = E\left[e^{\lambda X}\right]E\left[f(X + \lambda\sigma^2)\right] \text{ if } X \sim \phi(\mu,\sigma^2).$$

The first term is then given by

$$E\left[S(T)\chi_{S(T)>K}\right] = E\left[S(t)e^{\left(r-\frac{\sigma^2}{2}\right)(T-t)+\sigma Z(T-t)}\chi_{S(t)e^{\left(r-\frac{\sigma^2}{2}\right)(T-t)+\sigma Z(T-t)}>K}\right],$$

which we can simplify as

$$S(t)e^{\left(r-\frac{\sigma^2}{2}\right)(T-t)}E\left[e^{\sigma Z(T-t)}\right]E\left[\chi_{\left\{\ln\left(\frac{S(t)}{K}\right)+\left(r-\frac{\sigma^2}{2}\right)(T-t)+\sigma^2(T-t)\right\}>-Z(T-t)\sigma}\right],$$

giving

$$E\left[S(T)\chi_{S(T)>K} \right] = S(t)\,e^{r(T-t)}N(d_1),$$

where d_1 and d_2 is equal to

$$d_1 = \frac{\left\{ \ln\left(S(t)/K\right) + \left(r+\sigma^2/2\right)(T-t) \right\}}{\sigma\sqrt{T-t}},$$

$$d_2 = d_1 - \sigma\sqrt{T-t}$$

Thus, from Eq. (A.24) the Black–Scholes call option price is given by

$$P_{Call}(t,T) = S(t)N(d_1) - e^{-r(T-t)}K\,N(d_2). \qquad \text{(A.25)}$$

The value of the put option can be derived in a similar way and results in

$$P_{Put}(t,T) = e^{-r(T-t)}K\,N(-d_2) - S(t)\,N(-d_1). \qquad \text{(A.26)}$$

B.6 Black–Scholes with Continuous Dividends

From Eq. (2.13) for the forward price for an equity with dividend q we can see that we can replace $S(t)$ by $S(t)e^{-q(T-t)}$. This provides the Black–Scholes equations for an equity paying a continuous dividend q.

$$P_{call}(t,T) = S(t)e^{-q(T-t)}N(d_1) - e^{-r(T-t)}K\,N(d_2)$$

$$P_{Put}(t,T) = e^{-r(T-t)}K\,N(-d_2) - S(t)e^{-q(T-t)}N(-d_1), \qquad \text{(A.27)}$$

with modified d_1 and d_2

$$d_1 = \frac{\left\{ \ln\left(S(t)/K\right) + \left(r-q+\sigma^2/2\right)(T-t) \right\}}{\sigma\sqrt{T-t}}.$$

$$d_2 = d_1 - \sigma\sqrt{T-t}$$

B.7 Moment Generating Function and Girsanov's Theorem

Evaluating many closed form solutions for derivatives is made much easier with knowledge of the *moment generating function* and *Girsanov's theorem*. These theorems are easily derived. Consider a function $\eta(\lambda)$

$$\eta(\lambda) = E\left[e^{\lambda X}\right].$$

We can write this as

$$\eta(\lambda) = E\left[1 + \lambda X + \frac{\lambda^2 X^2}{2} + ...\right] = 1 + \lambda E[X] + \frac{\lambda^2}{2} E\left[X^2\right] + ...$$

Applying Taylor's series to $\eta(\lambda)$ directly we have
$$\eta(\lambda) = \eta(0) + \lambda\eta'(0) + \lambda^2\eta''(0)/2 + ...$$

Matching terms we can see that

$$\eta(0) = 1$$

$$\eta'(0) = E[X] \quad \text{the first moment}$$

$$\eta''(0) = E\left[X^2\right] \quad \text{the second moment.}$$

If X is a normally distributed variable so $X \sim \phi(\mu, \sigma^2)$ we have the *moment generating function* result

$$E\left[e^{\lambda X}\right] = e^{\lambda\mu + \sigma^2\lambda^2/2}. \tag{A.28}$$

Now we can extend this to arrive at *Girsanov's theorem*. Let there be a function $f(X) = e^{\omega X}$. From above result

$$E\left[e^{\lambda X} f(X)\right] = E\left[e^{\lambda X} e^{\omega X}\right]$$

$$= e^{(\lambda+\omega)\mu+\sigma^2(\lambda+\omega)^2/2} = E\left[e^{\lambda X}\right]E\left[e^{\omega X}\right]e^{\sigma^2\lambda\omega}$$

$$= E\left[e^{\lambda X}\right]E\left[f(X+\lambda\sigma^2)\right].$$

This is Girsanov's theorem

$$E\left[e^{\lambda X} f(X)\right] = E\left[e^{\lambda X}\right]E\left[f(X+\lambda\sigma^2)\right] \quad if \quad X \sim \phi(\mu,\sigma^2). \quad \text{(A.29)}$$

B.8 The "Greeks"

The price of any derivative P can be expanded as a Taylor's series to determine the first order sensitivities to various variables.

$$dP = \frac{\partial P}{\partial S}dS + \frac{\partial P}{\partial t}dt + \frac{\partial P}{\partial \sigma}d\sigma + \frac{\partial P}{\partial r}dr + \frac{1}{2}\frac{\partial^2 P}{\partial S^2}dS^2 + ...$$

These sensitivities have been given several well known names and are collectively known as the *greeks*.

- Delta – the sensitivity to changes in the underlying price

$$\Delta = \frac{\partial P}{\partial S}.$$

- Gamma – the change of delta with respect to changes in the underlying and thus the derivative of delta

$$\gamma = \frac{\partial^2 P}{\partial S^2}.$$

- Theta – the change of value of the option with time and thus a measure of the decay of time value. It is by convention defined as the negative of the partial derivative

$$\vartheta = -\frac{\partial P}{\partial t}.$$

- Vega – the sensitivity to changes in volatility

$$\nu = \frac{\partial P}{\partial \sigma}.$$

- Rho – the sensitivity to interest rates

$$\rho = \frac{\partial P}{\partial r}.$$

B.8.1 *Delta*

For a call option paying a continuous dividend q the delta is given by the simple differential of the Black–Scholes equation

$$\Delta_{call} = \frac{\partial P_{call}}{\partial S} = e^{-qT} N(d_1) > 0, \tag{A.30}$$

and for a put we have

$$\Delta_{put} = e^{-qT} \left(N(d_1) - 1 \right) < 0.$$

B.8.2 *Gamma*

The gamma is the second order differential and is the same for a call and a put option

$$\gamma_{call} = \frac{\partial^2 P_{call}}{\partial S^2} = \gamma_{put} = \frac{\partial^2 P_{put}}{\partial S^2},$$

so

$$\gamma_{call} = \gamma_{put} = \frac{\varphi(d_1)e^{-qT}}{S(0)\sigma\sqrt{T}}, \tag{A.31}$$

where the normal distribution or Gaussian probability density is

$$\varphi(x)=\frac{1}{\sqrt{2\pi}}e^{-x^2/2}.$$

B.8.3 *Vega*

The vega is the sensitivity to changes in the volatility and is the same for a call and a put option

$$v_{call}=\frac{\partial P_{call}}{\partial\sigma}=v_{put}=\frac{\partial P_{put}}{\partial\sigma},$$

which evaluates to

$$v_{call}=S(0)\,e^{-qT}\varphi(d_1)\sqrt{T}. \tag{A.32}$$

B.8.4 *Theta*

The theta is the sensitivity to changes in the time to maturity. As time to maturity decreases, the *time value* of the option decreases. It is convention to express this as the negative of the partial derivative.

$$\vartheta_{call}=-\frac{\partial P_{call}}{\partial T}=-\frac{S(0)\varphi(d_1)e^{-qT}\sigma}{2\sqrt{T}}+qS(0)e^{-qT}N(d_1) \\ -rKe^{-rT}N(d_2). \tag{A.33}$$

For puts we have

$$\vartheta_{put}=-\frac{S(0)\varphi(d_1)e^{-qT}\sigma}{2\sqrt{T}}-qS(0)e^{-qT}N(-d_1) \\ +rKe^{-rT}N(-d_2).$$

B.8.5 *Rho*

Rho is the sensitivity to changes in interest rate

$$\rho_{call} = \frac{\partial P_{call}}{\partial r} = K e^{-rT} N(d_2) T$$

$$\rho_{put} = -K e^{-rT} N(-d_2) T.$$

B.9 Binomial Trees

Consider the movement of a stock of price $S(t)$ at time t that can move with a *binomial process* to either a higher price $S(t)u$ with probability p or to a lower price $S(t)d$ with probability $(1-p)$ at a later time $t+\Delta t$. We can evaluate the branching probability p and the factors u and d by comparing the expected value and variance of this binomial process to that given by the Black–Scholes equation. The expected value is thus given by

$$E[S(t+\Delta t)] = S(t)e^{r\Delta t} = p S(t)u + (1-p)S(t)d,$$

and the variance by

$$E\left[S^2(t+\Delta t)\right] - \left(E[S(t+\Delta t)]\right)^2$$
$$= S^2(t)e^{2r\Delta t}\left(e^{\sigma^2 \Delta t} - 1\right)$$
$$= p S^2(t)u^2 + (1-p)S^2(t)d^2 - S^2(t)\left(pu + (1-p)d\right)^2,$$

so

$$e^{2r\Delta t}e^{\sigma^2 \Delta t} = pu^2 + (1-p)d^2.$$

To solve for p, u and d simultaneously we can impose the condition u $=1/d$. This condition allows the building of a recombining binomial tree since an up movement followed by a down movement is equivalent to a down then an up movement $Sud = Sdu$ etc. Solving the above simultaneous equations and ignoring terms higher than Δt we have

$$p = \frac{a-d}{u-d}, \qquad u = e^{\sigma\sqrt{\Delta t}}, \qquad d = e^{-\sigma\sqrt{\Delta t}}, \qquad a = e^{r\Delta t}. \tag{A.34}$$

Using this result we can build a binomial lattice or tree of stock prices $S(i,j)$ with time slices $i\Delta t$ $(i=0,...,N)$ and vertical nodes j $(j=0,1,...,i)$. Starting from node $S(0,0)$ at time $t=0$ the value of the other lattice nodes can be calculated using

$$S(i, j) = S(0,0)u^j d^{i-j}. \tag{A.35}$$

The probability of moving from $S(i,j)$ to $S(i+1,j+1)$ is given by probability p and from $S(i,j)$ to $S(i+1,j)$ by probability $(1-p)$.

Having built the lattice we now have a distribution of stock prices which maps on to the Black–Scholes PDE. This binomial tree can be used to value a range of different option contracts. Consider the valuation of a simple call option. Usually the terminal node is set equal to the option maturity T so that $T = N\Delta t$. At maturity $(i = N)$ the exercise value of the option is known and is given by

$$V(N, j) = Max(S(N, j) - K, 0) \quad i = N, \quad j = 0,1,2,...,N$$

The common technique is to "roll-back" the option value from the terminal slice and calculate this roll-back value $V_{RB}(i,j)$ at each node

$$V_{RB}(i, j) = [V(i+1, j+1) p + V(i+1, j)(1-p)]e^{-r\Delta t}. \tag{A.36}$$

For a European option this roll-back value gives the value of the call option at that particular node.

$$V(i, j) = V_{RB}(i, j).$$

For an American option early exercise can occur. At each node the roll-back value is compared with the intrinsic value to see whether it is more profitable for an investor to exercise at the node or continue to hold the option. Thus, the option value at the node is given for an American option by

$$V(i, j) = Max[V_{RB}(i, j), V_{IV}(i, j)],$$

where

$$V_{IV}(i,j) = Max(S(i,j) - K,0).$$

Continuing to roll-back through the tree the option value at time today ($t=0$) is given by $V(0,0)$, the value at the first node where the stock price is $S(0,0)$. Thus the valuation process is one where the stock tree is first built forwards in time from $S(0,0)$ and then rolled backwards in time to calculate the option value and to take into account any early exercise.

From the binomial tree we can directly approximate some of the greek hedging parameters. For example, the delta can be approximated by

$$\Delta = \frac{\delta V}{\delta S} \sim \frac{V(1,1) - V(1,0)}{S(1,1) - S(1,0)}.$$

To include equity dividends on the tree we must rebuild the tree slightly. Different approaches are available depending on whether we wish to use known continuous dividends, proportional dividends or absolute dividends. The simplest is for continuous dividends where the drift parameter a must be modified to include a continuous dividend q

$$a = e^{(r-q)\Delta t}.$$

The method for tree building above assumes that interest rates are flat and constant over time. Although this is a good approximation when equity volatilities are high and are the dominant feature in pricing it is sometimes important to include some form of term structure for interest rates. The simplest way to include non-constant rates is to substitute the constant interest rate r at the ith time slice with the forward rate.

$$r = r(i,j) \sim f(0, i\Delta t, (i+1)\Delta t).$$

American and Bermudan barrier options can be priced on binomial trees. However, the discrete nature of the tree means that barriers will be mispriced if they lie between nodes of the tree. It is possible to use interpolation techniques across nodes adjacent to the barrier or adjust the number of time steps to make the barrier fall close or on the nodes.

B.10 Pricing Convertible Bonds on a Binomial Tree

Convertible bonds are issued by a company and the bondholder has the option to exchange the bonds for the company's equity at certain times in the future. Usually *convertibles* are callable by the issuer and sometimes include complex features such as being callable after a specified number of years (a non-call period) or callable if the equity is above a certain strike. A conversion ratio CR is pre-specified, which is the number of shares of stock exchangeable for one bond on conversion. The conversion ratio is not always fixed and can vary with time $CR(t)$. The conventional convertible model uses a binomial tree and has only one stochastic factor – the equity price. As an approximation this works quite well since the equity volatility dominates the rate and credit volatility as a factor in pricing.

We have the bond price $B(i,j)$ for a T maturity bond at the maturity node $i = N$ on the tree paying a final coupon c as

$$B(N, j) = Max(100\% + c, S(N, j)CR(N)). \qquad (A.37)$$

We discount back through the tree looking to see if (i) conversion is optimal $B(i, j) < S(i, j)CR(i)$ or (ii) the issuer will call if

$$B(i, j) > K_{call}(i, j),$$

where K_{call} is the call price. Thus, at a node

$$B(i, j) = Max(Min(B_{RB}(i, j), K_{call}(i, j)), S(i, j)CR(i)),$$

with the rolled back bond price given as

$$B_{RB}(i, j) = [B(i+1, j+1) p + B(i+1, j)(1-p)]e^{-(r(i\Delta t)+s(i\Delta t))\Delta t} + c_{RB},$$

where c_{RB} is the rolled back coupon if one was paid in the interval present valued to the nearest node and $s(i\Delta t)$ the effective credit spread of the convertible.

Another common technique to include the credit risk is to include a default process at each node. Assuming a Poisson default process with hazard rate λ that is introduced in Chapter 8 the branching probabilities become

$$p_u = \frac{a - de^{-\lambda \Delta t}}{u - d}, \qquad p_d = \frac{ue^{-\lambda \Delta t} - a}{u - d},$$

$$u = e^{\sqrt{(\sigma^2 - \lambda)\Delta t}}, \qquad d = 1/u, \quad a = e^{(r-q)\Delta t}. \tag{A.38}$$

B.11 Three-Dimensional Binomial Trees

A *three-dimensional* tree or *3D tree* allows modelling of options with two stochastic variables, with correlation ρ, such as spread options and exchange options. In a 3D binomial tree each node at time t branches into four nodes at time $t+\Delta t$. The two main routes are either (i) keeping the tree rectangular and modifying branching probabilities or (ii) having similar branching probabilities and deforming the tree. Here we will consider the latter approach. Each node holds two equity values (S_1, S_2) let there be a 0.25 probability of moving to the following four nodes

$$(S_1 u_1, S_2 A) \quad (S_1 u_1, S_2 B) \quad (S_1 v_1, S_2 C) \quad (S_1 v_1, S_2 D),$$

where

$$u_1 = \exp[(r - q_1 - \sigma_1^2 / 2)\Delta t + \sigma_1 \sqrt{\Delta t}]$$
$$v_1 = \exp[(r - q_1 - \sigma_1^2 / 2)\Delta t - \sigma_1 \sqrt{\Delta t}]$$,

with

$$A = \exp[(r - q_2 - \sigma_2^2 / 2)\Delta t + \sigma_2 \sqrt{\Delta t}(\rho + \sqrt{1 - \rho^2})]$$
$$B = \exp[(r - q_2 - \sigma_2^2 / 2)\Delta t + \sigma_2 \sqrt{\Delta t}(\rho - \sqrt{1 - \rho^2})]$$
$$C = \exp[(r - q_2 - \sigma_2^2 / 2)\Delta t - \sigma_2 \sqrt{\Delta t}(\rho - \sqrt{1 - \rho^2})]$$
$$D = \exp[(r - q_2 - \sigma_2^2 / 2)\Delta t - \sigma_2 \sqrt{\Delta t}(\rho + \sqrt{1 - \rho^2})]. \tag{A.39}$$

A 3D tree allows pricing of European and American options including the following payoffs.

Spread options: $Max(Q_1 S_1 - Q_2 S_2 - K, 0)$.

Options on the maximum (or minimum): $Max(Max(Q_1 S_1, Q_2 S_2) - K, 0)$.

Exchange options: $Max(Q_1 S_1 - Q_2 S_2, 0)$.

Dual strike options: $Max((Q_1 S_1 - K_1), (Q_2 S_2 - K_2), 0)$.

Closed form solutions are available for European versions of these options.

B.12 Monte Carlo Simulation

In the simplest form of Monte Carlo the basic Black–Scholes lognormal stock process is discretised into time steps. If we assume that each simulation path contains N time steps t_i $(i=1,...,N)$ such that at the maturity of the option $T = t_N$. We simulate each path by generating a series of independent normally distributed random variables $Z_i \sim \phi(0,1)$. A technique that allows us to "jump" large distances in time is to use

$$S(t_i) = S(t_{i-1}) e^{(r-q-\sigma^2/2)(t_i - t_{i-1}) + \sigma\sqrt{(t_i - t_{i-1})}Z_i} . \qquad (A.40)$$

Probably the easiest way to generate normal random variables on a computer is to generate pairs of uniformly distributed random variables (U_1, U_2) and transform them using the Box–Muller transformation.

$$Z_1 = \sqrt{-2\ln U_1} \cos 2\pi U_2 \qquad (A.41)$$
$$Z_2 = \sqrt{-2\ln U_1} \sin 2\pi U_2.$$

For a call at maturity the payoff is then given by

$$V(N) = Max\left[S(N) - K, 0\right].$$

We then continue the simulation for M paths or "runs", calculating the jth $(j=1,...,M)$ payoffs in each case $V(j,N)$. The value of the call is then given by the discounted expected payoff.

$$P_{Call}(0,T) = D(0,T)E\big[Max[S(N) - K, 0]\big]$$

$$\sim D(0,T)\sum_{j}^{M}\frac{V(j,N)}{M}.$$

Valuing puts and calls is trivial and the real power of Monte Carlo is calculating path dependent options and options with path dependent resets and barriers. Below we shall look at a couple of examples:

B.12.1 *Monte Carlo simulation of maximum lookback call options*

For a *maximum lookback* call option the terminal payoff is

$$Max\left[S_{Max}(T) - K, 0\right].$$

Where S_{Max} is the maximum stock price attained before maturity. With a Monte Carlo we can store the maximum stock price attained along any path. Thus for the jth path we calculate

$$S_{Max}(j,i) = Max\{S(j,0),S(j,1),...,S(j,N)\},$$

and the payoff for the jth path is

$$V(j,N) = Max\left[S_{Max}(j,N) - K, 0\right],$$

which allows us to approximate the expectation

$$P_{\substack{lookback \\ call}}(0,T) = D(0,T)E\left[Max[S_{Max}(T) - K, 0]\right].$$

Obviously, the observation frequency (daily, monthly, quarterly...) is documented in the option contract. Ideally, we should run the Monte Carlo so that the time-step Δt corresponds to at least this observation period. With intraday (or even daily) observations this may prove computationally impossible and the Monte Carlo will provide only an approximation to the true value. Convergence tests by changing the value of Δt can provide an idea of the computational error involved with running the simulation with different lattice sizes.

B.12.2 *Monte Carlo simulation of average rate call options*

Average rate (or Asian) options are very common. By averaging the final stock price over a period of time we can reduce the effective volatility of the option and hence the option price. For an *average rate call option* with averaging periodicity Δt_{obs} and *averaging-out* over the last L periods we have a terminal payoff of

$$Max\left[S_{Avg}(T) - K, 0 \right],$$

or

$$Max\left[\frac{1}{L}\sum_{l}^{L} S(T - l\,\Delta t_{obs}) - K, 0 \right],$$

which can be evaluated if $\Delta t = \Delta t_{obs}$ as

$$V(j,N) = Max\left[\frac{1}{L}\sum_{l}^{L} S(j, N-l) - K, 0 \right].$$

B.13 Finite Difference Methods

A finite difference technique allows us to solve the Black–Scholes *partial differential equation* (PDE) directly on a finite difference grid. Various techniques exist but the main idea is that in the limit of small spacing the grid should converge to the continuous PDE calculation. The continuous Black–Scholes PDE equation for an option f is given by Eq. (A.20).

$$\frac{\partial f}{\partial t} + (r-q)S\,\frac{\partial f}{\partial S} + \frac{1}{2}\sigma^2 S^2 \frac{\partial^2 f}{\partial S^2} = r f.$$

Now we could easily build a grid in $S(t)$ and t but it is computationally more efficient to build a grid in a transformed variable $Y(t) = \ln S(t)$.

$$\frac{\partial f}{\partial t} + (r - q - \frac{\sigma^2}{2})\frac{\partial f}{\partial Y} + \frac{1}{2}\sigma^2\frac{\partial^2 f}{\partial Y^2} = rf.$$

We build a rectangular grid with $t = i\Delta T$ ($i=0,1,...N$) with $\Delta T = T/N$ versus $Y = j\Delta Y$ ($j=0,1,...M$). Using finite differences we can approximate the derivatives using an *explicit scheme* – that is working from future times when the option payout is known backwards to the present.

$$\frac{\partial f}{\partial t} \sim \frac{f_{i+1,j} - f_{i,j}}{\Delta t}$$

$$\frac{\partial f}{\partial Y} \sim \frac{f_{i+1,j+1} - f_{i+1,j-1}}{2\Delta Y}$$

$$\frac{\partial^2 f}{\partial Y^2} \sim \frac{f_{i+1,j+1} - 2f_{i+1,j} + f_{i+1,j-1}}{\Delta Y^2},$$

which reduces the PDE to

$$a_j f_{i+1,j-1} + b_j f_{i+1,j} + c_j f_{i+1,j+1} = f_{i,j}, \qquad (A.42)$$

with

$$a_j = \frac{1}{1+r\Delta t}\left\{-\frac{\Delta t}{2\Delta Y}(r - q - \sigma^2/2) + \frac{\Delta t}{2\Delta Y^2}\sigma^2\right\}$$

$$b_j = \frac{1}{1+r\Delta t}\left\{1 - \frac{\Delta t}{2\Delta Y^2}\sigma^2\right\}$$

$$c_j = \frac{1}{1+r\Delta t}\left\{\frac{\Delta t}{2\Delta Y}(r - q - \sigma^2/2) + \frac{\Delta t}{2\Delta Y^2}\sigma^2\right\}.$$

A good choice of spacing is $\Delta Y = \sigma\sqrt{3\Delta t}$ for convergence purposes. The evaluation of an option depends only on the boundary conditions imposed. Considering a call option and evaluating the payoff at the maturity slice so $f(N,j)=Max(S(N,j)-K,0)$ we can work backwards using this finite difference equation to find the initial option values $f_{0,j}$ for a range of initial equity values.

Greeks (delta, gamma, theta) can be calculated directly using the $f_{i,j}$ values and the technique can be readily extended to include a couple of stochastic underlying variables by increasing the dimensionality of the lattice.

B.14 Alternatives to the Black–Scholes Model

There exist various (although little used) alternatives to Black–Scholes and we shall detail a couple of these here.

B.14.1 *The CEV model*

Constant elasticity of variance (CEV) model where the equity follows the process

$$dS = S(r-q)dt + S^{\alpha}\sigma dz, \qquad (A.43)$$

where α is a positive constant. If $\alpha = 1$ we recover the Black–Scholes equation but if $\alpha \neq 1$ then the tail of the probability distribution shifts to left or right since for example if $\alpha > 1$ then the volatility increases as stock price increases. It produces a form of volatility smile and allows closed form solutions with a *chi-squared distribution* rather than a cumulative normal distribution. The model parameters can be determined by minimising squares between market and model prices.

B.14.2 *The Merton model*

In the *Merton model* equity price "jumps" are combined with a Black–Scholes process. The jumps are described by a *Poisson process dp* with λ as the average number of jumps/year and k the average jump size as a percentage of stock price.

$$dS = S(r-q-\lambda k)dt + S\sigma dz + Sdp. \qquad (A.44)$$

The diffusion process dz and the jump process dp are assumed uncorrelated. If the assumption is made that the logarithm of the size of the percentage jump is normally distributed then simple closed forms exist.

B.15 Implied Volatility Model

To fit completely the implied volatility surface an *implied volatility function model* (IVF) or *implied tree model* can be used. Market vanilla option prices for different maturities and strikes can be used to compute a local volatility function $\sigma(S,t)$ so the effective stochastic process is

$$dS = S\,(r(t) - q(t))\,dt + S\sigma(S,t)\,dz. \qquad (A.45)$$

The technique for finding the volatility function is relatively easy in theory but fairly hard in practice unless a complete, smooth implied volatility surface is present. The Black–Scholes or diffusion process has a "reverse" function called the Folker–Planck equation. A call option for zero interest rates and dividends is valued as

$$P_{Call}(K,T) = \int_0^\infty Max(S(T) - K)\,\varphi(S(T))\,dS(T),$$

where φ is the probability density as Eq. (3.6). Differentiating twice with respect to K we have

$$\phi(S(T)) = \frac{\partial^2 P_{Call}(K,T)}{\partial K^2}.$$

Which, using the Folker–Planck equation, leads to

$$\sigma(K,T)^2 \frac{K^2}{2} \frac{\partial^2 P_{call}(K,T)}{\partial K^2} = \frac{\partial P_{Call}(K,T)}{\partial T}. \qquad (A.46)$$

This can in theory be evaluated to provide the local volatility $\sigma(K,T)$ since

$$\frac{\partial^2 P_{call}(K,T)}{\partial K^2} \text{ and } \frac{\partial P_{call}(K,T)}{\partial T}$$

are known from the volatility surface. If we include non-zero rates and dividends we have the more complex but similar function

$$\sigma(K,T)^2 = 2\frac{\left(\begin{array}{c}\dfrac{\partial P_{Call}(K,T)}{\partial T} + q(T)P_{call}(K,T) \\[2mm] + K[r(T)-q(T)]\dfrac{\partial P_{call}(K,T)}{\partial K}\end{array}\right)}{\dfrac{\partial^2 P_{call}(K,T)}{\partial K^2}}.$$

If we have a well defined and smoothly interpolated volatility surface we can estimate the local volatility surface $\sigma(K,T)$ and use it within a finite difference calculation or *implied tree* to price options which match the market.

The implied volatility model correctly prices simple exotic options, for example it provides the same price for a digital as a tight call spread with different strikes. Unfortunately, care must be taken with implied trees since they are not very useful at pricing exotic options that have payoffs or events at more than one maturity. By fitting today's term structure of volatilities it does not mean it correctly captures the future evolution of volatilities. To do this requires a structural model of volatility which can describe why the volatility surface is as it is today and describe its future evolution.

B.16 Stochastic Equity Volatility Models

B.16.1 *The Heston model*

In an attempt to solve the shortcoming of implied volatility models, much research has been carried out into stochastic volatility models. The most popular of these is the *Heston model* where the equity process is

$$dS = S(r-q)dt + S\sqrt{\xi(t)}\,dz_1, \qquad (A.47)$$

and the stochastic volatility (or actually variance) process is given by

$$d\xi = \kappa(\xi_L - \xi)dt + \upsilon\sqrt{\xi}dz_2, \qquad (A.48)$$

where dz_1 and dz_2 have correlation ρ

$$dz_1 = \rho\, dz_2 + \sqrt{1-\rho^2}\, dz_3.$$

The volatility process has "vol of vol" given by υ, a long term variance ξ_L, a reversion speed controlled by κ and an initial *spot-rate* variance $\xi(0)$ that must be specified. The volatility smile is controlled primarily by the parameter υ and the correlation ρ. A correct form of smile is generated for negative correlations in the range -50 to -80%.

The advantages of the Heston model are pseudo closed form solutions for vanilla options since ξ follows a squared *Bessel distribution* that allow rapid calibration and the ability to fit quite well index volatilities. Pricing of more complex options can be performed using two factor Monte Carlo or 2+1 dimensional finite difference schemes.

The downside of the Heston model is that it cannot fit all volatility surfaces (particularly short dated options) and the fact that equity volatility can in fact go negative in the model (the same problem exists for rates in the not too dissimilar Hull–White equation). Corrections can be made to disallow negative volatilities. An extension to the model is to allow ξ_L to have a term structure and to be a function of t. Other similar volatility processes can be specified but most do not allow simple, approximate closed forms for vanilla options.

B.16.2 *The SABR model*

The SABR model (Stochastic Alpha, Beta, Rho) is a form of Black's model for forward rates (see Section 6.3.1). The model can be used for equities and interest rates and includes a stochastic volatility process $\alpha(t)$ with volatility v and correlation ρ to the forward rate process. If $F(t)$ is the forward (price or rate) then

$$dF(t) = \alpha(t)F^\beta dz_1$$
$$d\alpha(t) = v\,\alpha(t)dz_2.$$

The model can produce a range of "realistic" smiles and has the advantage over a simple local volatility model that the smile evolves in the same direction as the asset price as obviously observed in the market.

The parameter v controls the curvature of the volatility skew and ρ the volatility slope. Using $\beta=1$ corresponds to a lognormal type model. Using an approximation, for small relative v, the model can provide an adjusted Black–Scholes volatility that can be simply "plugged" in the Black–Scholes option equations. The major disadvantage is that, unlike the Heston model, the volatility has no mean reversion and is unbounded so pricing long dated options can be problematic. However, modifications can be made to account for this effect and a version of the LIBOR market model (Appx E.10) for interest rates can be developed using this approach.

B.17 Effects of Transaction Costs and Discrete Hedging

The effect of transaction costs on delta hedging a vanilla option can provide a change in the effective volatility as

$$\sigma_{effective} = \sigma \sqrt{\left(1 \pm \sqrt{\frac{2}{\pi}} \frac{C}{\sigma \sqrt{\Delta t}}\right)}, \qquad (A.49)$$

where the sign depends on whether the option has a (+) convex payoff (hedging a sale of a call) or a (−) concave payoff (hedging purchase of a call). Here C is the round trip transaction costs as a ratio of the equity price and Δt the re-hedging or rebalancing interval. So, for a convex function the effective volatility is higher than the theoretical volatility.

It is also possible to quantify the uncertainty in the theoretical price from a strategy of discrete hedging. Under the Black–Scholes assumption of continuous delta hedging the expected hedging costs are equal to the option value. Consider the sale of a vanilla call of maturity T. The hedging error is given approximately by

$$\sigma_{error} \sim \frac{(0.354)}{\sqrt{N}} S(0) \sigma \sqrt{T} e^{-d_1^2}, \qquad (A.50)$$

with N the number of times the option is re-hedged, $S(0)$ the initial equity price and d_1 is given by Eq. (3.8). For an at-the-money option this can be simplified as

$$\sigma_{error} \sim \frac{(0.89)}{\sqrt{N}} P_{call}(0,T),$$

where $P_{call}(0,T)$ is the initial call option value. Thus for 1 year maturity call option rehedged monthly the volatility error is 25%.

B.18 Effect of Realised Volatility and Variance Swaps

The Black–Scholes model assumes constant volatility throughout the life of the option. If volatility is stochastic but uncorrelated with the equity price the value of a European vanilla option is given by the Black–Scholes price integrated over the probability distribution $\psi(\overline{\sigma})$ of the average variance rate $\overline{\sigma}$ until maturity of the option

$$P_{call \atop effective} = \int_0^{\infty} P_{call}(\overline{\sigma})\psi(\overline{\sigma})d\overline{\sigma}.$$

More generally, an investor that buys an option originally priced with a volatility σ_0 and then delta hedges the option all later times t using a volatility σ_a, the P&L of the strategy is given by

$$P\&L = \left[P_{call}(\sigma_0) - P_{call}(\sigma_a)\right]e^{rT} + \int_0^T e^{r(T-t)}\left(\sigma_a^2 - \sigma_0^2\right)\Gamma(t,\sigma_a)\frac{S(t)^2}{2}dt,$$

where Γ is the gamma of the option. Thus, if σ_a is equal to σ_0 (the initial volatility) the pricing error is zero but in general it is equity path dependent.

Volatility swaps are forward contracts that provide payoffs at maturity equal to the difference between realised volatility σ_r and a strike K_{Vol} (say, the initial implied volatility) over the life of the swap.

$$Payoff_{Volatility \atop swap} = \left(\sigma_r(T) - K_{Vol}\right).$$

From the above discussion on volatility hedging error we can see that a replication hedging strategy in the variance, rather than volatility, is perhaps easier, and indeed in practice *variance swaps* are more widely traded. The payoff of a variance swap is then given as

$$Payoff_{\substack{Variance \\ swap}} = \left(\sigma_r(T)^2 - K_{Var}^2 \right),$$

where the M day realised variance is usually defined as

$$\sigma_r(T)^2 = \frac{252}{n-2} \sum_i^{M-1} \left(\ln \frac{S_{i+1}}{S_i} \right)^2.$$

This is an artificial definition of variance that is effectively the second moment only (see Section B.1). The variance swap has a closed form solution given by

$$P_{\substack{Variance \\ swap}}(T) = \frac{2}{T} \left[rT - \ln\left(\frac{F(0,T)}{S(0)} \right) - \left(\frac{S(0)}{F(0,T)} e^{rT} - 1 \right) \right]$$

$$+ e^{rT} \left(\int_0^{F(0,T)} \frac{P_{Put}(K,T)}{K^2} dK + \int_{F(0,T)}^{\infty} \frac{P_{Call}(K,T)}{K^2} dK \right),$$

where $F(0,T)$ is the at-the-money forward. The integrals can be easily discretised for evaluation and hedging using a series of vanilla options. The notional of a variance swap is usually expressed in points of variance and usually in practice a cap is included in the documentation to limit risk and the size of payments made in case of a volatility "blow-out". Trading variance swaps is widely carried out by hedge funds who wish to trade pure volatility in large size (I have used them to trade against credit spreads) but exchange traded VIX index contracts now also exist.

B.19 Pricing FX Options Using Black–Scholes

A modified Black–Scholes model can be used to price currency options if we recognise that an investor in a foreign currency receives a yield equal to r_f the foreign currency risk free rate which is analogous to holding a dividend paying equity. The currency forward for spot rate $X(0)$ is given

$$F(T) = X(0)e^{(r-r_f)T}.$$

Thus, the FX call and put option price is given by

$$
\begin{aligned}
P_{FX\ call} &= X(0)e^{-r_f T}N(d_1) - e^{-rT}K N(d_2) \\
P_{FX\ put} &= e^{-rT}K N(-d_2) - X(0)e^{-r_f T} N(-d_1),
\end{aligned}
\qquad \text{(A.51)}
$$

with

$$
d_1 = \frac{\left\{ \ln\left(X(0)/K \right) + \left(r - r_f + \sigma^2/2 \right)T \right\}}{\sigma\sqrt{T}}
$$
$$
d_2 = d_1 - \sigma\sqrt{T}.
$$

B.20 Quanto Corrections

Fixed exchange rate options or *quanto* options are very common. The underlying equity exposure in one currency (say an index measured in JPY) is currency hedged into the investor's domestic currency (say USD). It allows the currency risk to be eliminated for investors in many investments.

To understand the origin of the *quanto correction* we must consider the processes for domestic and foreign equities together with the FX process and evaluate what the risk neutral process is for a domestic investor investing in a foreign asset. The process for a domestic denominated equity (with no dividend) for a domestic investor is

$$dS_d = S_d\, r_d\, dt + S_d\sigma_d\, dz_d.$$

Similarly, the process for the foreign denominated equity as viewed by a foreign investor must have a similar form

$$dS_f = S_f\, r_f\, dt + S_f\sigma_f\, d\hat{z}_f.$$

For the domestic investor the foreign asset will follow a risk adjusted stochastic process with a different *risk premium* λ_f or drift to remain risk neutral

$$d\hat{z}_f = \lambda_f dt + dz_f.$$

If the FX process follows

$$dX = X(r_d - r_f)dt + X\sigma_{FX} dz_{FX},$$

then the value of the foreign asset for the domestic investor is XS_f. Using Ito's lemma we have

$$d(XS_f) = S_f dX + X dS_f + dX dS_f + \ldots$$

This gives to first order

$$\frac{d(XS_f)}{(XS_f)} = (r_d - r_f)dt + (r_f + \lambda_f \sigma_f)dt$$

$$+ \sigma_f \sigma_{FX} dz_f dz_{FX} + \sigma_{FX} dz_{FX} + \sigma_f dz_f.$$

The expectation of the $\sigma_f \sigma_{FX} dz_f dz_{FX}$ term introduces a correlation term $\rho\sigma_f\sigma_{FX}$. Comparing with the process for the domestic asset we can see that a foreign asset viewed by the domestic investor has a risk premium given by $\lambda_f = -\sigma_{FX}\rho$. A foreign *quantoed* asset thus is equivalent to a domestic asset with an effective dividend of

$$q = r_d - r_f + \rho\sigma_{FX}\sigma_f. \tag{A.52}$$

We can use this effective dividend and substitute it directly into the Black–Scholes equations to provide a quanto option. If the foreign equity actually pays an actual dividend we must obviously include this in the usual way as Eq. (3.16).

Appendix C

Equity Structured Products

C.1 Reverse Convertibles

The redemption amount at maturity for a reverse convertible is given by

$$R_{\substack{reverse \\ convert}} = 100\% - Max(K - S(T),0), \qquad (A.53)$$

where K is the initial strike and $S(T)$ the final stock price at maturity T. The issuer swap structure is valued as

$$V(0,T) = Issuer\,funding + Put\,option - Coupons$$

$$= \sum_{i}^{T} D(0,t_i)\left[f(0,t_i,t_i + h_i) + x\right]h_i + P_{put}(0,T,K)$$

$$- C\sum_{j}^{T} D(0,t_j)l_j,$$

where P_{put} is the value of the put option, $f(0,t_i,t_i+h_i)$ are the forward rates representing the floating swap payments fixing at times t_i and x the issuer spread. The annualised fixed coupon C is paid with accrual periods l_j.

C.2 Discount Reverse Convertibles

The swap structure is valued with no fixed coupons since it is a discount or zero coupon note

$$V(0,T) = Issuer\,funding + Put\,option$$

$$= \sum_{i}^{T} D(0,t_i)\left[f(0,t_i,t_i + h_i) + x\right]h_i + P_{put}(0,T,K), \qquad (A.54)$$

which is initially positive and provides the initial issue price of

$$P_{\substack{reverse \\ discount}} (0,T) = 100\% - V(0,T) \ < 100\%.$$

C.3 Knock-in Reverse Convertibles

For a K_1 strike put with K_2 *knock-in* level the expected payoff can be written as

$$P_{\substack{KI \\ put}} = E\Big[D(0,T) \ Max(K_1 - S(T),0)\chi_{S(t)\leq K_2} \Big], \qquad (A.55)$$

Here we have used the indicator function $\chi = 1$ if $(S(t) \leq K_2)$ and zero otherwise, so the put with strike K_1 is activated if the barrier is triggered before maturity $(0 < t \leq T)$. The closed form solution is given as a barrier option (Appx C.6).

C.4 Lock-up Reverse Convertibles

The "lock-up" feature is obtained by the investor effectively selling a *knock-out put*. For a K_1 strike put with barrier or knock-out level K_2 ($K_2 > K_1$) the expected payout is

$$P_{\substack{KO \\ put}} = E\Big[D(0,T) \ Max(K_1 - S(T),0)\chi_{S(t)<K_2} \Big] \qquad (A.56)$$

As with the knock-in put a closed form solution is possible (Appx C.6). It however, only applies to an abrupt, continuously observed barrier.

C.5 Digital Options

Digital call options or binaries pay a cash amount Q if the underlying equity finishes above the strike K on the maturity date T. The Black–Scholes closed form is very simple and can be written

$$P_{BinaryCall} = E[Q\,D(0,T)\,\chi_{S(T)>K}] = Qe^{-rT}N(d_2).$$

Similarly a digital put is

$$P_{BinaryPut} = E[Q\,D(0,T)\,\chi_{S(T)<K}] = Qe^{-rT}N(-d_2). \qquad \text{(A.57)}$$

C.6 Barrier Options

Knock-in and *knock-out* puts are two forms of standard barrier options commonly used in structured products. A standard knock-in put with K_1 strike and barrier or knock-in level K_2 ($K_2 < K_1$) is also known as a *down-and-in put* and is given by the closed form

$$\begin{aligned}
P_{KI\atop put} = &-S(0)N(-x_1)e^{-qT} + K_1e^{-rT}N(-x_1+\sigma\sqrt{T}) \\
&+ S(0)e^{-qT}\left(\frac{K_2}{S(0)}\right)^{2\lambda}[N(y)-N(y_1)] \\
&+ K_1e^{-rT}\left(\frac{K_2}{S(0)}\right)^{2\lambda-2}[N(y-\sigma\sqrt{T})-N(y_1-\sigma\sqrt{T})],
\end{aligned} \qquad \text{(A.58)}$$

where

$$\lambda = \frac{r-q+\sigma^2/2}{\sigma^2}$$

$$y = \frac{\ln[K_2^2/(S(0)K_1)]}{\sigma\sqrt{T}} + \lambda\sigma\sqrt{T}$$

$$y_1 = \frac{\ln[K_2/S(0)]}{\sigma\sqrt{T}} + \lambda\sigma\sqrt{T}$$

$$x_1 = \frac{\ln[S(0)/K_2)]}{\sigma\sqrt{T}} + \lambda\sigma\sqrt{T}.$$

A knock-out put where $K_2 > K_1$ is also known as an *up-and-out put* and is given by

$$P_{KO \atop put} = P_{put}(0,T,K_1) + S(0)e^{-qT}\left(\frac{K_2}{S(0)}\right)^{2\lambda} N(-y)$$

$$- K_1 e^{-rT}\left(\frac{K_2}{S(0)}\right)^{2\lambda-2} N(y+\sigma\sqrt{T}).$$

(A.59)

Black–Scholes closed form solutions for standard barrier options equations are widely published and several permutations of call/put, down/up and in/out barriers are possible.

The above equations are for continuous barriers. An approximation for discretely sampled (for example daily) barriers is possible where the barrier level K_2 is replaced with

$$K_{2discrete} = K_2 e^{\pm\beta\sigma\sqrt{\Delta t}},$$

where $\pm$ relates to a barrier above/below the underlying security. Δt is the barrier monitoring interval and $\beta = \zeta(1/2)/\sqrt{2\pi} \sim 0.5826$ where here ζ is the *Reimann zeta* function.

C.7 Leveraged Reverse Convertibles

From Example 4.5 the redemption amount for the leveraged reverse convertible is a sum of three different possible put payouts

$$R_{reverse \atop leveraged} = 100\% - Max(K_1 - S(T),0) - Max(K_2 - S(T),0)$$
$$+ 2Max(K_3 - S(T),0).$$

The swap can be thus decomposed with strikes $K_1 = 100\%$, $K_2 = 75\%$, $K_3 = 37.5\%$ as

$$V(0,T) = \sum_{i}^{T} D(0,t_i) \big[f(0,t_i,t_i+h_i)+x \big] h_i + P_{KI\,put}(0,T,K_1,K_2)$$
$$+ P_{KI\,put}(0,T,K_2,K_2) - 2P_{KI\,put}(0,T,K_3,K_2)$$
$$- C \sum_{j}^{T} D(0,t_j) l_j.$$

C.8 Protected Bull Notes

The issuer swap can be written as

$$V(0) = \textit{Issuer funding } - \textit{Call option}$$
$$= \sum_{i}^{T} D(0,t_i)\big[f(0,t_i,t_i+h_i)+x\big]h_i - \alpha P_{call}(0,T,K), \qquad \text{(A.60)}$$

where α is the participation. For an upfront margin of m, the participation is given by

$$\alpha = \frac{\displaystyle\sum_{i}^{T} D(0,t_i)\big[f(0,t_i,t_i+h_i)+x\big]h_i - m}{P_{call}(0,T,K)}.$$

C.9 Average Protected Bull Notes

The T maturity *average spot* call or *Asian* call is priced as the arithmetic average over the last M fixing dates t_i ($i=1,...,M$).

$$P_{\substack{Asian \\ call}}(0,T,t_i,K) = E\Big[D(0,T)\,Max\Big(\frac{1}{M}\sum_{i=1}^{M} \frac{S(t_i)}{S(0)} - K,0 \Big) \Big]. \qquad \text{(A.61)}$$

C.10 Pricing Average Rate Options

There is no closed form solution for pricing an *arithmetic average rate option* or *Asian option* since if the asset is modelled as lognormal the arithmetic average will not have a lognormal distribution. Analytical approximations can be used, for example fitting the mean drift and volatility to the exact moments of the arithmetic average (as below).

$$P_{\substack{average \\ call}} \sim S(0)e^{(b_A - r)T_2} N(d_1) - Ke^{-rT_2} N(d_2)$$

$$\text{(A.62)}$$

$$P_{\substack{average \\ put}} \sim Ke^{-rT_2} N(d_2) - S(0)e^{(b_A - r)T_2} N(d_1).$$

Here T_2 is the time remaining to maturity and

$$d_1 = \frac{\ln(S/K) + \left(b_A + \sigma_A^2/2\right)T_2}{\sigma_A\sqrt{T_2}}, \qquad d_2 = d_1 - \sigma_A\sqrt{T_2}.$$

The effective volatility and mean drift are given by

$$\sigma_A = \sqrt{\frac{\ln(M_2)}{T} - 2b_A}, \qquad b_A = \frac{\ln(M_1)}{T}$$

where T is the original time to maturity. If τ is the time to the beginning of the averaging period then the first and second arithmetic average moments are given by

$$M_1 = \frac{e^{(r-q)T} - e^{(r-q)\tau}}{(r-q)(T-\tau)},$$

$$\text{(A.63)}$$

$$M_2 = \frac{2e^{(2(r-q)+\sigma^2)T}}{(r-q+\sigma^2)(2(r-q)+\sigma^2)(T-\tau)^2}$$

$$+ \frac{2e^{(2(r-q)+\sigma^2)\tau}}{(r-q)(T-\tau)^2}\left[\frac{1}{2(r-q)+\sigma^2} - \frac{e^{(r-q)(T-\tau)}}{(r-q)+\sigma^2}\right].$$

If the option is already in the average period, we must, of course, replace the original strike price with a weighted average of the strike and the average asset price.

C.11 Capped Protected Bull Notes

For the capped protected bull notes the final redemption value is

$$R_{\substack{capped \\ bull}} = 100\% + \alpha \left\{ Max\left(\frac{S(T)}{S(0)} - K_1, 0 \right) - Max\left(\frac{S(T)}{S(0)} - K_2, 0 \right) \right\},$$

and is priceds a call spread with strikes K_1 and K_2.

$$V(0,T) = \sum_i^T D(0,t_i)\left[f(0,t_i,t_i + h_i) + x \right] h_i$$
$$- \alpha \left\{ P_{call}(0,T,K_1) - P_{call}(0,T,K_2) \right\}. \tag{A.64}$$

C.12 Protected Cliquet Notes

For a simple *cliquet* call with cliquet period between t_{i-1} and t_i and paying out at time T the present value of the payoff can be written as

$$P_{\substack{cliquet \\ call}}(0,t_{i-1},t_i,T) = E[D(0,T)\, Max\left(\frac{S(t_i)}{S(t_{i-1})} - K, 0 \right)], \tag{A.65}$$

where usually the strike K is 100% for an at-the-money cliquet call. Often performance caps and floors are added. Thus the typical redemption amount for an N period protected cliquet note with a cap of K_1 and floor of K_2 on each period performance would be

$$R_{\substack{protected \\ cliquet \\ capfloor}} = 100\% + \sum_i^N Max\left(K_2, Min\left(\frac{S(t_i)}{S(t_{i-1})} - 100\%, K_1 \right) \right),$$

which is priced as a sum of *cliquet call-spreads*

$$\sum_i^N \left[P_{\substack{cliquet \\ call}}(0,t_{i-1},t_i,K_2,\sigma_{i,K_2}) - P_{\substack{cliquet \\ call}}(0,t_{i-1},t_i,K_1,\sigma_{i,K_1}) \right],$$

where the individual volatilities used are modified to accommodate smile effects and the forward volatility.

C.13 Forward Start and Cliquet Options

A *forward start* call and put with final maturity T and starting at future time t with strike $\beta S(t)$ (where β is a constant) can be written as

$$P_{\substack{forward \\ start \\ call}} (0,t,T) = S(0)e^{-qt}\left\{e^{-q(T-t)}N(d_1) - \beta e^{-r(T-t)}N(d_2)\right\}$$

$$P_{\substack{foward \\ start \\ put}} (0,t,T) = S(0)e^{-qt}\left\{\beta e^{-r(T-t)}N(-d_2) - e^{-q(T-t)}N(-d_1)\right\} \qquad (A.66)$$

$$d_1 = \frac{\ln(1/\beta) + (r - q + \sigma^2/2)(T-t)}{\sigma\sqrt{T-t}}, \qquad d_2 = d_1 - \sigma\sqrt{T-t}.$$

A cliquet option (or *ratchet* option) consists of a series of forward starting options, where the strike for the next period is set equal to a constant times the final equity price of the last period. For M periods we can then write a cliquet call as

$$P_{\substack{cliquet \\ call}} (0,T) = \sum_{j=1}^{M} S(0)e^{-qt_j}\left\{\begin{array}{l} e^{-q(t_{j+1}-t_j)}N(d_1) \\ \qquad - \beta e^{-r(t_{j+1}-t_j)}N(d_2)\end{array}\right\}.$$

C.14 Multi-Barrier Protected Notes

For the Example 4.15 the annual coupon can be written as a series of forward start barrier options for which closed forms are available with in this case $a_0 = 9.0\%$, $a_1 = 4.0\%$, $a_2 = 2.0\%$, $a_3 = 3.0\%$.

$$C_i = a_0 - a_1 \chi_{S(t) \leq K_1} - a_2 \chi_{S(t) \leq K_2} - a_3 \chi_{S(t) \leq K_3}$$

$$i = 1,...,N; \quad K_1 > K_2 > K_3; \quad t_{i-1} < t < t_i. \qquad (A.67)$$

Appendix D

Equity Basket Products

D.1 Equity Correlation

The realised correlation ρ_{12} for two equities (j=1,2) can be calculated from time series data using daily log returns $y_{j,i}$ (i=1,...,M) (see Appx B.1).

$$\rho_{12} = \frac{\sum_{i=1}^{M}(y_{1,i} - \overline{y}_1)(y_{2,i} - \overline{y}_2)}{\sqrt{\sum_{i=1}^{M}(y_{1,i} - \overline{y}_1)\sum_{i=1}^{M}(y_{2,i} - \overline{y}_2)}}.$$

D.2 Protected Basket Notes

The basket value $B(t)$ of N_B equities at time t is given by the sum of the weighted equity prices

$$B(t) = \sum_{i=1}^{N_B} \hat{\omega}_i S_i(t),$$

with weights $\hat{\omega}_i$. The redemption amount at maturity T of the notes is

$$R_{\substack{basket \\ protected}} = 100\% + \alpha Max\left(\sum_{i=1}^{N_B} \hat{\omega}_i S_i(T) - K, 0\right),$$

where α is the participation and K is the strike. The weights can be redefined as ω_i such that the payoff represents performance

295

$$R_{\substack{basket \\ protected}} = 100\% + \alpha\, Max\left(\sum_{i=1}^{N_B} \omega_i \frac{S_i(T)}{S_i(0)} - K, 0\right)$$

(A.68)

$$= 100\% + \alpha\, Max(B(T) - K, 0).$$

We can price the issuer swap as the funding leg minus the basket call cost

$$V(0,T) = V_{funding}(0,T) - \alpha\, P_{\substack{basket \\ call}}(0,T,K).$$

D.3 Basket Pricing Using a Single Factor Approximation

The sum of lognormal distributions is unfortunately not a lognormal distribution. We can, however, value a basket using a single factor approximation by matching the first two moments (effectively mean and variance) of the basket distribution to a lognormal distribution. This allows us to use the Black–Scholes approach for valuing basket options.

Consider a basket with N_B stocks and an option contract with maturity T. The basket value at time T is given by

$$B(T) = \sum_{i=1}^{N_B} \hat{\omega}_i S_i(T).$$

The forward for each stock is

$$F_i(T) = E[S_i(T)] = S_i(0)e^{(r-q_i)T}.$$

The first two moments are

$$M_1 = E[B(T)] \qquad\qquad M_2 = E[B(T)^2].$$

So equating with the lognormal distribution we have

$$M_1 = \sum_{i=1}^{N_B} \hat{\omega}_i F_i(T), \qquad (A.69)$$

and

$$E[S_i(T)S_j(T)] = F_i(T)F_j(T)e^{\rho_{ij}\sigma_i\sigma_i T}$$

where ρ_{ij} is the correlation between the ith and jth stock so we have the second moment as

$$M_2 = \sum_{i=1}^{N_B} \sum_{j=1}^{N_B} \hat{\omega}_i \hat{\omega}_j F_i(T)F_j(T)e^{\rho_{ij}\sigma_i\sigma_j T}. \qquad (A.70)$$

D.4 Basket Monte Carlo Pricing

If we have a basket of underlying equities then each individual equity can be modelled as the following Black–Scholes process:

$$dS_j = S_j(r_j - q_j)dt + S_j\sigma_j dz_j,$$

where $j=1,...,N_B$ the total number of equities in the basket. Discretising in steps of Δt gives the following equity prices at each time step of the Monte Carlo path

$$S_j(t_i) = S_j(t_{i-1})e^{(r_j - q_j - \sigma_j^2/2)\Delta t + \sigma_j\sqrt{\Delta t}Z_j(t_i)}. \qquad (A.71)$$

The normal random variables Z_j for the different equities are correlated. If the covariance matrix is given as Σ we can, provided it is symmetric positive definite, express (using Cholseky decomposition) as a function of the diagonal matrix A such that $\Sigma = AA^T$. This allows a vector of uncorrelated random variables $\underline{X}$ to be simulated and converted into correlated variables $\underline{Z}=A\underline{X}$.

Generally, however, we can simplify and use a single factor approximation with one overall constant correlation and a common independent random factor F with

$$Z_j = \sqrt{\rho}F + \sqrt{1-\rho}X_i,$$

where $E[Z_j Z_k] = \rho$.

D.5 Average Protected Basket Bull Notes

The basket call option for M fixings of the basket price before the maturity date is calculated as

$$P_{\substack{basket \\ average \\ call}}(0,T) = E\left[D(0,T)Max\left(\sum_{j=1}^{M}\frac{B(t_j)}{M} - K, 0\right)\right], \quad \text{(A.72)}$$

D.6 Protected Basket Cliquet Notes

The N period basket cliquet option can be written as

$$P_{\substack{basket \\ cliquet}}(0,T) = E\left[D(0,T)\sum_{k=1}^{N}Max\left(\frac{B(t_k)}{B(t_{k-1})} - K, 0\right)\right], \quad \text{(A.73)}$$

where k denotes the cliquet period. This can be evaluated as the sum of individual cliquet basket call options, using a single factor approximation for the basket and then applying a forward starting option closed form or using Monte Carlo.

D.7 Protected Multiple Binary Notes

The double binary notes can be composed as a sum of a series of double binaries with one for each coupon period. The value of each double binary with coupon C can be given as

$$P_{\substack{double \\ binary}}(0,t_i) = E\left[D(0,t_i)C\chi_{\frac{S_1(t_i)}{S_1(t_{i-1})}>K_1}\chi_{\frac{S_2(t_i)}{S_2(t_{i-1})}>K_2}\right]. \quad \text{(A.74)}$$

A single double binary can be evaluated using a closed form solution using the bivariate normal distribution $M(x,y,\rho)$ with correlation ρ.

$$P_{\substack{double \\ binary}}(0,T) = D(0,T)CM(d_1(T),d_2(T),\rho), \qquad (A.75)$$

where the $d_i(T)$ with $i = 1,2$ are defined here by

$$d_i(T) = \frac{\left\{\ln\left(S_i(0)/K\right)+\left(r-q_i-\sigma^2/2\right)T\right\}}{\sigma_i\sqrt{T}},$$

and the cumulative bivariate normal distribution is

$$M(a,b,\rho) = \frac{1}{2\pi\sqrt{1-\rho^2}}\int_{-\infty}^{a}\int_{-\infty}^{b}\exp\left[\frac{x^2-2\rho xy+y^2}{2(1-\rho^2)}\right]dxdy.$$

This gives a theoretical valuation but in practice it proves better to smooth the discontinuity in the product by pricing as a worst-of call spread.

D.8 Rainbow Notes

For a rainbow note the realised performances of the N_B stocks in the basket are sorted from the *worst-of* to the *best-of*

$$Min\left(\frac{S_1(T)}{S_1(0)},\frac{S_2(T)}{S_2(0)},...,\frac{S_{N_B}(T)}{S_{N_B}(0)}\right) = \bar{S}_1(T)$$

$$< \bar{S}_2(T)<...<\bar{S}_{N_B-1}(T)$$

$$... < \bar{S}_{N_B}(T) = Max\left(\frac{S_1(T)}{S_1(0)},\frac{S_2(T)}{S_2(0)},...,\frac{S_{N_B}(T)}{S_{N_B}(0)}\right),$$

where $\bar{S}_i(T)$ is the ith worst performance. The rainbow option pays a sum of the weighted prices at maturity T and the redemption amount is

$$R_{rainbow} = \sum_{k=1}^{N_B}\omega_k\frac{\bar{S}_k(T)}{\bar{S}_k(0)}, \qquad (A.76)$$

and is priced as

$$P_{rainbow}(0,T) = E\left[D(0,T) \sum_{k=1}^{N_B} \omega_k \frac{\overline{S}_k(T)}{\overline{S}_k(0)} \right].$$

The rainbow call is calculated as

$$P_{rainbow \atop call}(0,T) = E\left[D(0,T)\, Max\left(\sum_{k=1}^{N_B} \omega_k \overline{S}_k(T) - K, 0 \right) \right]. \qquad (A.77)$$

D.9 Worst-of Protected Notes

The most common form of the worst-of option pays the worst performance in the basket and has no strike (strike set at zero) and is effectively the forward of the worst-of. The value of the option is thus

$$P_{worst\,of}(0,T) = E\left[D(0,T)\, Min\left(\frac{S_1(T)}{S_1(0)}, \frac{S_2(T)}{S_2(0)}, ..., \frac{S_{N_B}(T)}{S_{N_B}(0)} \right) \right]. \qquad (A.78)$$

D.10 Best-of and Worst-of Closed Form on Two Assets

The payoff of the best-of option on two assets can be written as the well known *exchange option* on two assets. Writing the payoff as

$$Max\left(\frac{S_1(T)}{S_1(0)}, \frac{S_2(T)}{S_2(0)} \right) = \frac{S_2(T)}{S_2(0)} + Max\left(\frac{S_1(T)}{S_1(0)} - \frac{S_2(T)}{S_2(0)}, 0 \right).$$

Now $Max(Q_1 S_1 - Q_2 S_2, 0)$ is an exchange option, where Q_1 is the amount of asset 1 and Q_2 is the amount of asset 2.

$$P_{exchange \atop option} = Q_1 S_1 e^{-q_1 T} N(d_1) - Q_2 S_2 e^{-q_2 T} N(d_2), \qquad (A.79)$$

with

$$d_1 = \frac{\ln(Q_1 S_1 / Q_2 S_2) + (q_2 - q_1 + \hat{\sigma}^2 / 2)T}{\hat{\sigma}\sqrt{T}}$$

$$d_2 = d_1 - \hat{\sigma}\sqrt{T}$$

$$\hat{\sigma} = \sqrt{\sigma_1^2 + \sigma_2^2 - 2\rho\sigma_1\sigma_2}.$$

The payoff of the worst-of option on two assets can also be written as an exchange option on two assets since

$$Min\left(\frac{S_1(T)}{S_1(0)}, \frac{S_2(T)}{S_2(0)}\right) = \frac{S_1(T)}{S_1(0)} - Max\left(\frac{S_1(T)}{S_1(0)} - \frac{S_2(T)}{S_2(0)}, 0\right).$$

For more than two assets a normal copula approach similar to first-to-default pricing can be used.

D.11 Everest Protected Notes

The Everest option on a basket N_B underlyings and paying fixed coupon C can be decomposed into a series of worst-of options for the M annual coupon dates

$$P_{Everest}(0,T) = E\left[\sum_{i=1}^{M} D(0,t_i) \, C \, Min\left(\frac{S_1(t_i)}{S_1(0)}, \frac{S_2(t_i)}{S_2(0)}, ..., \frac{S_{N_B}(t_i)}{S_{N_B}(0)}\right)\right]$$

$$= C\sum_{i=1}^{M} P_{worst\,of}(0,t_i). \qquad\qquad (A.80)$$

D.12 Power Reverse Convertibles

The power reverse convertible payoff ignoring coupons is given as

$$R_{\substack{power \\ reverse}} = 100\% - Max(K - Min\left(\frac{S_1(T)}{S_1(0)}, \frac{S_2(T)}{S_2(0)}, ..., \frac{S_{N_B}(T)}{S_{N_B}(0)}\right), 0),$$

and the worst-of put is valued as

$$P_{\substack{worst\,of \\ put}}(0,T) = E\left[D(0,T)\,Max\left\{K - Min\left(\frac{S_1(T)}{S_1(0)},...,\frac{S_{N_B}(T)}{S_{N_B}(0)}\right),0\right\}\right].$$

$$\text{(A.81)}$$

For two stocks it is usual to value with a worst-of closed form solution whilst for a larger basket a Monte Carlo or copula method is required.

D.13 Pulsar Protected Notes

The Pulsar product in Example 5.15 can be decomposed into:

(i)   a zero-coupon bond redeeming 100% at maturity
(ii)   a worst-of, knock-out binary paying $B = 200\%$ with a barrier at $K=40\%$ of the initial stock price of each stock
(iii)   a worst-of, knock-in forward on the worst-of with a knock-in at 40% and forward strike at the initial stock price

$$R_{Pulsar} = 100\% + B\,\chi_{\left\{\left(\frac{S_i(t)}{S_i(0)}\right)_{Min} > K\right\}}$$

$$+ Min\left(\frac{S_1(T)}{S_1(0)},\frac{S_2(T)}{S_2(0)},...,\frac{S_{N_B}(T)}{S_{N_B}(0)}\right)\chi_{\left\{\left(\frac{S_i(t)}{S_i(0)}\right)_{Min} < K\right\}} \qquad \text{(A.82)}$$

$$t_1 < t \leq T.$$

D.14 Altiplano and Neptune Protected Notes

The Altiplano is a basket capital guaranteed product based on a single worst-of, knock-out coupon C_1 which is paid at maturity. If a knock-out occurs, a smaller coupon C_2 is paid. This is priced with barrier strike K as

$$P_{Altiplano}(0,T) = E\left[D(0,T)\left\{C_1\,\chi_{\left\{\left(\frac{S_i(t)}{S_i(0)}\right)_{Min} > K\right\}} + C_2\,\chi_{\left\{\left(\frac{S_i(t)}{S_i(0)}\right)_{Min} \leq K\right\}}\right\}\right].$$

The Neptune comprises of a strip of M of these barrier options

$$P_{Neptune} = E\left[\sum_{j=1}^{M} D(0,t_j)C_1\,\chi_{\left\{\left(\frac{S_i(t)}{S_i(0)}\right)_{Min} > K\right\}}\right]. \qquad \text{(A.83)}$$

Appendix E

Pricing Interest Rate Products

E.1 Different Types of Interest Rate Models

There exist many types of interest rate model with different stochastic processes used to describe the future evolution of interest rates. An overview of the equations of state for several major models is provided in Table E.1. Models can be roughly divided into whether they are:

(i)   Spot rate or forward rate underlying
(ii)   Normal, lognormal or other distribution of underlying
(iii)   Arbitrage free
(iv)   Mean reverting
(v)   Number of stochastic factors
(vi)   Analytically tractable and provide closed forms or numerical solutions required

E.2 Black's Model for Forward Rates

If $f(t,T,T+h)$ is the forward rate between T and $T+h$ at time t the evolution of the forward rate is given by Eq. (6.1)

$$\frac{df(t,T,T+h)}{f(t,T,T+h)} = -\sigma(T,T+h)\,dz(t). \qquad (A.84)$$

Now let $f_t = f(t,T,T+h)$ so we can expand as

$$d(\ln f_t) = \frac{\partial(\ln f_t)}{\partial f_t}df_t + \frac{1}{2}\frac{\partial^2(\ln f_t)}{\partial f_t^2}df_t^2 + \dots$$

Table E.1: A few different types of interest rate model.

Model	Type	Equation of State	Comment
Black	One factor forward rate or swap rate	$$\frac{df(t,T,T+h)}{f(t,T,T+h)} = -\sigma(T,T+h)\,dz(t)$$	Forward rates are lognormally distributed. Market standard for caps/floors.
Vasicek	One factor spot rate	$$dr(t) = a\big[b - r(t)\big]dt + \sigma\,dz(t)$$	Normal spot rate. Mean reversion. Closed form solutions.
CIR (Cox, Ingersoll, Ross)	One factor spot rate	$$dr(t) = a\big[b - r(t)\big]dt + \sigma\sqrt{r(t)}\,dz(t)$$	Mean reversion. Closed forms.
Ho–Lee	One factor spot rate	$$dr(t) = \theta(t)\,dt + \sigma\,dz(t)$$	Arbitrage free. Normal spot rate. Closed forms.
Hull–White	One factor spot rate	$$dr(t) = \big[\theta(t) - a\,r(t)\big]dt + \sigma\,dz(t)$$	Arbitrage free. Normal spot rate with mean reversion. Closed forms.
Black Karasinki	One factor spot rate	$$d\ln r(t) = \big[\theta(t) - a\ln r(t)\big]dt + \sigma\,dz(t)$$	Arbitrage free. Lognormal spot-rate. No analytic closed forms.
LIBOR Market	1+ factor forward rate	$$\frac{df_k(t)}{f_k(t)} = \sum_{i=m(t)}^{k} \frac{hf_i(t)\sigma_i(t)\sigma_k(t)}{1+hf_i(t)}dt + \sigma_k(t)dz(t)$$	Arbitrage free. Lognormal forward rates. Closed form approximations.
Hull–White (two factor)	2+ factor spot rate	$$dr(t) = \big[\theta(t) - u(t) - a\,r(t)\big]dt + \sigma_1\,dz_1(t)$$ $$du(t) = -bu(t)\,dt + \sigma_2\,dz_2(t)$$	Arbitrage free. Mean reversion. Richer volatility structure.
HJM (Heath, Jarrow and Morton)	1+ factor forward rate	$$df(t,T) = m(t,T)dt + \sum_{k}\sigma_k(t,T)dz_k(t)$$	Arbitrage free. Richer volatility structure. Analytically intractable.

$$d \left(\ln f_t \right) = \frac{df_t}{f_t} - \frac{\sigma^2}{2} dt.$$

Integrating over time from time $t = 0$ gives

$$\ln f_t = \ln f_0 + \int_0^t d(\ln f_t)$$

$$= \ln f_0 - \frac{\sigma^2}{2} t - \sigma \int_0^t dz,$$

where $f_0 = f(0,T,T+h)$ is the initial forward rate at $t = 0$. Rearranging and using the standard normal distribution $Z \sim \phi(0,1)$ we have

$$f_t = f_0 e^{-\frac{\sigma^2}{2} t - \sigma \sqrt{t} Z}, \qquad (A.85)$$

which can be more generally written as

$$f(t,T,T+h) = f(0,T,T+h) \, e^{-\frac{v^2}{2} - vZ}, \qquad (A.86)$$

where $v = \sigma(T,T+h)\sqrt{t}$.

E.3 Black's Cap

Each caplet fixing at t and paying at $t+h$ can be evaluated as the expectation

$$P_{caplet}(0,t,t+h) = E[h \, D(0,t+h) Max\big(f(t,t,t+h) - K, 0 \big)]. \qquad (A.87)$$

Using Black's model Eq. (A.86) we can write this as

$$P_{caplet} = h \, D(0,t+h) \, E \left[\left(f(0,t,t+h) e^{-\frac{v^2}{2} - vZ} - K \right) \chi_{f(0,t,t+h) e^{-\frac{v^2}{2} - vZ} > K} \right],$$

with $v = \sigma(t,t+h)\sqrt{t}$ and the discount factor $D(0,t+h)$ is deterministic (non-stochastic). Here we have 2 terms to evaluate. The second term is given by

$$K E\left[\chi_{f(0,t,t+h)e^{\frac{v^2}{2}-vZ}>K} \right] = K E\left[\chi_{Z<\frac{1}{v}\ln\frac{f_0}{K}-\frac{v}{2}} \right] = K\, N(d_2),$$

with

$$d_2 = \frac{1}{v}\ln\frac{f_0}{K}-\frac{v}{2},$$

For the first term we need Girsanov's theorem Eq. (A.29) to solve

$$E\left[f(0,t,t+h)e^{-\frac{v^2}{2}-vZ}\, \chi_{vZ<\ln\frac{f_0}{K}-\frac{v^2}{2}} \right]$$

$$= f(0,t,t+h)e^{\frac{v^2}{2}}E\left[e^{-vZ} \right]E\left[\chi_{v(Z-v)<\ln\frac{f_0}{K}-\frac{v^2}{2}} \right]$$

$$= f(0,t,t+h)\,N(d_1),$$

with

$$d_1 = \frac{1}{v}\ln\frac{f_0}{K}+\frac{v}{2}$$

The solution for the caplet is thus

$$P_{caplet}(0,t,t+h) = h\,D(0,t+h)\left[f(0,t,t+h)N(d_1)-K\,N(d_2) \right]. \quad (A.88)$$

The floorlet can be derived in a similar fashion.

E.4 The Hull–White Model

The Hull–White model equation for the spot rate $r(t)$ is given by

$$dr(t) = \left[\theta(t)-a\,r(t)\right]dt + \sigma\,dz(t), \quad (A.89)$$

where a is the mean reversion parameter and σ the volatility. Applying the method of integrating factors to this equation we have

$$r(t) = r(0)e^{-at} + e^{-at}\int_0^t \theta(u)e^{au}\,du \ + \sigma\,e^{-at}\int_0^t e^{au}\,dz.$$

So the expectation of the spot rate $r(t)$ and the variance are given by

$$E[r(t)] = r(0)e^{-at} + e^{-at}\int_0^t \theta(u)e^{au}\,du, \quad Var[r(t)] = \frac{\sigma^2}{2a}\left[1 - e^{-2at}\right].$$

We can obtain an analytical form for $\theta(t)$

$$\begin{aligned}
\theta(t) &= \frac{\partial f(0,t)}{\partial t} + af(0,t) + \frac{\sigma^2}{2a}(1 - e^{-2at}) \\
&\sim \frac{\partial f(0,t)}{\partial t} + af(0,t).
\end{aligned} \tag{A.90}$$

This shows the spot rate drift is approximately

$$\frac{\partial f(0,t)}{\partial t} + a\big[f(0,t) - r\big].$$

and therefore mean reverts when moves away from the forward rate. In a similar manner to the Black–Scholes PDE it is possible to derive for the Hull–White model a PDE dependent on the variation of the spot rate

$$\frac{\partial V(r,t)}{\partial t} + \frac{1}{2}\sigma^2\frac{\partial^2 V(r,t)}{\partial r^2} + \big(\theta(t) - ar\big)\frac{\partial V(r,t)}{\partial r} - rV(r,t) = 0, \tag{A.91}$$

for which the solution for a discount bond at time t maturing at time T can be shown to be

$$D(r,t,T) = A(t,T)e^{-B(t,T)r(t)}. \tag{A.92}$$

Thus, the discount factor is stochastic and depends on the level of the spot rate. This form can be verified by direct substitution into Eq. (A.91). Here $B(t,T)$ is

$$B(t,T) = \frac{1-e^{-a(T-t)}}{a},$$

and $A(t,T)$ is given by

$$\ln A(t,T) = \ln \frac{D(0,T)}{D(0,t)} + B(t,T) f(0,t)$$

$$-\frac{1}{4a^3}\sigma^2(e^{-aT}-e^{-at})^2(e^{2at}-1).$$

From Eq. (A.92) we can see that although the spot value r follows a normal process the discount bond value has a lognormal process. A useful result that is used in the derivation of many closed forms is the stochastic value of a forward discount bond price at time t bought at a future time s and maturing at a later time T ($t < s \leq T$). This is given by

$$D(t,s,T) = \frac{D(0,t,T)}{D(0,t,s)} e^{-\frac{1}{2}v^2(t,s,T)-v(t,s,T)Z}, \qquad (A.93)$$

where $Z \sim \phi(0,1)$ and $v(t,T,s)$ is the volatility of the discount bond.

$$v^2(t,s,T) = \sigma^2 \left(\frac{1-e^{-a(T-s)}}{a}\right)^2 \left[\frac{1-e^{-2a(s-t)}}{2a}\right]. \qquad (A.94)$$

This result is useful in establishing the closed forms for caps/floors and swaptions.

E.5 The Hull–White Caplet

As shown previously a cap is a sum of caplets. Consider the caplet fixing at time t and paying at time $t+h$. Today at time $t = 0$ the present value is given by

$$P_{HW \atop caplet}(0,t,t+h)=E_0\left[e^{-\int_0^{t+h}r(u)du}Max\big(f(t,t,t+h)-K\big)\right]. \qquad (A.95)$$

Notice in contrast with Black's formula the discounting of the payoff is now stochastic. Rearranging we can write as the expectation from 0 to t (the fixing time) and from t to $t+h$ (when the payment is made). We can write

$$P_{HW \atop caplet}(0,t,t+h)=E_0\left[e^{-\int_0^t r(u)du}\big(f(t,t,t+h)-K\big)^+E_t\left[e^{-\int_t^{t+h}r(u)du}\right]\right]$$

$$=E_0\left[e^{-\int_0^t r(u)du}\right]E_0\left[\left(\frac{1}{D(t,t+h)}-(1+K)\right)^+D(t,t+h)\right]$$

$$=D(0,t)E_0\left[\big(1-(1+K)D(t,t,t+h)\big)\chi_{1>(1+K)D(t,t,t+h)}\right].$$

Substituting, using Eq. (A.93), with

$$D(t,t,t+h)=\frac{D(0,0,t+h)}{D(0,0,t)}e^{-\frac{1}{2}v^2(0,t,t+h)-v(0,t,t+h)Z},$$

we can show the simplified result for a caplet

$$P_{HW \atop caplet}(0,t,t+h)=D(0,t)\big[1-N(d^-)\big]-D(0,t+h)(1+K)\big[1-N(d^+)\big],$$

$$\qquad (A.96)$$

with

$$d^{\pm}=\frac{1}{v(0,t,t+h)}\ln\left[\frac{D(0,t+h)}{D(0,t)}(1+K)\right]\pm\frac{v(0,t,t+h)}{2}.$$

Similarly a floorlet is given by

$$P_{HW \atop floorlet}(0,t,t+h)=D(0,t+h)(1+K)N(d^+)-D(0,t)N(d^-).$$

E.6 Black's Model for European Swaptions

Consider the valuation of a *payers' swaption*. If exercised, the holder will enter at $t = T$ the forward swap value $V(T,T,T_M)$ if it has value by paying the fixed rate K and receiving the floating rate. The swaption is only exercised if the swap has positive payout so

$$
Max\left(V(T,T,T_M),0\right) = \left(\sum_{t_j > T}^{T_M} f(T,t_j,t_j+h)D(T,t_j)h - K\sum_{t_i > T}^{T_M} D(T,t_i)h,0\right)^+
$$

$$
= \left(R(T,T,T_M) - K\right)^+ \sum_{t_i > T}^{T_M} D(T,t_i)h,
$$

where we have assumed accrual periods h. Thus, on date T the swaption will be exercised if the swap rate on that date R lies above the strike K. The value of a European payers' swaption if exercised can be written as

$$
P_{BS \atop Swaption}(0,T,T_M) = E\left[D(0,T)\left(R(T,T,T_M) - K\right)^+ \sum_{t_t}^{T_M} D(T,t_i)h_i\right]
$$

$$
= E\left[\left(R(T,T,T_M) - K\right)^+\right] \sum_{t_t}^{T_M} D(0,t_i)h_i,
$$

Using the Black's swap model this reduces to

$$
P_{BS \atop Swaption}(0,T,T_M) = \left(R(0,T,T_M)N(d_1) - KN(d_2)\right)\sum_{t_t}^{T_M} D(0,t_i)h_i,
$$

$$(A.97)$$

with

$$
d_{1,2} = \frac{\ln\left[R(0,T,T_m)/K\right] \pm \sigma_R^2 T/2}{\sigma_R\sqrt{T}},
$$

and $R(0,T,T_M)$ is the forward starting swap rate.

E.7 Hull–White Swaptions

A fairly simple closed form pricing formula for swaptions can be obtained in the Hull–White model. Having a closed form solution is important since it allows for fast volatility calibration. Within the Hull–White model the swaption price is given as the expected payoff discounted using stochastic discount factor.

$$
\begin{aligned}
P_{HW\atop swaption}(0,T,T_M) &= E\left[D(0,T)\left(R(T,T,T_M)-K\right)^{+}\sum_{t_i>T}^{T_M}D(T,t_i)h_i \right] \\[2mm]
&= E\left[e^{-\int_0^T r\,du}\left(R(T,T,T_M)-K\right)^{+}\sum_{t_i>T}^{T_M}e^{-\int_T^{t_i} r\,du}h_i \right] \\[2mm]
&= D(0,T)E\left[\left(\begin{array}{c}(1-D(T,T_M)) \\[2mm] -K\sum_{t_i>T}^{T_M}D(T,t_i)h_i \end{array} \right)\chi_{R(T,T,T_M)>K} \right].
\end{aligned}
$$

Substituting for the volatilities of the discount bonds

$$
D(T,T_M) = \frac{D(0,T_M)}{D(0,T)}e^{-\frac{1}{2}v_M-v_M Z} = \lambda(T_M,Z),
$$

and

$$
D(T,t_i) = \frac{D(0,t_i)}{D(0,T)}e^{-\frac{1}{2}v_i-v_i Z} = \lambda(t_i,Z),
$$

where

$$
v_M = v(0,T,T_M), \qquad v_i = v(0,T,t_i).
$$

We can see that the option is exercised for $R(T,T,T_M)>K$ or

$$
1-D(T,T_M) > K\sum_{t_i>T}^{T_M}D(T,t_i)h_i.
$$

If we write the specific discount factors $D(T,T_M)=\lambda(T,Z)$ for exercise, then the boundary for exercise occurs for a particular value of $Z=Z*$ given by the solution to

$$\left[1-\lambda(T_M,Z*)\right] = K\sum_{t_i>T}^{T_M}\lambda(t_i,Z*)h_i. \qquad (A.98)$$

By integrating the payoff we can show that the swaption value is

$$P_{HW\,Swaption}\,(0,T,T_M) = D(0,T)N(-Z*) - D(0,T_M)N(-Z*-v_M)$$

$$- K\sum_{t_i>T}^{T_M}D(T,t_i)h_iN(-Z*-v_i).$$

$$(A.99)$$

Thus, to calculate the swaption price, we must first calculate the value $Z*$ for optimal exercise from Eq. (A.98) through a root finding process and then use Eq. (A.99) to find the price.

E.8 Hull–White Model Trinomial Trees

The Hull–White trinomial tree has been widely documented and here we shall merely detail the major features and certain important aspects of its implementation that are often neglected. It is equivalent to a PDE finite difference grid. The Hull–White model base equation in discrete form for a time period Δt is

$$\Delta r(t) = \left[\theta(t)-ar(t)\right]\Delta t + \sigma\,\Delta z(t).$$

To build a discrete lattice we follow the following recipe:

(a) Build a lattice for the spot rate

Initially ignore the interest rate term-structure and consider the simpler process $r*$

$$dr* = -a\,r*\,dt + \sigma\,dz.$$

For this process we build a tree with lattice nodes (i,j) with $i=(0,1,2,...,N)$ and $-i \le j \le i$ for variable $r*(i,j)$

$$r * (i, j) = j \; \Delta r, \qquad r * (0,0) = 0.$$

The horizontal time spacing between the nodes is $\Delta t = T/N$, where T is the longest maturity of the underlying instrument and the spacing $\Delta r = \sigma\sqrt{3\Delta t}$ to maximise convergence and minimise error. This builds a tree as shown in Fig. 6.10(b).

(b) Assign branching probabilities

To account for the drift term $-ar(t)$ different branching probabilities must be applied for movements forward in time through the lattice. Thus,

$$\begin{aligned}
\Pr((i, j) \rightarrow (i+1, j+1)) &= p_u \quad (up) \\
\Pr((i, j) \rightarrow (i+1, j)) &= p_m \quad (middle) \\
\Pr((i, j) \rightarrow (i+1, j-1)) &= p_d \quad (down).
\end{aligned}$$

The values for these three probabilities can be found by matching the expected drift and variance of $r*$ (the first and second moments)

$$\begin{aligned}
E[\Delta r *] &= p_u \Delta r - p_d \Delta r = - a \, j \, \Delta r \, \Delta t \\
E[\Delta r *^2] &= p_u \Delta r^2 - p_d \Delta r^2 = \sigma^2 \Delta t^2 + a^2 j^2 \Delta r^2 \Delta t^2.
\end{aligned}$$

With $p_u + p_m + p_d = 1$ and $\Delta r = \sigma\sqrt{3\Delta t}$ this gives as a solution

$$\begin{aligned}
p_u &= \frac{1}{6} + \frac{a^2 j^2 \Delta t^2 - aj\Delta t}{2} \\
p_m &= \frac{2}{3} - a^2 j^2 \Delta t^2 \qquad \text{(A.100)} \\
p_d &= \frac{1}{6} + \frac{a^2 j^2 \Delta t^2 + aj\Delta t}{2}.
\end{aligned}$$

(c) Include the interest rate term-structure

Up to now we have ignored the interest rate term-structure factor $\theta(t)$. We must displace the nodes $r*(i,j)$ on the tree so that the market term-structure is satisfied. This can be done for most purposes when the term-structure is well defined with an analytical formula for the displacement. The rate $r*(i,j)$ is displaced vertically by the factor $\alpha(i\Delta t)$ to give the market spot rate tree $r(i,j)$

$$r(i, j) = r*(i, j) + \alpha(i \Delta t).$$

The displacement factor is given analytically by

$$\alpha(t) = r(t) - r*(t)$$

$$= e^{-at}\left[r(0) + \int_0^t \theta(u)e^{-au}du \right] \qquad (A.101)$$

$$= f(0,t) + \frac{\sigma^2}{2a^2}\left(1-e^{-at}\right)^2,$$

where $f(0,t)$ is the instantaneous forward rate. This technique is sufficient when the zero curve is well defined, smooth and can be interpolated over the node times. An alternative numerical technique exists by fitting the displacement factor to the discount factors of known points of today's zero curve through a numerical "bootstrapping" technique.

(d) Implementation issues

1. Tree "pruning"
"Pruning" the tree to exclude low probability nodes can lead to increased computational efficiency. Typically, nodes that provide very high or very low rates are low probability events that can be excluded from the calculation without influencing the results of any valuation but we must take care to conserve probability adjacent to nodes that are excluded.

2. Valuation of fixed cash-flows and bonds

To value a bond or a leg of a swap on the tree we place the cash-flows (coupon and principal payments) on the on the tree at the correct times and then "roll-back" in time discounting the cash-flows using the spot rate r at each node. Thus for a bond paying a cash-flow $c(t_k)$ at time t_k we discount onto the closest node

$$c(i, j) = c(t_k)\, e^{-r(i,j)(t_k - i\Delta t)}, \quad if \ \ i\Delta t \le t_k < (i+1)\Delta t.$$

The value of the bond on each node is given by $V_{bond}(i,j)$ and is given by discounting back the expected value of the bond from nodes on the next time slice and including the relevant adjusted cash-flow $c(i,j)$ if one falls in the ith period.

$$V_{bond}(i, j) = \left[\begin{array}{c} V_{bond}(i+1, j+1)\, p_u + V_{bond}(i+1, j)\, p_m \\ + V_{bond}(i+1, j-1)\, p_d \end{array} \right] e^{-r(i,j)\Delta t}$$
$$+ c(i, j).$$

The present value of the bond today is given by $V_{bond}(0,0)$.

3. Valuation of American bond option

We can use the above valuation of fixed cash-flows to calculate an option to call (or put) a fixed rate bond at any time (American *bond option*). Calculating American options using a closed form solution is fairly intractable and a tree renders the problem very simple. Consider the case of an issuer call at strike K. The bond values $V_{bond}(i,j)$ at each node point are calculated and the option value at the option maturity date $T_{option} = M\Delta t$ calculated as

$$V_{option}(M, j) = V_{Intrinsic}(M, j) = Max[V_{bond}(M, j) - K, 0].$$

The value of the call option at earlier times is calculated by "rolling back" through the tree. At each node, the intrinsic value of the option is calculated along with the rolled-back value of the option from an earlier time slice. At any tree node if the intrinsic value is higher than the expected future value of the option, represented by the rolled-back value the option will rationally be exercised. Thus, the option value is

$$V_{option}(i,j) = Max \left\{ \left[\begin{array}{c} V_{option}(i+1,j+1)\, p_u \\ +V_{option}(i+1,j)\, p_m \\ +V_{option}(i+1,j-1)\, p_d \end{array} \right] e^{-r(i,j)\Delta t} \\ , V_{Intrinsic}(i,j) \right\},$$

where

$$V_{Intrinsic}(i,j) = Max(V_{bond}(i,j) - K, 0).$$

The final option value is given by $V_{option}(0,0)$.

4. Use of closed forms on the tree

Continuously compounded spot rates $r(t)$ are used in the Hull–White closed forms. The tree we have constructed actually uses Δt period spot rates which are slightly different. To be exact on each node we must correct to the continuously compounded spot rates r_{spot} using the equations $A(t,T)$ and $B(t,T)$ from Eq. (A.92) the spot values on the tree r_{tree}.

$$r_{spot}(i,j) = \frac{r_{tree}(i,j)\Delta t + \ln\left[A(i\Delta t,(i+1)\Delta t)\right]}{B(i\Delta t,(i+1)\Delta t)}. \qquad (A.102)$$

Once we have the true continuously compounded rates at each node we can take advantage all the Hull–White closed forms to make things easier. For example, the T maturity discount factor can be calculated at each node using Eq. (A.92). This can be further used to calculate the forward rate at a given node.

5. Valuation of swaps

We can value swaps by rolling-back from the terminal node and including either the fixed rate coupon or the floating rate coupon if they fall within the current time slice

$$V_{swap}(i,j) = \left[\begin{array}{c} V_{swap}(i+1,j+1)\,p_u + V_{swap}(i+1,j)\,p_m \\ + V_{swap}(i+1,j-1)\,p_d \end{array} \right] e^{-r(i,j)\Delta t}$$
$$+ c_{fixed}(i,j) + c_{float}(i,j),$$

with the fixed rate paid at time t_k as

$$c_{fixed}(i,j) = c(t_k)\, e^{-r(i,j)(t_k - i\Delta t)} \qquad i\Delta t \le t_k < (i+1)\Delta t,$$

and floating rate fixing at time t_l

$$c_{float}(i,j) = h_l\, f(t_l, t_l + h_l)\, e^{-r(i,j)(t_l + h_l - i\Delta t)} \quad i\Delta t \le t_l + h_l < (i+1)\Delta t.$$

Another alternative method is to simply calculate the value of the closed form for the swap at each node directly. At each node we can use the closed form to calculate all the forward rates and discount factors required to calculate the swap value at each node without a roll-back.

6. Calculation of American swaptions

Swaptions with American and Bermudan features have been very popular over the last few years. In particular, swaps which pay a high fixed rate coupon but are callable or cancellable at any time after a fixed time period for example 5 years. As with the bond option, the value of the call feature can be calculated by rolling-back from the final option exercise date and calculating whether exercise into the swap is optimal on each possible exercise date.

$$V_{option}(i,j) = Max \left\{ \begin{array}{c} \left[\begin{array}{c} V_{option}(i+1,j+1)\,p_u + V_{option}(i+1,j)\,p_m \\ + V_{option}(i+1,j-1)\,p_d \end{array} \right] e^{-r(i,j)\Delta t}, \\ Max[V_{swap}(i,j) - K, 0] \end{array} \right\}.$$

E.9 The Heath, Jarrow and Morton Model

The Heath, Jarrow and Morton model (HJM) provides a general framework for a range of non-arbitrage yield curve models. If we assume zero coupon bonds (or discount factors) $P(t,T)$ are lognormal then

$$dP(t,T) = r(t)P(t,T)dt + \upsilon(t,T)P(t,T)dz(t),$$

where $\upsilon(t,T)$ is the discount bond volatility. The continuous definition of the forward rate is Eq. (A.5).

$$f(t,T_1,T_2) = \frac{\ln[P(t,T_1)] - \ln[P(t,T_2)]}{T_2 - T_1}.$$

Applying Ito's lemma to the bond process gives

$$d\ln[P(t,T_1)] = [r(t) - \upsilon(t,T_1)^2/2]dt + \upsilon(t,T_1)dz(t)$$
$$d\ln[P(t,T_1)] = [r(t) - \upsilon(t,T_2)^2/2]dt + \upsilon(t,T_2)dz(t).$$

Substituting into the forward rate definition gives

$$df(t,T_1,T_2) = \frac{[\upsilon(t,T_2)^2 - \upsilon(t,T_1)^2]}{2(T_2 - T_1)}dt + \frac{[\upsilon(t,T_1) - \upsilon(t,T_2)]}{(T_2 - T_1)}dz(t).$$

This very general result shows that the forward rate process is completely dependent on the volatilities of the discount factors. As we take limits, so as $T_2 \rightarrow T_1$ we have the continuous time result and can replace $f(t,T_1,T_2)$ with $f(t,T)$ the instantaneous forward rate

$$\underset{T_2 \rightarrow T_1}{Lim} \frac{[\upsilon(t,T_2)^2 - \upsilon(t,T_1)^2]}{2(T_2 - T_1)} = \frac{1}{2}\frac{\partial \upsilon(t,T)^2}{\partial T} = \upsilon(t,T)\upsilon_T(t,T),$$

where $\upsilon_T(t,T)$ is the partial derivative with respect to T.

$$df(t,T) = \upsilon(t,T)\upsilon_T(t,T)dt + \upsilon_T(t,T)dz(t).$$

Integrating the partial derivatives we can write

$$v(t,T) = \int_t^T v_s(t,s)ds.$$

The final HJM result is then

$$df(t,T) = m(t,T)dt + \sigma(t,T)dz(t), \qquad (A.103)$$

with the drift $m(t,T)$ completely specified by the forward rate volatility $\sigma(t,T)$

$$m(t,T) = \sigma(t,T) \int_t^T \sigma(t,s)ds.$$

This can be extended to N stochastic factors

$$df(t,T) = m(t,T)dt + \sum_k^N \sigma_k(t,T)dz_k(t),$$

with

$$m(t,T) = \sum_k^N \sigma_k(t,T) \int_t^T \sigma_k(t,s)\,ds.$$

The main problem with the HJM model is that, in general, paths are non-Markov and hence non-recombining so it cannot be used in a recombining tree and Monte Carlo simulation is the only real practical valuation method. Generally, it is best to assume a particular simple exponential functional form for $\sigma(t,T)$ so the drift term $m(t,T)$ is a closed form analytical expression.

E.10 The LIBOR Market Model

The *LIBOR market model* (LMM) avoids the problem of instantaneous forward rates $f(t,T)$ of the HJM model and builds a model in terms of the h period forward rates $f(t,T,T+h)$ actually traded in the market (say, $h = 3$ months). If the kth forward rate is given by

$$f_k = f(t, t_k, t_k + h) = f(t, t_k, t_{k+1}),$$

then in the world that is *forward risk neutral* with respect to the zero coupon bond $P(t, t_{k+1})$ maturing at t_{k+1} we assume the lognormal process

$$df_k(t) = f_k(t)\sigma_k(t)dz(t). \qquad (A.104)$$

If the index for the next LIBOR fixing date is $m(t)$ such that $t \le t_{m(t)}$ we have in the "rolling forward risk neutral world" with respect to $P(t, t_{m(t)})$ an effective drift term included

$$df_k(t) = \sigma_k(t)[V_{m(t)}(t) - V_{k+1}(t)]f_k(t)dt + \sigma_k(t)f_k(t)dz(t).$$

Here $v_k(t)$ is the volatility of $P(t, t_k)$. The forward rate is defined as Eq. (A.4)

$$\frac{P(t, t_i)}{P(t, t_{i+1})} = 1 + hf_k(t),$$

which, using Ito's lemma, we can relate the volatility of the discount factors and the forward rates to give

$$v_i(t) - v_{i+1}(t) = \frac{hf_i(t)\sigma_i(t)}{1 + hf_i(t)}.$$

Substituting these bond volatilities we arrive at

$$\frac{df_k(t)}{f_k(t)} = \sum_{i=m(t)}^{k} \frac{hf_i(t)\sigma_i(t)\sigma_k(t)}{1 + hf_i(t)}dt + \sigma_k(t)dz(t). \qquad (A.105)$$

Thus, the model is lognormal in the forward rate and superficially very similar to Black's model, except for the complex drift term. The model can be implemented using a Monte Carlo simulation and with a few approximations closed forms for caps, floors and swaptions can be produced. The volatility parameters for the forward rates can be calibrated from market data for vanilla caps and swaptions. In addition, as with HJM model, extension to two or three stochastic factors is possible. Also, it is possible to implement a SABR model version of the LMM with stochastic volatility to allow better fitting of volatility smiles.

Interest Rate Products

F.1 Capped/Floored Notes

The capped note pays a floating coupon of $f(t,t,t+h)$ plus a fixed spread q. If the market floating rate (LIBOR) rises the total coupon cannot exceed the cap level K. We can write this as two terms: (i) where the coupon is less than, or equal to K and (ii) where capped at K

$$P_{capped \atop FRN} = E\left[\sum_{i=1}^{N} D(0,t_i+h)\begin{cases}\left(f(t_i,t_i,t_i+h)+q\right)\chi_{f(t_i,t_i,t_i+h)+q\leq K} \\ +K\chi_{f(t_i,t_i,t_i+h)+q>K}\end{cases} + D(0,T)\right]$$

$$=\sum_{i=1}^{N} D(0,t_i+h)\left(f(0,t_i,t_i+h)+q\right) - P_{cap}(0,\underline{t},h,K-q) + D(0,T).$$

The value of the capped FRN is thus just a FRN minus a cap with strike $(K-q)$. Here we have written $\underline{t}$ to denote all the series of payment dates t_i for the cap. The issuer swap with a funding leg at LIBOR + x bp per annum, if we assume the same periodicity on both legs, is

$$V(0,T) = \sum_{i=1}^{N} D(0,t_i+h)\left(x-q\right) + P_{Cap}(0,\underline{t},h,K-q). \quad (A.106)$$

The cap can be evaluated using a closed form under Black's model or the Hull–White model described in Chapter 6.

F.2 Reverse Floating Rate Note

A reverse floating rate note or *inverse floater* pays a floating coupon that increases as interest rates decrease (and vice versa). For a reverse FRN paying a fixed coupon C minus the floating rate we can model as

$$
P_{\substack{reverse \\ FRN}} = E\left[\sum_{i=1}^{N} h D(0,t_i+h)\big(C - f(t_i,t_i,t_i+h)\big)\chi_{f(t_i,t_i,t_i+h)<C} + D(0,T) \right]
$$

$$
= P_{floor}(0,\underline{t},h,C) + D(0,T).
$$
(A.107)

Thus, a reverse FRN is simply a deeply in-the-money floor plus principal payment.

F.3 Digital Barrier Note

For a barrier note where an enhanced coupon is paid provided the interest rate fixing lies below the barrier level K at each rate fixing until maturity. This can be written as

$$
P_{\substack{barrier \\ note}} = E\left[\sum_{i=1}^{N} D(0,t_i+h)\big(f(t_i,t_i,t_i+h)+q\big)\chi_{f(t_i,t_i,t_i+h)<K} + D(0,T) \right]
$$

$$
= \sum_{i=1}^{N} D(0,t_i+h)\big(f(0,t_i,t_i+h)+q\big)+D(0,T)
$$

$$
- P_{cap}(0,\underline{t},h,K) - P_{\substack{digital \\ cap}}(0,\underline{t},h,B,K).
$$
(A.108)

The structure can be decomposed as: (i) buying an FRN paying a spread q, (ii) selling a cap strike K and (iii) selling a *digital cap* strike K with payout $B = q+K$. The digital cap can be priced using a closed form with an abrupt barrier, although applying an option spread as with equity options is more practical for hedging purposes.

F.4 Minimum Payoff Range Note

The minimum payoff range note where floating rate coupon $(f(t_i,t_i,t_i+h)+q)$ is paid if the LIBOR rate fixes in the range L to U and otherwise pays a fixed coupon a coupon C can be written as

$$P_{\substack{Range\\Note}} = E\left[\sum_{i=1}^{N} D(0,t_i+h)\left\{\begin{array}{l}(f(t_i,t_i,t_i+h)+q)\chi_{L<f(t_i,t_i,t_i+h)<U}\\+C\chi_{f(t_i,t_i,t_i+h)>U}+C\chi_{L>f(t_i,t_i,t_i+h)}\end{array}\right\}+D(0,T)\right]$$

$$=\sum_{i=1}^{N} D(0,t_i+h)\big(f(0,t_i,t_i+h)+q\big)-P_{cap}(0,\underline{t},h,U)+P_{floor}(0,\underline{t},h,L)$$

$$+P_{\substack{digital\\cap}}(0,\underline{t},h,B_1,U)+P_{\substack{digital\\floor}}(0,\underline{t},h,B_2,L)+D(0,T),$$

(A.109)

where $B_1= C-U-q$ and $B_2= C-L-q$. Closed forms can be used for the digital cap and floor.

F.5 Digital Caps and Floors

A *digital caplet* is given by the expectation

$$P_{\substack{digital\\caplet}}=E[B\,D(0,t)\chi_{f(t,t,t+h)>K}].$$

Similarly, the digital floorlet pays at time t if the forward sets at time t below the strike K. These can be evaluated using the Hull–White model to give the closed forms

$$P_{\substack{digital\\caplet}}=B\,D(0,t)\big[1-N(d^-)\big]$$ (A.110)

$$P_{\substack{digital\\floorlet}}=B\,D(0,t)N(d^-),$$

where

$$d^\pm=\frac{1}{v(0,t,t+h)}\ln\left[\frac{D(0,t+h)}{D(0,t)}(1+K)\right]\pm\frac{v(0,t,t+h)}{2},$$

using the Hull–White volatility function Eq. (A.94)

$$v^2(t,s,T) = \sigma^2 \left(\frac{1-e^{-a(T-s)}}{a} \right) \left(\frac{1-e^{-2a(s-t)}}{2a} \right).$$

F.6 Digital Accrual Note

If the coupon is defined as a fraction $C \times$ (Number of days below strike)/ (Number of days in year) then we can price as a series of daily digital floorlets. If we approximate using a continuous form we have an integral equation

$$P_{\substack{digital \\ accrual \\ note}} = E \left[\sum_{i=1}^{N} D(0,t_i+h) \left\{ \int_{t_i}^{t_i+h} \frac{C}{h} \chi_{f(s,s,s+h)<K} \, ds \right\} + D(0,T) \right].$$

We can write each individual *notelet* paying at t_i+h as

$$P_{\substack{digital \\ accrual \\ notelet}} = E \left[e^{-\int_0^{t_i+h} r \, du} \int_{t_i}^{t_i+h} \frac{C}{h} \chi_{f(s,s,s+h)<K} \, ds \right].$$

This continuous form can be solved using the Hull–White model to give a closed form solution

$$P_{\substack{digital \\ accrual \\ notelet}} = D(0,t_i+h) \frac{C}{h} \int_{t_i}^{t_i+h} N(\psi_1) \, ds, \qquad (A.111)$$

with

$$\psi_1 = \frac{\left\{ \ln\left[\dfrac{D(0,s+h)(1+K)}{D(0,s)} \right] + [v_4 - v_5][v_3 - v_5/2 + v_4] + v_2[v_1 - v_2/2] \right\}}{\sqrt{v_2^2 + [v_4 - v_5]^2}},$$

and volatility functions

$$v_1 = v(t_i,s,t_i+h) \quad v_2 = v(t_i,s,s+h) \quad v_3 = v(0,t_i,t_i+h)$$
$$v_4 = v(0,t_i,s+h) \quad v_5 = v(0,t_i,s).$$

F.7 Barrier Accrual Floating Rate Note

Similar to the fixed rate barrier accrual notes but instead a floating rate (fixed at the beginning of the period) plus spread q accrues if the daily fixing of LIBOR is below the barrier. Approximating the daily fixing with a continuous fixing for each notelet this gives

$$
P_{\substack{barrier \\ accrual \\ floater}} = E\left[e^{-\int_0^{t_i+h} r\, du} \int_{t_i}^{t_i+h} \frac{\left(f\left(s,s,s+h\right)+q \right)}{h} \chi_{f(s,s,s+h)<K}\, ds \right].
$$

This has the following closed form for a notelet under the Hull–White model.

$$
P_{\substack{barrier \\ accrual \\ floater}} = D(0,t_i) \int_{t_i}^{t_i+h} N(\psi_2)\, ds - \frac{(1-q)}{h} D(0,t_i+h) \int_{t_i}^{t_i+h} N(\psi_1)\, ds, \qquad (A.112)
$$

where ψ_1 is given as above and ψ_2 is

$$
\psi_2 = \left\{ \frac{\ln\left[\dfrac{D(0,s+h)(1+K)}{D(0,s)} \right] + v_5^2/2 - v_4^2\left[v_1 v_2 - v_2/2 \right]/2}{\sqrt{v_2^2 + \left[v_4 - v_5 \right]^2}} \right\}.
$$

F.8 Minimum Payoff Range Accrual Notes

A variant on the above two structures is one which pays a floating rate accrual coupon within a specified range and smaller fixed coupon when it lies outside the range.

$$
P_{\substack{range \\ accrual \\ floater}} = E\left[\sum_{i=1}^{N} D(0,t_i+h) \left\{ \int_{t_i}^{t_i+h} \left\{ \frac{\left(f\left(t_i,t_i,t_i+h\right)+q \right)}{h} \chi_{L<f(s,s,s+h)<U} + \frac{C}{h}\left(\chi_{f(s,s,s+h)<L} + \chi_{U<f(s,s,s+h)} \right) \right\} ds \right\} + D(0,T) \right].
$$

This can be priced using the same principles as the previous couple of examples.

F.9 Chooser Notes

To value such options we assume that investor is rational and will set the range to optimise his expected payout at the start of each period. This requires us to calculate the expected payout and maximise with respect to where the barrier is placed. This requires a calculation for each ith period, which involves a differential of the expected payout to determine the strike K_i of the form

$$\frac{\partial}{\partial K_i} E\left[D(0,t_i+h)h\left\{ \left(f\left(t_i,t_i,t_i+h\right)+q\right) \int_{t_i}^{t_i+h} \chi_{K_i<f(s,s,s+h)<K_i+U} ds \right\} \right].$$

This provides a solution for the *chooser accrual notelets* of the form

$$P_{\substack{chooser \\ accrual \\ notelet}} = D(0,t_i) \int_{-\infty}^{\infty} \int_{t_i}^{t_i+h} \left[N(d_2(K^*(Z),s)) - N(d_1(K^*(Z),s)) \right] ds \frac{e^{-Z^2/2}}{\sqrt{2\pi}} dZ$$

$$- D(0,t_i+h)(1-hq) \int_{-\infty}^{\infty} \int_{t_i}^{t_i+h} \left[N(d_2(K^*(Z-v_3),s)) - N(d_1(K^*(Z-v_3),s)) \right] ds \frac{e^{-Z^2/2}}{\sqrt{2\pi}} dZ,$$

$$(A.113)$$

with

$$d_1(K(Z),s) = \frac{1}{v_2} \ln\left[\frac{D(0,s+h)(1+Kh)}{D(0,t)} \right] - \frac{(v_4^2-v_5^2)}{2v_2} - v_2/2 + v_1 - \frac{v_4-v_5}{v_2} Z$$

$$d_2(K(Z),s) = \frac{1}{v2} \ln\left[\frac{D(0,s+h)(1+h(K+U))}{D(0,t)} \right] - \frac{(v_4^2-v_5^2)}{2v2} - v2/2 + v_1 - \frac{(v_4-v_5)}{v_2} Z,$$

and K^*, the optimised barrier level, is the solution for a particular Z to

$$\int_{t_i}^{t_i+h} \frac{1}{v_1} \left[\frac{e^{-d_2^2(K(Z),s)/2}}{1+h(K(Z)+U)} - \frac{e^{-d_1^2(K(Z),s)/2}}{1+hK(Z)} \right] ds = 0.$$

Appendix G

Pricing Credit Derivatives

G.1 Par Asset Swap

In a *par asset swap* the buyer purchases a fixed rate bond at an effective price of par (100%) and swaps it into a floating rate coupon. Importantly the market price of the underlying bond is probably not exactly par. Thus the *asset swap buyer* pays 100% and receives a bond plus a swap contract. Under the swap the buyer pays a fixed coupon c (plus principal) and receives a floating rate LIBOR plus spread s_{Par} from the *seller*. The value of the swap transaction for the buyer is

$$
V_{\substack{par \\ ASW}}(0,T) = (P_{bond}(0,T) - 100\%) - c\sum_{j=1}^{M} D(0,t_j)l_j
$$
$$
+ \sum_{i=1}^{N} D(0,t_i)\big[f(0,t_i,t_i+h_i) + s_{Par}(0,T)\big]h_i
$$

(A.114)

where $P_{bond}(0,T)$ is the market bond price for a bond of maturity T. Here the floating leg payments are received on dates t_i ($i=1,2,\ldots,N$) with daycount h_i and the fixed leg bond payments are made on dates t_j ($j=1,2,\ldots,M$) with daycount factor l_j. To balance the swap $V(0,T)=0$ and $s_{Par}(0,T)$ is the *par asset swap level* and we can rearrange to give

$$
s_{Par}(0,T) = \frac{D(0,T) - P_{bond}(0,T) + c\sum_{j=1}^{M} D(0,t_j)l_j}{\sum_{i=1}^{N} D(0,t_i)h_i}.
$$

(A.115)

G.2 Market Value Asset Swap

In a *market value asset swap* the value of the asset swap package is equal to the market bond price $P_{bond}(0,T)$. Thus the buyer pays the bond price $P_{bond}(0,T)$, receives the bond and pays the coupon c and principal to the seller. The seller pays floating rate LIBOR plus asset swap spread s_{Mar} on $P_{bond}(0,T)$ notional and makes a principal payment of $P_{bond}(0,T)$ at maturity. The value of the overall swap package is given by

$$
\begin{aligned}
V_{Market \atop ASW}(0,T) = P_{bond}(0,T)&\left\{ 1 + \sum_{i=1}^{N} D(0,t_i)\, s_{Mar}(0,T)\, h_i \right\} \\
&-\left\{ c\sum_{j=1}^{M} D(0,t_j)\, l_j + D(0,T) \right\}.
\end{aligned} \tag{A.116}
$$

For most circumstances where the bond price is close to 100% the par and market asset swap spreads are virtually identical. Notice also that the actual asset swap spread in both cases depends slightly on the coupon of the bond.

G.3 Z-Spread

In recent years *Z-spread* is more commonly used as a measure of the credit spread. It is equal to the flat spread over the zero curve used to reproduce the market price of a bond. Thus, for a bond with annual coupon C for annualised spread Z-spread s_Z we have

$$
P_{bond}(0,T) = \sum_{i}^{N} \frac{Ch_i}{\left(1+z(0,t_i)+s_Z\right)^{t_i}} + \frac{1}{\left(1+z(0,T)+s_Z\right)^{T}}. \tag{A.117}
$$

G.4 Stochastic Firm Value Models

G.4.1 *Simple maturity default model*

A default occurs when the *firm value* $A(t)$ (or *enterprise value*) falls below the value of the company's debt B at maturity T so $A(T) < B$. The debt can be considered as zero coupon so no default can occur prior to T. In the simplest case the company firm value can be modelled by the process

$$\frac{dA(t)}{A(t)} = \mu_A dt + \sigma_A \, dz. \tag{A.118}$$

The probability of default at time T using Black–Scholes formulation is

$$\Pr(A(T) < B) = \Pr\left(\left(\mu_A - \sigma_A^2 / 2\right)T + \sigma_A Z(T) < \ln\frac{B}{A(0)} \right),$$

which gives

$$\Pr(A(T) < B) = N\left(\frac{\ln(B/A(0)) - \left(\mu_A - \sigma_A^2 / 2\right)T}{\sigma_A \sqrt{T}} \right).$$

We can consider the leverage ratio to be $L = B/A(0)$ and at maturity the value of the debt is given by

$$Min(A(T), B) = B - Max(B - A(T), 0)$$

which is equivalent to long a bond of value B and short a put on the company value $A(t)$. The equity value $E(T)$ is given by a call on the firm value with strike B.

$$E(T) = Max(A(T) - B, 0).$$

The initial bond value is given by

$$B(0,T) = D(0,T)\left(e^{\mu T} A(0)N(-d_1) + BN(d_2) \right),$$

and the equity value

$$E(0,T) = D(0,T)\left(e^{\mu T} A(0)N(d_1) - BN(d_2) \right),$$

with

$$d_1 = \frac{\ln(A(0)/B) + \left(\mu_A + \sigma_A^2/2\right)T}{\sigma_A \sqrt{T}} \qquad d_2 = d_1 - \sigma_A \sqrt{T}.$$

The effective credit spread s is

$$s(0,T) = -\frac{1}{T}\ln\left(\frac{B(0,T)}{D(0,T)B}\right)$$

$$= -\frac{1}{T}\ln\left(\frac{e^{\mu T}A(0)N(-d_1)}{B} + N(d_2)\right).$$

(A.119)

The above model can be extended so that potential default occurs when the firm value $A(t)$ falls below a barrier at any time before the maturity date T. This is called the *first passage* or barrier model.

G.4.2 *CreditGrades model*

JP Morgan published a variant of the above model in 2002 for credit risk analysis which was widely adapted for capital structure and market spread analysis by many market participants. It was clearly demonstrated that such models are often a leading indicator of ratings changes, credit deterioration and default. The major shortcoming of the previous models is that default is represented by a diffusion process so cannot model well the level of short term spreads – predicted short term default rates are too low. There cannot be a sudden default of a company in a diffusion based model. The CreditGrades model addresses this problem by assuming the recovery rate $R(t)$ follows a lognormal distribution with mean R^* and percentage standard deviation λ. With an uncertain recovery rate the default barrier can be unexpectedly hit even for short maturities. The diffusion process for the firm value follows Eq. (A.118) but with zero drift. The default in the model is given by a first time hitting of the barrier given by $R(t)D_S$ where D_S is defined as debt per share. The survival probability is then

$$L(0,T) = N\left(-\frac{\hat{\sigma}(t)}{2} + \frac{\ln(d)}{\hat{\sigma}(t)}\right) - d\,N\left(-\frac{\hat{\sigma}(t)}{2} - \frac{\ln(d)}{\hat{\sigma}(t)}\right),$$

where

$$d = \frac{S(0)+R^*D_S}{R^*D_S}e^{\lambda^2} \qquad\qquad \hat{\sigma}(t)^2 = \sigma_A^2 t + \lambda^2.$$

Assuming that the equity volatility and the firm value volatility are related by

$$\sigma_S = \sigma_A \frac{A}{S}\frac{\partial S}{\partial A}.$$

We can estimate the asset volatility from the equity volatility

$$\sigma_A = \sigma_S \frac{S}{S+R^*D_S}. \qquad (A.120)$$

G.5 The Reduced Form Model and Poisson Default Processes

For a Poisson default process the probability of default in time t to $t+dt$ (given no default has already occurred) is given by $\lambda(t)dt$. $\lambda(t)$ is known as the hazard rate or default intensity so considering this conditional probability we have

$$\Pr\left[t < \tau \le t+dt | \tau > t\right] = \lambda(t)dt,$$

where τ is the actual time of default. From the definition of the Poisson distribution the survival probability $L(0,t)$ or the probability of no default occurring between 0 and time t is given by

$$L(0,t) = \Pr\left[\tau > t\right] = e^{-\int_0^t \lambda(u)du}. \qquad (A.121)$$

The probability of a default occurring between time t and dt is thus given by the default probability density

$$\Pr\left[t < \tau \le t+dt\right] = \lambda(t)e^{-\int_0^t \lambda(u)du}\,dt = L(0,t)\lambda(t)dt.$$

G.6 Pricing Credit Default Swaps (CDS)

Using the *reduced form model* outlined above a valuation formula for a typical vanilla CDS can be derived. A *par recovery* framework is assumed where the bondholder on default is owed an amount equal to par plus accrued interest.

A CDS can be considered as (i) a premium flow, typically paid quarterly, that terminates on a credit event and (ii) a payment of (100%–recovery rate) on a credit event. In Section 8.10 we detailed a simplified calculation where default occurs on coupon dates. If we instead consider a continuous time calculation, we can value the CDS of maturity T as the expectation of the value of the premium flows, which terminate at default time τ if $\tau < T$, minus the credit event payment which only occurs if default occurs before maturity so time $\tau < T$. The CDS value is given by the expectation

$$V_{CDS}(0,T) = E\left[q \int_0^T D(0,u)\, \chi_{\tau > u} du \right]$$

$$- E\left[\int_0^T (1 - R(u))D(0,u)\, \chi_{\tau = u} du \right].$$

If the recovery rate $R(u) = R$ is a constant we can simplify assuming that the default intensity and interest rates are non-stochastic. The effect of introducing these as stochastic processes can be shown to be very small. Also including correlation between rates and default intensity has negligible effect for reasonable correlation levels. This gives

$$V_{CDS}(0,T) = q \int_0^T D(0,u)\, L(0,u) du$$

$$\qquad\qquad (A.122)$$

$$- \int_0^T (1 - R)D(0,u)\, \lambda(u) L(0,u) du.$$

This can easily be solved numerically but a quick closed form can be derived for $r(t) = r = $ constant and $\lambda(t) = \lambda = $ constant.

$$V_{CDS}(0,T) = \frac{(1-e^{-(r+\lambda)T})}{(r+\lambda)}\{q-\lambda(1-R)\}. \qquad (A.123)$$

Now for a market value CDS the swap value $V_{CDS}(0,T)=0$ and thus the fair value premium is

$$q(0,T) = q = \lambda(1-R). \qquad (A.124)$$

In reality, premium payment are made on a discrete (semiannual or quarterly) basis and the continuous time equations must be slightly modified. On a credit event all accrued premium is normally paid, so

$$V_{CDS}(0,T) = q \sum_{i=1}^{N} D(0,t_i)\, L(0,t_i) h_i$$

$$+ q \sum_{i=1}^{N} \int_{t_{i-1}}^{t_i} \left(\frac{u-t_{i-1}}{t_i - t_{i-1}}\right) D(0,u)\, \lambda(u) L(0,u) du$$

$$- \int_{0}^{T} (1-R(u)) D(0,u)\, \lambda(u)\, L(0,u) du.$$

Here, premium payments are made on dates t_i $(i=1,...,N)$ with accrual period h_i.

G.7 Building a Simple Hazard Rate Curve

Building a default intensity curve requires a "bootstrapping" technique similar to that used in constructing a zero curve. Usually, a single recovery rate assumption R is made for all maturities and the default intensity curve is built starting with the shortest maturities. Thus if $q(0,T_1)$ is the shortest maturity CDS premium and $q(0,T_2)$ is the next higher maturity CDS premium $(T_1 < T_2)$ we can solve first to find $\lambda(T_1)$ and then $\lambda(T_2)$ and so on until a curve is built. Illustrating, using the continuous time equations and building a flat hazard rate curve for simplicity, we have for the first CDS

$$V_{CDS}(0,T_1) = q(0,T_1) \int_0^{T_1} D(0,u)e^{-\lambda(T_1)u}du$$

$$-(1-R)\int_0^{T_1} D(0,u)\lambda(T_1)e^{-\lambda(T_1)u}du = 0.$$

This provides $\lambda(T_1)$ given $q(0,T_1)$. The next CDS has maturity T_2 and

$$V(0,T_2) = q(0,T_2) \left\{ \begin{array}{l} \int_0^{T_1} D(0,u)e^{-\lambda(T_1)u}du \\[2ex] + \int_{T_1}^{T_2} D(0,u)e^{-\lambda(T_1)T_1 - \lambda(T_2)(u-T_1)}du \end{array} \right\}$$

$$- \left\{ \begin{array}{l} (1-R)\int_0^{T_1} D(0,u)\lambda(T_1)e^{-\lambda(T_1)u}du \\[2ex] + \int_{T_1}^{T_2} D(0,u)\lambda(T_2)e^{-\lambda(T_1)T_1 - \lambda(T_2)(u-T_1)}du \end{array} \right\} = 0,$$

so we can "bootstrap" to find $\lambda(T_2)$.

G.8 Modelling "Risky" Bonds

Bonds subject to credit risk or "risky" bonds can be priced in a similar manner to CDS. However, several important effects must be considered. Technically on a default a bond holder is owed par (100%) plus accrued interest by the issuer. Also bonds trade at a basis (positive or negative) to CDS, so to allow both cash and CDS to be priced consistently, the basis effect can be accommodated by the use of a *market financing* or *effective repo* curve $m(0,t)$ and a corresponding financing discount factor $M(0,t)$. Under most circumstances the value of $m(0,t)$ is small 25 to -25 bp and $M(0,t)$ is close to unity. Under continuous time we can thus value a credit risky bond paying a coupon c as

$$P_{\substack{risky \\ bond}}(0,T) = E\left[\begin{array}{l} c\int_0^T D(0,u)\,M(0,u)\,\chi_{\tau>u}du \\ \\ + D(0,T)\,M(0,T)\chi_{\tau>T} + R\int_0^T D(0,u)\,M(0,u)\,\chi_{\tau=u}du \end{array}\right].$$

Here the first term represents the coupon, the second term the principal if no default occurs and the third term the recovery rate if a default occurs. We ignore any effective recovery on the coupons. Including the effect of discrete coupons c paid at times t_i with accrual factors h_i we have

$$P_{\substack{risky \\ bond}}(0,T) = c\sum_i^N h_i\, D(0,t_i)\,L(0,t_i)M(0,t_i)$$

$$+ Rc\sum_i^N \int_{t_{i-1}}^{t_i}\frac{u-t_{i-1}}{h_i}\,D(0,u)\,M(0,u)\,\lambda(u)\,L(0,u)\,du \quad \text{(A.125)}$$

$$+ D(0,T)\,M(0,T)\,L(0,T)$$

$$+ R\int_0^T D(0,u)\,M(0,u)\,\lambda(u)\,L(0,u)\,du.$$

It could be argued that since an average recovery rate is fixed by the market for CDS cash settlement for all issues then for consistency with CDS we should ignore the coupon effect and assume an "average" accrued coupon is included in the average determined recovery rate.

G.9 Digital CDS

The digital CDS can be modelled as a CDS with zero recovery.

$$V_{\substack{digital \\ CDS}}(0,T) = q_{\substack{dig \\ CDS}}\int_0^T D(0,u)\,L(0,u)du$$

$$-\int_0^T D(0,u)\,\lambda(u)\,L(0,u)du,$$

where for flat interest rates r and hazard rates λ the market value digital CDS premium is given by

$$q_{\substack{dig \\ CDS}} = \lambda = \frac{q_{CDS}}{(1-R)}. \quad \text{(A.126)}$$

G.10 Correlated Credit Default Swap

Consider the correlated default swap. One way of calculating the effect of correlation is by considering the *joint survival probability* for the reference entity (credit 1) and the protection provider (credit 2).

$$L_J(0,T) = \Pr[\tau_1 > T, \tau_2 > T] = E\left[\chi_{\tau_1 > T, \tau_2 > T}\right].$$

The probability both names default together is given by the joint default distribution

$$\begin{aligned} Q_J(0,T)\,dt &= \Pr[T < \tau_1 \leq T + dt, T < \tau_2 \leq T + dt] \\ &= E\left[\chi_{T < \tau_1 \leq T + dt, T < \tau_2 \leq T + dt}\,dt\right]. \end{aligned}$$

The value of the correlated CDS can be written as

$$\begin{aligned} V_{\substack{correlated \\ CDS}}(0,T) = &\ q \int_0^T D(0,u)\ L_J(0,u)du \\ &- (1 - R_1)\int_0^T D(0,u)\ \lambda_1^{LF}(u)L_J(0,u)du, \end{aligned} \qquad (\text{A.127})$$

where λ_1^{LF} is the *lone-first* default probability which is the probability that credit 1 defaults before credit 2. Thus the premium is paid up to the point where both credits 1 and 2 survive and the credit payment $(1-R_1)$ is paid if credit 1 defaults first. The correlated CDS can be evaluated using the normal copula model below.

G.11 Normal Copula Model for Correlated Default Times

The standard market model for introducing correlation in default processes is the *normal copula model* where default times are correlated. Consider a basket of M reference entities. Define $Q_i(t) = \Pr(\tau_i \leq t)$ with $(i = 1,\dots,M)$ as the cumulative probability of a credit event of the ith credit by time t, where

$$Q_i(t) = \Pr(\tau_i \leq t) = 1 - e^{-\int_0^t \lambda_i(u)\,du} = 1 - L_i(0,t).$$

We can define a variable x_i such that $N(x_i) < Q_i(t)$ with inverse

$$x_i < N^{-1}(Q_i(t_i)), \qquad (A.128)$$

where N^{-1} is the *inverse cumulative normal distribution*. The joint distribution of x_i is *multivariate normal*. To simulate defaults by time t we must generate M correlated normal random variables x_i and if the condition $x_i < N^{-1}(Q_i(t))$ is true then there has been a default of the ith credit in the period (see Fig. 8.14). This allows us to price baskets and via simulation other correlated default products such as CDOs.

Usually a single factor approximation is applied where each credit has a correlated random variable x_i formed by its own uncorrelated random variable Z_i and an independent single factor F. In this model the pair-wise correlation coefficient is $\rho_{ij} = a_i a_j$ which is often be set to a constant $\rho = a^2$.

$$x_i = a_i F + \sqrt{1 - a_i^2}\, Z_i.$$

G.12 Synthetic CDO Valuation

To illustrate consider a simplified model where $n_i(t_j)$ is the expected notional of the ith tranche at time t_j ($j=1,2,...,M$). Assume these dates correspond to equal coupon periods so $h=t_j-t_{j-1}$. If the spread of the tranche is q_i the present value of all spread payments on the tranche is given by

$$Spread\ Paid = q_i \sum_{j=1}^{M} D(0,t_j) n_i(t_j) h$$

$$+ q_i \sum_{j=1}^{M} D(0,t_j - h/2)(n_i(t_j) - n_i(t_{j-1}))(h/2),$$

where the second term assumes that accrued spread is paid until on average half-way through the coupon period. For a fair value spread this must equal the expected payout or principal loss on the tranche. Assuming again that the loss occurs half-way through the coupon period.

$$Payout = \sum_{j=1}^{M} D(0, t_j - h/2)(n_i(t_j) - n_i(t_{j-1})).$$

By simulating the timing and amount of credit losses on the underlying reference portfolio using the normal copula model we are able to calculate the expected principle for each time period and determine the fair value spread q_i on the tranches.

In reality, it is a bit more complicated since we must for each credit in the underlying portfolio determine the implied market default probability curve from CDS spreads. This could involve a couple of hundred credit curves. From these curves we must perform a Monte Carlo simulation to determine the correlated default times for each credit for each simulation path. The loss distribution must be determined and the losses apportioned to each tranche on each simulation run to tranches with different *attachment points* and thicknesses. From this the expected loss for each tranche can be determined and the fair value spread for the individual tranches calculated.

Often simplifications, such as flat credit curves, constant recovery rates and single factor constant correlation are used to ease calculation. To determine greeks, such as deltas, to individual spread curve changes, sensitivity to correlation change and instantaneous *jump-to-default* (JTD) risk requires perturbation of the inputs and recalculation. For accurate greeks this is very computationally intensive, especially if each credit curve in the underlying portfolio is to be perturbated. To allow faster calculations simplified closed form approximations can be used for homogenous portfolios where we can use the average hazard rate, recovery rate and correlation (Appx G.13).

The normal copula model with a single factor approximation is a market standard model but implies a market correlation smile across the capital structure (see Fig. 9.14). We can introduce more complex models with multiple random factors or different copulas such as the Student-t distribution or even an implied copula model where the probability distribution is implied from the market in a similar fashion to implied volatility distributions from equity prices.

G.13 Extending the Normal Copula Approach

Monte Carlo simulation is usually the best route to pricing CDO and FTD baskets but the normal copula approach can be extended to provide closed forms for homogenous portfolios. The results can also be applied to simplified equity basket products (Altiplano, Everest…).

If, as before, the cumulative probability of default of the ith name in a basket of M names is $Q_i(t) = \Pr(\tau_i \leq t)$ then under the single factor approximation we can write for a given random variate F the conditional probability

$$Q_i(\tau_i \leq t|F) = N\left(\frac{N^{-1}(Q_i(t)) - a_i F}{\sqrt{1 - a_i^2}}\right).$$

The joint distribution function ψ can be written as

$$\psi(t_1, t_2, ..., t_M) = \int_{-\infty}^{\infty} \prod_{j=1}^{M} Q_j(\tau_j \leq t_j|F) \, \varphi(F) dF,$$

where the integral is over the Gaussian density $\varphi(F)$. This can be used to readily determine $\hat{N}(t)$ the total number of defaulting assets by time t if we assume a constant uniform correlation ρ. To price a CDO we require the further assumption that all assets in the portfolio have the same notional n_0, recovery rate R and maturity. If we impose a uniform default probability, so $Q_i(t) = Q(t)$, this allows us to simplify the *conditional* joint default probability distribution using a Binomial distribution

$$\Pr(\hat{N}(t) = k|F) = \binom{M}{k} Q(t|F)^k (1 - Q(t|F))^{M-k}.$$

To obtain the unconditional probabilities we must integrate over all possible values of the variate F using the Gaussian density by employing an integration technique called *Gaussian quadrature*. In the limit of a large homogenous portfolio (large M) we can further apply the *central limit theorem* and approximate the Binomial distribution with Gaussian probability distribution.

If a particular CDO tranche has a lower *attachment point* corresponding to k_L defaults and an upper *detachment point* of k_U defaults, so the tranche thickness is $n_0(1-R)(k_U-k_L)$ the expected loss at time t on the tranche is approximated as

$$E[Loss(t)] = n_0(1-R)D(0,t)\left(\sum_{k=k_L}^{k_U} P(\hat{N}(t)=k) + (k_U - k_L)\sum_{k=k_U}^{M} P(\hat{N}(t)=k)\right).$$

The first sum corresponds to losses "eating through" the tranche and the last sum refers to losses that completely destroy the tranche. Summing the expected loss over time we can evaluate CDOs as Appx (G.12).

Another application of the above approach is in pricing certain equity basket products. Consider a simplified, generic version of a product such as the Altiplano or Everest which pays a coupon $C_k(t_l)$ if k equities of a basket of M equities have breached a barrier by coupon time t_l ($l=1,2,...,L$). By analogy with the above if we assume equity barrier hitting times correspond to default times in CDOs we can price the equity basket option as

$$P_{\substack{generic \\ Altiplano}} = \sum_{l=1}^{L}\sum_{k=0}^{M} D(0,t_l)C_k(t_l)P(\hat{N}(t_l)=k).$$

Applying the single factor joint distribution function ψ we can produce closed forms for many equity products such as worst-of, rainbows, etc. Although these solutions require numerical integration they can provide faster convergence than Monte Carlo, although simulation techniques are generally preferred since they provide greater flexibility in product design.

Appendix H

Structured Credit Products

H.1 Fixed Rate Credit Linked Note

A credit linked note (CLN) that pays a fixed rate coupon c will often include a CDS plus a fixed/floating interest rate swap which will be terminated early on a credit event. Alternatively, the swap risk can be embedded in the structure and the funding leg becomes contingent on no credit event occurring. The swap for maturity T is then priced in continuous time as

$$
V_{fixed \atop CLN}(0,T) = \int_0^T (c - f(0,u) - x)L(0,u)D(0,u)\,du
$$
$$
- (1-R)\int_0^T \lambda(u)L(0,u)D(0,u)\,du. \tag{A.129}
$$

H.2 Basket Credit Linked Note

Example 9.2 shows a four name digital basket CLN where the nominal and coupon steps down by 25% after each credit event. This product can be composed of a series of four digital CDS ($i=1,\ldots,4$) each with a hazard rate curve $\lambda_i(t)$. The structured swap that pays a credit linked coupon c is given by

$$
V_{digital \atop basket \atop CLN}(0,T) = \frac{1}{4}\sum_{i=1}^4 \int_0^T (c - f(0,u) - x)L_i(0,u)D(0,u)\,du
$$
$$
- \frac{1}{4}\sum_{i=1}^4 \int_0^T \lambda_i(u)L_i(0,u)D(0,u)\,du. \tag{A.130}
$$

H.3 Principal Protected Credit Linked Note

The structure can be modelled as an issuer guaranteeing the principal and paying a funding leg until the maturity date and the swap counterparty paying a coupon c until a credit event. On a continuous time basis we can write

$$V_{\substack{protected \\ CLN}}(0,T) = c \int_0^T L(0,u) D(0,u) \, du$$

$$- \int_0^T (f(0,u) + x) D(0,u) \, du. \tag{A.131}$$

H.4 Basket Principal Protected Note

Diversification and risk reduction can be obtained by including several high yielding credits and a coupon that steps down after a credit event. For Example 9.4 with three eastern European credits in a basket the coupon steps down by one third on each credit event.

$$V_{\substack{basket \\ protected \\ CLN}}(0,T) = \frac{c}{3} \sum_{i=1}^3 \int_0^T L_i(0,u) D(0,u) \, du$$

$$- \int_0^T (f(0,u) + x) D(0,u) \, du. \tag{A.132}$$

H.5 First-to-Default Notes

Standard *first-to-default* swap valuation uses the joint survival rate L_J for all the N names in the basket and the hazard rate for the first credit event in the basket to default. To be exact this hazard rate must take into account the fact that several credit events may happen simultaneously and is effectively the *joint-first* hazard rate λ^{JF}

$$V_{\substack{FTD \\ CDS}}(0,T) = q_{FTD} \int_0^T L_J(0,u) D(0,u) \, du$$

$$- \sum_{i=1}^N (1 - R_i) \int_0^T \lambda_i^{JF}(u) L_J(0,u) D(0,u) \, du, \tag{A.133}$$

where q_{FTD} is the first-to-default CDS premium. The swap can be evaluated using the normal copula model (Appx G.11).

Appendix I

Fund Options and Hybrids

I.1 CPPI Methodology

Constant proportion portfolio insurance (CPPI) is a trading strategy where a constant proportional exposure to a risky asset or index is maintained whilst guaranteeing a minimum value of the portfolio until maturity.

The value of the CPPI is given by a mixture of the *risky asset V* and the *floor FLR*. Typically rebalancing between the risky asset and the floor is carried out on a daily basis. In the simplest case we can consider the floor to be a zero coupon bond. The effective participation, here capped at 100%, for time period t_i is given by

$$\alpha(t_i) = Min \left\{ 100\%, G\left(\frac{CPPI(t_i) - FLR(t_i)}{CPPI(t_i)} \right) \right\}, \qquad (A.134)$$

where G is the gearing level (typically 200–500%). The CPPI value from one period to the next is given by the weighted return of the risky asset and the floor.

$$CPPI(t_i) = CPPI(t_{i-1}) \left[\begin{array}{l} 1 + \alpha(t_{i-1})\left(\dfrac{V(t_i)}{V(t_{i-1})} - 1 \right) \\[2ex] \quad + (1 - \alpha(t_{i-1}))\left(\dfrac{FLR(t_i)}{FLR(t_{i-1})} - 1 \right) \end{array} \right].$$

$$(A.135)$$

I.2 Pricing Hybrids

A simple pricing model for equities, rates and credit can be given by assuming a Hull–White system of diffusions for the short interest rate $r(t)$ and the hazard rate $\lambda(t)$.

$$dr(t) = \left[\theta_r(t) - a_r\, r(t)\right]dt + \sigma_r\, dz_r(t)$$

$$d\lambda(t) = \left[\theta_\lambda(t) - a_\lambda\, \lambda(t)\right]dt + \sigma_\lambda dz_\lambda(t).$$

(A.136)

A Black–Scholes process can be used for equity prices $S(t)$ with an extra term as an uncorrelated jump process $N(t) = 1_{\tau \leq t}$ for the default time and the deterministic drift $\lambda(t)dt$ to retain risk neutrality.

$$\frac{dS(t)}{S(t)} = (r(t) - q(t))\,dt + \sigma_S\, dz_S(t) + (\lambda(t)dt - dN(t)).$$

(A.137)

The stochastic processes can correlated as required in this basic framework. In addition, an FX process $X(t)$ or other underlying can be included as a Black–Scholes process.

$$\frac{dX(t)}{X(t)} = (r_d(t) - r_f(t))\,dt + \sigma_{FX}\, dz_{FX}(t).$$

(A.138)

Hybrid options can be priced with Monte Carlo, multi-dimensional finite difference and in some rare exceptions closed form.

Further Reading

On interest rate curves and convexity.

Baz, J. and Pascutti, M. (1996) Alternative Swap Contracts Analysis and Pricing, *Journal of Derivatives*, 4, 2, p. 7.

Brotherton-Ratcliffe, R. and Iben, B. (1993) *Yield Curve Applications of Swap Products, Advanced Strategies in Financial Risk Management* (New York Institute of Finance).

Fabozzi, F.J. (2006) *Fixed Income Mathematics: Analytical and Statistical Techniques*, 4th Edition (New York, McGraw-Hill).

Flavell, R. (2002) *Swaps and Other Instruments* (Chichester, Wiley).

Hull, J.C. (2009) *Options, Futures and Other Derivatives*, 7th Edition (New Jersey, Pearson, Prentice-Hall).

Litzenberger, R.H. (1992) Swaps: Plain and Fanciful, *Journal of Finance*, 47, 3, p. 831.

On stock returns, risk neutral valuation and volatility.

Bramwell, S.T., Holdsworth, P.C.W. and Pinton, J.F. (1998) Universality of Rare Fluctuations in Turbulence and Critical Phenomena, *Nature*, 396, p. 552.

Cox, J.C. and Ross, S.A. (1976) The Valuation of Options for Alternative Stochastic Processes, *Journal of Financial Economics*, 3, p. 145.

Fama, E.F. (1965) The Behaviour of Stock Market Prices, *Journal of Business*, 38, 1, p. 34.

French, K.R. and Roll, R. (1986) Stock Return Variances: The Arrival of Information and the Reaction of Traders, *Journal of Financial Economics*, 17, p. 5.

Kon, S.J. (1984) Models of Stock Returns – A Comparison, *Journal of Finance*, 39, 1, p. 147.

Richardson, M. and Smith, T. (1993) A Test for Multivariate Normality in Stock Returns, *Journal of Business*, 66, 2, p. 295.

On the Black–Scholes equation.

Black, F. (1989) How We Came Up with the Option Pricing Formula, *Journal of Portfolio Management*, 15, 2, p. 4.
Black, F. and Scholes, M. (1973) The Pricing of Options and Corporate Liabilities, *Journal of Political Economy*, 81, p. 637.
Merton, R.C. (1973) Theory of Rational Option Pricing, *Bell Journal of Economics and Management*, 4, 1, p. 141.

On hedging and volatility smiles.

Andersen, L. and Brotherton-Ratcliffe, R. (1997) The Equity Option Volatility Smile: An Implicit Finite Difference Approach, *Journal of Computational Finance*, 1, 2, p. 5.
Dupire, B. (1994) Pricing with a Smile, *Risk*, 7, 1, pp. 18–20.
Rubenstein, M. (1994) Implied Binomial Trees, *Journal of Finance*, 49, 3, p. 771.
Taleb, N.N. (1996) *Dynamic Hedging: Managing Vanilla and Exotic Options* (Chichester, Wiley).

On numerical methods.

Boyle, P.P. (1977) Options: A Monte Carlo Approach, *Journal of Financial Economics*, 4.
Cox, J.C., Ross, S.A. and Rubenstein, M. (1979) Option Pricing: A Simplified Approach, *Journal of Financial Economics*, 7, p. 229.
Glasserman, P. (2004) *Monte Carlo Methods in Financial Engineering* (Heidelberg, Springer).
Hull, J. and White, A. (1990) Valuing Derivative Securities Using the Explicit Finite Difference Method, *Journal of Financial and Quantitative Analysis*, 25, p. 87.
Press, W.H., Teukolsky, S.A., Vetterling, W.T. and Flannery, B.P. (1992) *Numerical Recipies in C: The Art of Scientific Computing*, 2nd Edition (Cambridge, Cambridge University Press).
Wilmott, P. (1990) *Derivatives: The Theory and Practice of Financial Engineering* (Chichester, Wiley).

On exotics, currency options and quantos.

Garman, M.B. and Kohlhagen, S.W. (1983) Foreign Currency Option Values, *Journal of International Money and Finance*, 2, p. 231.
Haug, E.G. (1998) *The Complete Guide to Option Pricing Formulas* (New York, McGraw-Hill).
Jamshidian, F. (1994) Corralling Quantos, *Risk*, 7, p. 71.
Kat, H.M. (1998) *Structured Equity Derivatives* (Chichester, Wiley).

Reiner, E. and Rubenstein, M. (1991) Breaking Down the Barriers, *Risk*, 4, 8, pp. 28–35.

On other equity pricing models.

Carr, P. and Madan, D. (2002) Towards a Theory of Volatility Trading, Robert Jarrow Ed. (London, Risk).

Cox, J.C. and Ross, S.A. (1976) The Valuation of Options for Alternative Stochastic Processes, *Journal of Financial Economics*, 3, p. 145.

Heston, S. (1976) A Closed-form Solution for Options with Stochastic Volatility with Applications to Bond and Currency Options, *Review of Financial Studies*, 6, p. 327.

Merton, R.C. (1976) Option Pricing When the Underlying Stock Returns are Discontinuous, *Journal of Financial Economics*, 3, p. 125.

Scott, L. (1987) Option Pricing when the Variance Changes Randomly: Theory, Estimation and an Application, *Journal of Financial and Quantitative Analysis*, 22, p. 419.

On Asian options, basket options, exchange options.

Kemma, A. and Vorst, A. (1990) A Pricing Method for Options Based on Average Asset Values, *Journal of Banking and Finance*, 14, p. 113.

Margrabe, W. (1978) The Value of an Option to Exchange One Asset for Another, *Journal of Finance*, 33, p. 177.

Turnbull, S.M and Wakeman, L.M. (1991) A Quick Algorithm for Pricing European Average Options, *Journal of Financial and Quantitative Analysis*, 26, p. 377.

On interest rate pricing models.

Black, F. (1976) The Pricing of Commodity Contracts, *Journal of Financial Economics*, 3, p. 167.

Brace, A., Gatarek, D. and Musiela, M. (1997) The Market Model of Interest Rate Dynamics, *Mathematical Finance*, 7, 2, p. 127.

Heath, D., Jarrow, R. and Morton, A. (1992) Bond Pricing and the Term Structure of Interest Rates: A New Methodology, *Econometrica*, 60, 1, p. 77.

Ho, T.S. and Lee, S.B. (1986) Term Structure Movements and Pricing Interest Rate Contingent Claims, *Journal of Finance*, 41, p. 1011.

Hull, J. and White, A. (1990) Pricing Interest Rate Derivative Securities, *Review of Financial Studies*, 4, p. 573.

Hull, J. And White, A. (1993) The Pricing of Options on Interest Rate Caps and Floors using the Hull–White Model, *Journal of Financial Engineering*, 2, p. 287.

Hull J. and White, A. (2000) Forward Rate Volatilities, Swap Rate Volatilities and the Implementation of the LIBOR Market Model, *Journal of Fixed Income*, 10, 2, p. 46.

Jamshidian, F. (1997) LIBOR and Swap Market Models and Measures, *Finance and Stochastics*, 1, p. 293.

Vasicek, O. (1977) An Equilibrium Characterisation of the Term Structure, *Journal of Financial Economics*, 5, p. 177.

On credit risk and credit pricing models.

Altman, E.I. (1989) Measuring Corporate Bond Mortality and Performance, *Journal of Finance*, 44, p. 902.

Duffie, D. and Singleton, K. (1999) Modeling Term Structures of Defaultable Bonds, *Review of Financial Studies*, 12, p. 687.

Finger, C.C. (2000) A Comparison of Stochastic Default Rate Models, *RiskMetrics Journal*, 1, p. 49.

Merton, R. (1974) On the Pricing of Corporate Debt: The Risk Structure of Interest Rates, *Journal of Finance*, 29, p. 449.

Pan, G. (2001) Equity to Credit Pricing, *Risk*, p. 99, November.

Schonbucher, P.J. (2003) *Credit Derivative Pricing Models* (Chichester, Wiley).

On credit correlation.

Andersen, L., Sidenius, J. and Basu, S. (2003) All Your Hedges in One Basket, *Risk*, p. 67, November.

Hull, J. and White, A. (2004) Valuation of a CDO and nth to Default Swap without Monte Carlo Simulation, *Journal of Derivatives*, 12, p. 2.

Hull, J. and White, A. (2006) Valuing Credit Derivatives Using an Implied Copula Approach, *Journal of Derivatives*, 14, p. 8.

Li, D.X. (2000), On Default Correlation: A Copula Approach, *Journal of Fixed Income*, 9, 4, p. 43, March.

On hybrids.

Overhaus, M., Bermúdez, A., Buehler, H. *et al.* (2007) *Equity Hybrid Derivatives* (Chichester, Wiley).

Index

volatility smile, 45
volatility swap, 282

worst-of closed form, 300, 339
worst-of option, 110
worst-of protected notes, 114

XOVER, 189

yield curve, 25
yield curve model, 130
yield curve note, 169

zero coupon bond, 22
zero curve, 22
zero curve building, 33
z-spread, 328